Deleuze's Hume

Deleuze's Hume

Philosophy, Culture and the Scottish Enlightenment

Jeffrey A. Bell

Edinburgh University Press

© Jeffrey A. Bell, 2009, 2020

Edinburgh University Press Ltd
22 George Square, Edinburgh
www.euppublishing.com

First published in hardback by Edinburgh University Press 2009

Typeset in Sabon and Futura
by Servis Filmsetting Ltd, Stockport, Cheshire

A CIP record for this book is available from the British Library

ISBN 978 0 7486 3439 2 (hardback)
ISBN 978 1 4744 7456 6 (paperback)

The right of Jeffrey A. Bell
to be identified as author of this work
has been asserted in accordance with
the Copyright, Designs and Patents Act 1988.

Contents

Acknowledgements	vii
Abbreviations	ix
Introduction	1
1. Staging the Mind: From Multiplicity to Belief	9
I. Ideas and Impressions	10
II. Transcendental Empiricism	15
III. Radical Empiricism	18
IV. Reality of the Virtual	22
V. Belief	26
2. Becoming Who We Are	34
I. Historical Ontology	36
II. Personal Identity	42
III. Creative Evolution and Pragmatics	49
3. The Time of our Life: Historical Ontology and Creative Events	59
I. Problematizing History	60
II. Creative Events and Counter-causality	64
III. Kafka: a Life, an Event . . .	73
4. Becoming Civil: History and the Discipline of Institutions	82
I. Hume and History	84
II. The Rise of Arts and Sciences	89
III. Commerce and Schizophrenia	94
IV. Institutions, Power, and Culture	97
5. Creating Culture: The Case of the Scottish Enlightenment	106
I. Cultural Preconscious	107

	II. Instituting Culture	112
	III. Scottish Enlightenment	117
	IV. From Culture to Canon	122
6.	Beyond Belief: Deleuze's Hume and the Fear of Politics	131
	I. Speech and Event	132
	II. Beyond Belief	135
	III. Speaking for the Multitude	139
	IV. Becoming-imperceptible	147

Bibliography 156
Index 167

Acknowledgements

Much of the initial research for this book was conducted while I was a Visiting Research Fellow at the Institute for Advanced Studies in the Humanities in Edinburgh. The convivial, stimulating environment of the Institute and of Edinburgh contributed mightily to this project, but of special significance was the helpful feedback, guidance, and generosity of Susan Manning, Tony Lavopa, and Anthea Taylor. I am also especially indebted to Innes Kennedy for pointing me in the direction of the Institute as well as for his many incisive suggestions for furthering my project, and last but not least for his exceptional musical taste! Further support for my research in Edinburgh was provided by Southeastern Louisiana University faculty development grants and by my department, where department head Bill Robison made available whatever resources he could. Above all, I want to thank James Williams and Claire Colebrook for their encouragement and support, along with Len Lawlor, John Protevi, and my colleague Pete Petrakis, who have all had a hand in alerting me to points I would have otherwise missed. I am indebted as well to the professional, thorough, and helpful comments the readers for Edinburgh University Press gave concerning the proposal for this book. I am especially thankful to Carol MacDonald at Edinburgh University Press for her willingness to take on this project and for adeptly ushering it to final publication, and to Tim Clark, whose copyediting skills gave this book greater polish than it had when he received it. An earlier version of Chapters 1 and 2 was published in *The Southern Journal of Philosophy* (44:3) under the title, 'Charting the Road of Inquiry: Deleuze's Humean Pragmatics and the Challenge of Badiou,' and the anonymous readers for the journal offered useful suggestions for improving this essay, suggestions that would later make their way into this book. In the end, whatever merits the book may be deemed to have, it would have had fewer had it not been for the support and help of those listed above, and for those not mentioned but who have, at various times and in untold ways, prompted me to pursue paths that would later become parts of this project – Ian Buchanan, Nick Phillipson, Cairns Craig, Eugene Holland, Joe Hughes, Manuel DeLanda, Simon Malpas, Alex Thomson, and ... AND ...

And finally, this book would not have been possible had it not been for the patience, support, and love of my wife, Liz, and my daughters, Leah and Rebecca. It is they who assure that I follow Hume's maxim: 'Be a philosopher; but, amidst all your philosophy, be still a man.'

Abbreviations

Works by Hume

A *An Abstract of a Treatise of Human Nature*. Oxford: Clarendon Press, 1978. In *A Treatise of Human Nature*, edited by L. A. Silby-Bigge, with text revised and notes by P. H. Nidditch.

DNR *Dialogues Concerning Natural Religion*. Indianapolis: Bobbs-Merrill, n.d. Edited by Norman Kemp Smith.

EHU *Enquiry Concerning Human Understanding*. Oxford: Oxford University Press, 2004. Edited by Tom Beauchamp.

EPM *Enquiry Concerning the Principles of Morals*. Oxford: Clarendon Press, 1975. Edited by L. A. Silby-Bigge, with text revised and notes by P. H. Nidditch.

EMPL *Essays, Moral, Political, and Literary*. Indianapolis: Liberty Fund, 1985. Edited by Eugene F. Miller.

L1, L2 *The Letters of David Hume*, 2 vols. Oxford: Oxford University Press, 1969. Edited by J. Y. T. Grieg. L1 and L2 will reference volumes one and two respectively.

T *A Treatise of Human Nature*. Oxford: Clarendon Press, 1978. Edited by L. A. Selby-Bigge, with text revised and notes by P. H. Nidditch.

Works by Deleuze

AO *Anti-Oedipus: Capitalism and Schizophrenia* (with Félix Guattari). New York: Viking Press, 1977. Translated by Robert Hurley, Mark Seem, and Helen R. Lane.

B *Bergsonism*. New York: Zone Books, 1988. Translated by Hugh Tomlinson and Barbara Habberjam.

CC	*Essays Critical and Clinical*. Minneapolis: University of Minnesota Press, 1997. Translated by Daniel W. Smith and Michael A. Greco.
D	*Dialogues* (with Claire Parnet). London: Athlone Press, 1987. Translated by Hugh Tomlinson and Barbara Habberjam.
DI	*Desert Islands and Other Texts 1953–1974*. New York: Semiotext(e), 2004. Translated by Mark Taormina.
DR	*Difference and Repetition*. New York: Columbia University Press, 1994. Translated by Paul Patton.
ES	*Empiricism and Subjectivity: An Essay on Hume's Theory of Human Nature*. New York: Columbia University Press, 1991. Translated by Constantin Boundas.
K	*Kafka: Toward a Minor Literature* (with Guattari). Minneapolis: University of Minnesota Press, 1986. Translated by Dana Polan.
LS	*Logic of Sense*. New York: Columbia University Press, 1990. Translated by Mark Lester, with Charles Stivale; edited by Constantin Boundas.
N	*Negotiations*. New York: Columbia University Press, 1995. Translated by Martin Joughin.
PI	*Pure Immanence*. New York: Zone Books, 2001. Translated by Anne Boyman.
TP	*A Thousand Plateaus: Capitalism and Schizophrenia* (with Guattari). Minneapolis: University of Minnesota Press, 1987. Translated by Brian Massumi.
2RM	*Two Regimes of Madness: Texts and Interviews 1975–1995*. New York: Semiotext(e), 2006. Translated by A. Hodges and Michael Taormina.
WP	*What is Philosophy?* (with Guattari). New York: Columbia University Press, 1994. Translated by Hugh Tomlinson and Graham Burchell.

Introduction

Deleuze begins the preface to the 1987 English language edition of *Dialogues* with the assertion 'I have always felt that I am an empiricist, that is, a pluralist' (D vii). A few lines later, Deleuze details what this means: a pluralist assumes that the abstract 'must itself be explained,' and explained so as to 'find the conditions under which something new is produced (creativeness)' (ibid.). Thirty-four years earlier, in his first published book, *Empiricism and Subjectivity*, Deleuze found just such an explanation in Hume.[1] With the premise that 'Mankind is an inventive species' (T 484), Hume set out in his *Treatise of Human Nature* to explain how the principles of human nature can account for this inventiveness. More precisely, Hume argues that the principles of association draw relationships between ideas in the mind, ideas that are themselves copies of corresponding impressions, and as a result of these relationships and the easy transition from one idea to another they facilitate, what is produced is the belief in causation and necessity, a belief that is irreducible to the impressions themselves. As Hume puts it, the belief in causal relations enables the mind to go 'beyond what is immediately present to the senses' (T 73).

Hume's approach, although profoundly influential, has nonetheless received significant criticism. For our purposes the most warranted of these criticisms are those of William James and Henri Bergson. For James, who like Deleuze claimed to be an empiricist and a pluralist, Hume was wrong to do 'away with the connections of things . . . [and to insist] most on the disjunctions' (James 1987, 1160). In particular, Hume wrongly insists upon the disjunctions between impressions, arguing that it is contrary to experience to assert, as Hume does, that 'as all distinct ideas are separable from each other, and as the ideas of cause and effect are evidently distinct,' there is consequently no intrinsic connection between these ideas (T 79). This was precisely why the belief in a causal connection goes 'beyond what is immediately present to the senses.' Hume's 'preposterous view,' as James characterizes it, is typical of the 'intellectualist method [which] pulverize[s] perception and triumph[s] over life' (James 1987, 1084). James argues that his radical empiricism 'does full justice to conjunctive relations' (ibid. 1161), relations that are experienced in what he calls 'pure experience.' Bergson also finds in Hume's approach a 'capital error' in that he substitutes for the 'continuity of becoming, which is the living reality, a discontinuous multiplicity of elements, inert and juxtaposed' (Bergson [1896] 1988, 134). For Bergson, a true empiricism is one that seeks 'to get as near to the original itself as possible, to search deeply into its life' (Bergson [1903] 1999, 36–7), and this is done by way of intuition, which is just 'the kind of intellectual sympathy by which one places oneself within an object in order to coincide with what is unique in it and consequently inexpressible' (ibid. 23–4).

Since it draws significantly on Hume's work, Deleuze's project might therefore be open to similar criticisms, which would be particularly troubling given the importance of Bergson's thought for Deleuze. Yet there is a further, perhaps more damning problem for Deleuze's empiricism, namely the dualism Deleuze readily admits is entailed by empiricism. Deleuze is quite forthright: 'empiricism,' he asserts in *Empiricism and Subjectivity*, 'will not be correctly defined except by means of dualism' (ES 108). Therein lies the problem, however, for a number of recent commentators on Deleuze's philosophy. Alain Badiou, for instance, finds the virtual/actual dualism in Deleuze's philosophy – what Badiou calls the 'unthinkable Two' (Badiou 2000, 53) – especially problematic.[2] In short, Deleuze ultimately fails in his effort to reconcile the dualism of empiricism with his assertion that being is univocal. We will address this and other criticisms in due course, but it must first be noted that despite the claim that empiricism will 'not be correctly defined except by means of dualism,' Deleuze will nonetheless argue, in his final published essay 'Immanence: a life . . .,' that transcendental empiricism is to be contrasted with 'everything that makes up the world of the subject and the object' (PI 25). Furthermore, in *Dialogues* Deleuze counters the charge that his work (along with his work with Félix Guattari) is dualistic by arguing that one avoids dualism only 'when you find between the terms . . . whether they are two or more, a narrow gorge like a border or a frontier which will turn the set into a multiplicity, independently of the number of parts' (D 132). Between identifiable terms, therefore, is a multiplicity, and with this multiplicity Deleuze's empiricism is remarkably similar to Hume's. Hume, as will be argued in the chapters to follow, does not presuppose the simple, discontinuous identities of impressions and ideas as the already individuated givens with which the principles of association work. Identity, on our reading of Hume, is fictioned from within a multiplicity. Understood in this way, Deleuze's Hume will be seen to be in line with the projects of James and Bergson, for Deleuze likewise proposes a multiplicity – namely, a transcendental field of pre-individual singularities – that comes to be drawn (fictioned) into a plane of consistency (in what Deleuze will call a first articulation) that is then actualized as identifiable, individuated entities and terms (in a second articulation). Between the identifiable terms of a dualism or set, therefore, there is a multiplicity, the AND, and this, for Deleuze, is in the end what empiricism is ultimately all about: 'Thinking with AND, instead of thinking IS, instead of thinking for IS: empiricism has never had another secret. Try it, it is a quite extraordinary thought, and yet it is life' (D 57).

Thinking with AND, however, is not a thinking about or of life, nor is it a thinking for the sake of life, but it is life. And yet in making this claim the thinking with AND has been individuated and identified, the *is* has returned – 'and yet it *is* life.' In thinking the nature of Deleuze's thought, in thinking what it *is* to be 'thinking with AND, instead of thinking IS,' this thinking itself becomes, as Deleuze affirms, immediately double.[3] The return of the *is* is thus double, hence an empiricism that seeks to determine and think the *real* 'conditions under which something new is produced,' will not 'be correctly defined except by means of dualism.' This is no less true when it comes to the efforts of Deleuze's commentators to think the nature of Deleuze's thought. We have on the one hand what could be called the *materialist* or *realist* Deleuze. Here the thinking with AND that is life is a life that is a dynamic system that draws associative connections within a multiplicity of elements, associations that then come to be actualized as an emergent property that is irreducible to the multiplicity of elements themselves. Whether this is the reciprocal relations among phonemes Deleuze refers to as 'a virtual system,' a system that is then 'incarnated in the actual terms and relations of diverse languages,' (DR 208) or any of a number of other ways in which materiality involves dynamic processes of self-organization, what is generally assumed here is that Deleuze's concepts enable us to comprehend and make sense of material processes that are nonetheless real and distinct from the conceptual activity that names and identifies them as the types of process they *already were* prior to being named.[4]

In contrast to the realist or materialist Deleuze, there is the *idealist, nominalist* Deleuze. On this reading, life is an Idea or problem, meaning, as these terms are discussed in *Difference and Repetition* and elsewhere, that life as an Idea or problematic is only identifiable as actualized within an entity that is a solution to this problem. Eyes, Deleuze notes, are the actualized solution of a light problem, a problem that becomes identifiable as such only after it has become actualized as eyesight.[5] Otherwise, the problematic (or virtual) does *not yet* exist as an identifiable state, and thus it is not an identifiably distinct state separate from the actual.[6] The *realist* Deleuze thus provides us with the conceptual tools to name that which *already is/was* identifiable, and the *nominalist* Deleuze gives us the means to name the manner in which something is *not yet* identifiable but becomes so when it becomes nameable – that is, when actualized. We have, in short, the event of Deleuze's thought, and as 'event,' as Deleuze defines it in *Logic of Sense*, 'there is indeed the present moment of its actualization,' but there is also, more importantly, 'the future and past of the event considered in itself, side-stepping each present, being free of the limitations of a state of affairs, impersonal, pre-individual, neutral' (LS 151).

These contrasting interpretations of Deleuze's work do not pose a problem for Deleuze scholarship; to the contrary, they highlight Deleuze's very claim that empiricism is only correctly defined by dualism. One need not choose between the realist or nominalist Deleuze. It is more accurate to state, instead, that there is a double movement of Deleuze's thought, a nominalist and realist movement, and this double movement becomes, as actualized and individuated within the thought that seeks to determine the nature of Deleuze's philosophy, two contrasting if not opposing interpretations. Moreover, a similar dualism is at work in Hume's thought, for with Hume as well – as Deleuze points out – there is the dualism between the causes of perception on the one hand and the causes of relations on the other (see ES 109, and Chapter 1 below). This in turn leads to two contrasting readings. There is the realist Hume who sees hidden causal powers that are already there and function as the basis upon which the order and regularity of our sense impressions depends; and then there is the nominalist Hume who claims that causal powers arise only after the association of ideas and custom. These two interpretations comprise what has come to be called the New Hume debate, which will be discussed at length in Chapter 1.

In the following study we will resist the temptation to identify Deleuze's philosophical approach as being either realist or nominalist. More to the point, we will pay heed to Deleuze's advice and study Deleuze AND Hume, thereby attempting to avoid a dualistic interpretation by finding the 'border' or 'frontier' that will turn Deleuze AND Hume, along with Deleuze the realist AND Deleuze the nominalist, 'into a multiplicity.' What this will mean, and as the arguments of subsequent chapters will show, is that a multiplicity is always already identified the more the multiplicity comes to be named and identified. Put in other terms, there is no *already* distinct, autonomous reality that Deleuzian concepts enable us to understand and identify; nor do Deleuzian concepts simply enable us to facilitate the emergence of a novel reality that has *not yet* occurred; rather, a distinct, autonomous reality is distinct and autonomous precisely insofar as it facilitates the emergence of novel realities that have not yet occurred. As Bruno Latour states this same point in *Pandora's Hope*, 'it is because it [autonomous reality] is constructed that it is so very real, so autonomous, so independent of our own hands' (Latour 1999, 275). What this means for Latour, and for Deleuze on the reading offered here, is that between the identifiable terms of a dualism – cause and effect, subject and object, autonomous and constructed, already and not yet – there is a multiplicity of singularities that allows for the possibility of identifying a distinct, autonomous reality the more this multiplicity is drawn into a network of collaborative associations. Latour uses the concept 'relative existence' to refer to this process, meaning that 'an entity . . . gains in reality if it is associated with many others that are viewed as collaborating with it. It loses in reality if, on the contrary, it has to shed associates or collaborators' (Latour 2000, 257). We thus do not begin with being, with what already or not yet *is*, but with processes whereby what *is* acquires and loses relative being and existence, and does so as the singularities acquire greater or lesser connections with other singularities. This is the sense then in which one should read Deleuze and Guattari's claim that 'politics precedes being' (TP 203)[7] – being, in short, cannot be thought as such without presupposing the processes of association that raise and lower the relative existence of that which is. We will refer to the relationship between this process and being as historical ontology.[8]

These themes will occupy us in the chapters to follow, but in order to indicate briefly the trajectory we will be pursuing we can return to Hume. Reading Hume in light of the concept of historical ontology, what this entails for Hume's notion of belief is that the more lively the belief in something is, the more reality is attributed to that which is believed. Thus the belief in the continued existence of independent objects is not a belief that is justified by the independence and autonomy of the objects of this belief; rather, the justification of belief is 'nothing but the vivacity of those perceptions they present' (T 86). The more associations are established through custom, the more lively the belief, and hence the more justified and reasonable the belief. A consequence of this position, as Deleuze notes, is the inseparability of delusional beliefs from reasonable ones.[9] There are, for Hume, no transcendent standards and limits that would enable us to differentiate between a lively idea that is reasonable and one that has become delusional; there are only immanent standards and limits, and thus the reasonableness of belief and the reality of that which is believed are differentiated precisely because of the immanent construction of these limits. And yet the excesses of delusion, the tendencies that may very well undermine and transform one's reasonable beliefs into fits of madness, remain presupposed by these very beliefs. Similarly for Deleuze, the reality of the actual, its identifiable essence and nature, is actual precisely because of the reality of the virtual. This is not, as Badiou implies, because the reality of the virtual is a distinct reality that determines the actualization of the actual;[10] to the contrary, the virtual is the *problematic* inseparable from the actualization of the actual, and by *inseparable* we mean simply that the reality of the actual is real because it can become problematized and become other AND still other actualities. This is the power of AND, the power of life, and the thinking of empiricism which 'has never had another secret.'[11] It is no wonder, then, that Deleuze always considered himself an empiricist, and it is also no surprise that Hume's project would provide an influential trajectory for Deleuze's thought, a trajectory Deleuze would follow from his first to his final writings.

The following chapters will detail the implications of thinking Deleuze AND Hume, implications that will provide connections between Hume and Deleuze and a number of issues to be found in William James, Henri Bergson, and political philosophy. To this end, Chapter 1 will explore the problematic Deleuze believes to be at work in Hume's philosophy, namely the problem of how a multiplicity of ideas and impressions in the mind comes to constitute a subject with beliefs that go 'beyond what is immediately present to the senses.' This problematic will become, in Deleuze's hands, transcendental empiricism, or the effort to think the conditions for the production of the new that does not reduce the identity of the new to these conditions. To clarify the nature of Deleuze's transcendental empiricism, we will then turn to address William James' criticisms of Hume (sketched above). Chapter 2 will address the problem of personal identity in Hume's philosophy, which will enable us to further elaborate our argument that for both Hume and Deleuze there is an historical ontology inseparable from each and every identity, including the identity of the self or person. With these arguments in place, we then show that Deleuze's work on Bergson, undertaken soon after his work on Hume, is not – despite Bergson's criticisms of Hume – a departure for Deleuze but is rather part of his continuing effort to develop a transcendental empiricism.

In Chapter 3 our focus will shift to history, and more precisely to a discussion of the relationship between creative, novel events and the already constituted historical conditions within which these events appear. Rather than providing a causal analysis of such events, a Deleuzian approach offers a counter-causal reading of history that does not seek to account for historical events by relating them to a preceding actuality that would function as a causal factor, but rather attempts to move from the actual to the virtual 'unhistorical vapour' (WP 140) that is inseparable from these actualities – a virtual that may very well, as was Deleuze's strategy, problematize the actualities of the present. Chapters 4 and 5 will explore how the deterritorializing tendencies of creative events come to be captured, for better AND for worse. Along these lines, we will discuss the important role institutions play, for Hume, in producing both a love for humanity and the belief that becoming cultured and polished will benefit humanity. Chapter 5 will take the

Scottish Enlightenment as a case study to assist us in clarifying the arguments of the preceding chapters. The sixth and final chapter will explore the political implications of Deleuze's transcendental empiricism, where it will be argued that there are indeed – despite the criticisms that claim Deleuze's project has no effective connection with the political – important political ramifications in his thought. In short, we shall show that becoming-imperceptible is for Deleuze an effective tool in becoming-revolutionary, and, more precisely, in resisting the powers of the capitalist societies of control, powers we have largely come to believe in and desire. In the spirit of Deleuze, therefore, we shall seek to find between the terms of this study, between the proper names David Hume and Gilles Deleuze, a multiplicity that is irreducible to these terms, and a multiplicity that may problematize these AND many other terms besides. We shall seek to think Deleuze's Hume.

Notes

1. In an interview with Antonio Negri, Deleuze claims that what first attracted him to the work of Hume was 'a very creative conception of institutions and law' (N 169).
2. Peter Hallward has also come down hard on Deleuze for being a dualistic philosopher, and even more for being a dualistic philosopher who stresses the virtual as nothing less than a movement or tendency out of this world, a freeing or escape from this world, over and against the actualities of this world. See Hallward 2006.
3. In his early essay on Bergson, Deleuze argued that 'virtuality exists in such a way that it actualizes itself as it dissociates itself; it must dissociate itself to actualize itself' (DI 40). And as this actualization unfolds, Deleuze adds a few pages later, 'what is differentiating itself in two divergent tendencies is a virtuality' (DI 42). The realist and nominalist Deleuze (to be discussed below) are thus the two divergent tendencies that arise as the event that is Deleuze's thought is actualized by the commentaries that set forth this thought.
4. Brian Massumi, for instance, uses the language of chaos theory (e.g., strange attractors, self-organization, dissipative structures, etc.) to clarify Deleuze and Guattari's philosophy (see Massumi 1992). A similar approach can be found in DeLanda (1997, 2002), who interprets Deleuze and Guattari as exemplars of the theory of nonlinear dynamics. John Protevi and Mark Bonta have pushed this scientific reading of Deleuze and Guattari even more forcefully, arguing that just as Kant's philosophy enabled us to make sense of a Euclidean world, so too Deleuze's work 'provides the philosophical concepts that make sense of our world of fragmented space (the fractals of Mandelbrot, the "patchworks" of Riemann), twisted time (the so-called anticipatory effects of systems that sense their approach to a threshold), and the non-linear effects of far-from-equilibrium thermodynamics' (Protevi and Bonta 2004, viii).
5. DR 211: 'An organism is nothing if not the solution to a problem, as are each of its differenciated organs, such as the eye which solves a light "problem."'

6. Dan Smith has stated this position most forcefully and persuasively in a series of articles, most recently in his essay 'The Conditions of the New' (Smith 2007). In showing how Deleuze extends Maimon's critique of Kant, Smith argues that the concept of the differential (as found in the calculus) enables Deleuze to think the conditions of real experience. More precisely, the differential is the unconditioned that enables the determination of a relation between a condition and the conditioned. As Smith puts it, the 'conditions of real experience must be determined at the same time as what they are conditioning' (13), and the differential, or the Idea as problem as Smith shows, is the unconditioned element or groundless ground for every determinate condition–conditioned relationship, but it is only identifiable 'at the same time as what they are conditioning.' It is only in this way that Deleuze can account for the new, for a conditioned that is not pre-determined by a condition that already contains it (as a possibility). This is in contrast, therefore, to the realist Deleuze, whereby Deleuzian concepts facilitate a better understanding and representation of what is already there. It should be noted, however, that Smith acknowledges the double movement in Deleuze's work, or what we have called the nominalist and realist movements, when citing the following passage from Deleuze: 'Sufficient reason or the ground . . . is strangely bent: on the one hand, it leans towards what it grounds, towards the forms of representation [realist direction]; on the other hand, it turns and plunges into a groundlessness beyond the ground which resists all forms and cannot be represented [nominalist direction]' (DR 274–5; cited by Smith, 7).
7. When this point is made Deleuze and Guattari are discussing the Body Without Organs (BwO) and the lines that are drawn upon this body. As will be discussed in the chapters to follow, the BwO is the multiplicity which is drawn into relations that then come to be actualized as identifiable, determinate beings, beliefs, etc.
8. Ian Hacking has recently written of historical ontology in a book of the same name (Hacking 2002). As Hacking uses the term, he is referring to the historicity of ways in which a subject can be. He gives the example of trauma to show that there is a history to the different ways in which a subject can be, such as a subject suffering from post-traumatic stress disorder (PTSD). We shall extend this concept and argue that Deleuze's Humean project calls for an historical ontology inseparable from each and every identifiable being.
9. See ES 83, for instance, where Deleuze comes to the following conclusion after discussing the importance of the fictioning of identity and unity for Hume: 'From the point of view of philosophy, the mind is no longer anything but delirium and madness. There is no complete system, synthesis, or cosmology that is not imaginary.'
10. In *Deleuze: The Clamour of Being*, Badiou is quite forthright in his criticism, arguing that 'the virtual [for Deleuze] is no better than the finality of which it is the inversion (it determines the destiny of everything, instead of being that to which everything is destined)' (Badiou 2000, 53).
11. We could also say this is the power of becoming. As Heraclitus notes in his famous fragment: 'As they step into the same rivers, different and <still> different waters flow upon them' (Fragment 12 in Heraclitus 1987, 17). It is important to note the 'and' in 'different and <still> different waters.' A multiplicity of 'different and <still> different waters' is presupposed by the identity and being of 'same rivers.'

Chapter 1

Staging the Mind: From Multiplicity to Belief

In Deleuze's first published book, *Empiricism and Subjectivity*, he lays out what he takes to be two central problems at work in the philosophy of David Hume. The first problem, as Deleuze reads Hume, is how the multiplicity of ideas in the imagination 'become[s] a system?' (ES 22). This problem arises for Hume, as we will see, because of the externality of relations between impressions and the ideas that are the copies of these impressions. 'The mind,' Hume says in his *Treatise*, 'is a kind of theatre,' but Hume immediately adds this caution: 'The comparison of the theatre must not mislead us. They are the successive perceptions only, that constitute the mind; nor have we the most distant notion of the place, where these senses are represented . . .' (T 253). As a collection of ideas that lacks any intrinsic basis for relating one to another, the mind is thus, as Deleuze puts it, 'a collection without an album, a play without a stage, a flux of perceptions' (ES 23). How then, to restate the problem, does this multiplicity come to form an integrated system? The second problem follows from the first: 'The problem,' Deleuze states, 'is as follows: how can a subject transcending the given be constituted in the given?', or how can the 'subject who invents and believes [be] constituted inside the given in such a way that it makes the given itself a synthesis and a system' (ES 86–7). The problem of transforming a multiplicity of ideas and impressions into a system is thus inseparable from the problem of accounting for the constitution of a subject within the given, and a subject that is irreducible to the given.

The effort to respond to these problems will be the work of what Deleuze will call transcendental empiricism. We will discuss this effort at length below, but before doing so we will first show how Hume's understanding of the relationship between impressions and ideas leads to the problems that are so central to Hume's project, and that emerge in Deleuze's work as the project of transcendental empiricism.

I. Ideas and Impressions

Hume begins his *Treatise* with what he takes to be an obvious distinction, namely the difference between thinking and feeling. 'Every one of himself,' Hume argues, 'will readily perceive the difference betwixt feeling and thinking' (T1–2). And it is precisely this obvious difference between feeling and thinking that underlies the distinction Hume makes between ideas and impressions. Impressions, Hume claims, are those 'perceptions, which enter with most force and violence,' and ideas are 'the faint images of these in thinking and reasoning' (T 1). Moreover, as a rule that Hume boldly asserts 'holds without any exception . . . every simple idea has a simple impression, which resembles it; and every simple impression a correspondent idea' (T 3). This relationship between ideas and impressions has come to be called the copy principle. As Hume states it, 'all our simple ideas in their first appearance are deriv'd from simple impressions, which are correspondent to them, and which they exactly represent' (T 4). Hume will readily admit that his philosophical system would crumble if one could successfully show that there are indeed ideas that are not copies of correspondent impressions. In a 1752 letter to Hugh Blair, responding to Thomas Reid's criticisms, Hume continues to affirm the copy principle: 'the Author [Reid] affirms I had been hasty, & not supported by any Colour of Argument when I affirm, that all our Ideas are copy'd from Impressions . . . If no exception can ever be found, the Principle must remain incontestible' (Reid [1764] 1997, 257).[1]

One need not turn to Reid, however, for a possible exception to the copy principle. Hume provides us with one, in the widely discussed case of the missing shade of blue. Could one who has never had an impression of this missing shade nonetheless come up with the idea of it if 'all the different shades of that colour, except that single one, be plac'd before him, descending gradually from the deepest to the lightest' (T 6)? Hume has no doubt that one would be able to do so, and yet rather than see this as 'proof, that the simple ideas are not always derived from the correspondent impressions,' he simply moves on, dismissing this case as 'so particular and singular, that 'tis scarce worth our observing' (ibid.). One could say that Hume is merely setting forth general rules and distinctions he believes hold despite the fact that there are occasional, singular exceptions to these rules.[2] Yet the fact that Hume repeatedly, and in numerous places throughout his life, upholds the principle as one that holds *without* exception, has led a number of commentators to take issue with Hume's complacent attitude towards the case of the missing shade of blue.

David Pears, for example, sees Hume's offhanded dismissal of the missing shade of blue as evidence of a fundamental error. In his book, *Hume's*

System, Pears sees in Hume's philosophy a 'general failure to mark the transition from his theory of ideas developed as a psychological analogue of a theory of meaning to its development as a theory of truth and evidence' (Pears 1990, 33). In other words, for Pears, Hume's adherence to the copy principle and its claim that all our simple ideas are 'deriv'd from simple impressions . . . which they exactly represent,' is the psychological analogue to a Fregean-Russellian theory of meaning which states that an utterance is meaningful if there is a content, x, which exactly corresponds to the utterance and gives the utterance a truth value – for example, x is the argument that makes the function 'x is the author of *Waverly*' both true and meaningful when 'x' is replaced by 'Scott.' There is certainly ample textual support for Pears' argument. Pears himself cites the following passage from Hume's *Abstract* to the *Treatise*: 'And when he [Hume anonymously referring to himself] suspects that any philosophical term has no idea annexed to it (as is too common) he always asks from what impression that presented idea is derived? And if no impression can be produced, he concludes that the term is altogether insignificant' (A 648–9). Hume will make this exact point again in his first *Enquiry*, and thus it appears one finds in Hume an anticipation of the critique of metaphysics one finds in the logical positivists – namely, a philosophical problem is a pseudo-problem if it cannot be referred to, or resolved by means of, a verifiable sense impression.

Turning to Hume's dismissal of the significance of the missing shade of blue, Pears argues that it should not be swept under the rug. To the contrary, if one insists on the externality of relations – that is, on the claim that there are no intrinsic relations between ideas and impressions, and that they constitute merely a collection of separable, distinct, simple, and indivisible impressions – then one such as Hume is led to a form of atomism that leaves them unable to account for the idea of the missing shade of blue. For Pears, both Russell and Wittgenstein attempted to do this as well, 'But genuine simplicity proved unattainable, and he [Wittgenstein] soon abandoned his atomism in favour of holism. Hume should have done the same' (Pears 1989, 27).

Jonathan Bennett has also faulted Hume for not taking the case of the missing shade of blue seriously. For Bennett, the difficulty for Hume arises from making vivacity the sole differentiator of impressions and ideas. In presenting an example to illustrate the difficulties this leads to, Bennett proposes the following:

> Here I am with an idea with a certain kind of sound. Being convinced [that all our ideas are derived from corresponding impressions] I conclude that I once had an impression of such a sound, though I have no memory of it. This conclusion is an idea [belief] of mine, which means that it has more vivacity than the idea [that is, the mere thought] had a moment ago. Where did the vivacity come from? (Bennett 2001, 206)

For Bennett, Hume never resolves this or other problems, one way out of which would have been to understand the copy thesis 'in terms not of phenomenological "vivacity," but rather of involving experience of an objective world' (ibid. 212). In short, Bennett argues that the best defense of Hume's system would be to understand Hume's use of the copy principle as an effort 'to offer meaning-criticism in the light of word–word and word–world relations,' even though, Bennett adds, Hume 'had not the theoretical and terminological tools to do this properly' (ibid. 216). Rather than analyzing the meanings of words in terms of both their interdependent relationships to other words in the language (*à la* Ferdinand de Saussure) and/or the world, Hume instead reduces everything to a hierarchy built upon independent, distinct, simple impressions. Echoing Pears' criticism of Hume's atomism, Bennett believes that in fact there 'are no "simple ideas" in Hume's sense,' hence the subsequent 'problem with the simple missing shade of blue' (ibid. 217). Had Hume developed an approach to meaning-criticism that accepted an *interdependence* of word–word and word–world relationships, the missing shade of blue could have been accounted for; as it is, however, Bennett concludes that there is 'no defense for Hume's complacent dismissal of what he ought to have seen as a serious problem' (ibid. 218).

In his defense of Hume, Don Garrett relies on a passage from the *Abstract* to the *Treatise* where Hume argues that 'even different simple ideas may have a similarity or resemblance to each other,' noting that 'Blue and green are different simple ideas, but are more resembling than blue and scarlet' (A 637).[3] The significance of this, for Garrett, is that it challenges the assumption of many commentators, such as Pears and Bennett, that Hume was a strict nominalist who reduced all simple ideas to the logically simple, independent impressions that must correspond to these ideas. In the case of blue and green and blue and scarlet, the greater resemblance of the former pair over the latter cannot be reduced to either of the simple impressions. The simple ideas, blue and green, can therefore be compared while remaining simple and distinct, and without bringing in a common third element to serve as a basis for comparison. In fact, Hume asserts that 'These [simple ideas] admit of infinite resemblances upon the general appearance and comparison, without having any common circumstance the same' (ibid.). Once this is admitted, Garrett argues, then resemblances among simple impressions of blue can form the basis for the idea of the missing shade of blue without violating the simplicity of the impressions that are being compared. Garrett thus concludes that 'although the idea of the missing shade of blue need not . . . be derived from an exactly corresponding impression, it is still ultimately derived from a set of very closely resembling impressions' (Garrett 1997, 52).[4] For Bennett, however, 'As soon as he [Garrett] admits that the copy thesis is false,' that there are indeed cases where a simple idea is not derived from a corresponding simple impression, then 'the game is up' (Bennett 2001, 220).

Central to the difficulties Pears and Bennett (among many others) have with Hume's 'complacent dismissal' of the missing shade of blue is the notion that simple ideas are derived from impressions that are autonomous, independent identities. In other words, the problem with the idea of the missing shade of blue is that it is an improper idea, an idea fabricated with no relationship to an independent impression that would give it validity. By Hume's own standards, such an idea is to be rejected, for 'if no impression can be produced' to back up a given idea, then the idea itself 'is altogether insignificant,' or, as the famous closing lines to Hume's first *Enquiry* have it: if a text of metaphysics and philosophy does not 'contain any experimental reasoning concerning matter of fact and existence,' then one ought to 'commit it then to the flames: for it can contain nothing but sophistry and illusion' (EHU 165). And in yet another, more relevant instance, Hume, in letters to friends regarding the blind poet Thomas Blacklock, claims that 'He is a very elegant, correct Poet: He even employs the Ideas of Light and Colors with great Propriety' (L1 195). In accounting for this Hume adds 'that as he [Blacklock] met so often both in books and conversation, with the terms expressing colours, he had formed some false associations, which supported him when he read, wrote, or talked of colours . . .' (L1 201). The moral Hume draws from the case of Blacklock is that ''Tis certain we always think in some language, viz. in that which is most familiar to us; and 'tis but too frequent to substitute words instead of ideas' (ibid.). In other words, Blacklock is using words whose associations are only with other words, and although Blacklock is able to utilize these associations with 'great Propriety,' they are still 'false associations' since they are not related to independent impressions. It is, therefore, the autonomous reality and identity of impressions that seems to be, for Hume, as for Pears and Bennett, the condition that allows for true, meaningful associations.

At the basis of this reading of Hume, however, is an understanding of simple impressions and ideas that presupposes their identity as an already constituted fact that serves as the given of Hume's system. Such an understanding does not stand up to a close reading of Hume's *Treatise*. The problem with this view is precisely the assumption that the atoms (simple impressions and ideas) are identities, identities that exist without the type of 'lateral relations' Pears believes would help explain the idea of the missing shade of blue.[5] Identity, however, is for Hume, as we will see, underdetermined; rather than being the determinate basis for Hume's theory, as Pears sees it, identity forever needs to be determined, constituted, systematized, and maintained.[6] There is no identity, then, inseparable from a constitutive process, an historical ontology, and thus, as will be argued, the duality between fictioning/fabricating on the one hand, and autonomous, independent reality and identity on the other, is a false duality. It is no wonder then that Deleuze, in his efforts to develop a philosophy of difference, found an initial inspiration in the work of Hume.

Hume's discussion of identity occurs at a crucial part of the *Treatise*, towards the end of Book I. After offering a summary of his system, and how it accounts for the 'idea of continu'd existence,' Hume claims that the principle of identity is crucial for the system. And yet, he admits, identity cannot arise from the perception of 'one single object,' for this 'conveys the idea of unity, not that of identity' – that is, not the continued identity of this object in time; nor can a multiplicity of objects convey this idea, for here one finds separable and distinct existences, not the continued self-identity of one and the same existence. Hume then offers the following solution:

> To remove this difficulty, let us have recourse to the idea of time or duration. I have already observ'd, that time, in a strict sense, implies succession, and that when we apply its idea to any unchangeable object [i.e., to a unity], 'tis only by a fiction of the imagination, by which the unchangeable object is suppos'd to participate of the changes of the co-existent objects, and in particular that of our perceptions. This fiction of the imagination almost universally takes place; and 'tis by means of it, that a single object, plac'd before us, and survey'd for any time without discovering in it any interruption or variation, is able to give us a notion of identity. (T 200–1)

As Hume will clarify a few lines later, this fiction creates a difference within the unchanging object, a difference that enables us to see the object as the same as itself at a *different* time. Identity, in other words, is the result of an artifice, a fiction, and thus the identity of any object, whether it is an indivisible atom, a self, and so on, is inseparable from a generative, systematizing process. As a fiction, however, identity is by no means false or lacking in reality; rather, the idea of continued existence through time is an idea that applies to that from which it cannot be derived – namely, sense impressions.[7] And it is precisely at this point that Deleuze's transcendental empiricism becomes most evident, for as Deleuze encapsulates his own project, it is to be contrasted with 'everything that makes up the world of the subject and the object' (PI 25). In other words, rather than presupposing the identity of a consciousness that is a consciousness of an identifiable object, transcendental empiricism concerns itself with what Deleuze will refer to as a transcendental field of pre-individual singularities and virtualities that are presupposed by the actualities of conscious experience. Thus, in the same way that the transcendental field of virtualities cannot be identified in the proper way – that is, by way of the subject–object distinction, or by way of identity period – so too for Hume, the idea of continued existence through time is presupposed by our concrete everyday, vulgar experience of the world, by our experience of objects as continued, self-identical objects separate from us as identifiable subjects, and yet this idea cannot be understood in the terms that it makes possible and to which it applies. Therefore, before returning to Hume's quick dismissal of the missing shade of blue, and to the criticisms this provoked, we will first address the transcendental empiricism Deleuze finds in Hume. In doing this, we will begin to set the stage for showing that Hume was quite right to pass over the missing shade of blue as an instance that 'is so particular and singular, that 'tis scarce worth our observing, and does not merit that for it alone we should alter our general maxim [i.e., the copy principle]' (T 6).

II. Transcendental Empiricism

In delineating the transcendental empiricism he sees at work in Hume, Deleuze claims that the transcendental component involves addressing the question, 'how can something be given to a subject, and how can the subject give something to itself?'; while the empiricist aspect addresses the question, 'how is the subject constituted in the given?' (ES 87). More to the point, for Deleuze the question becomes one of ascertaining how the subject can be constituted in the given without being reducible to it, and for Deleuze, Hume is quite clear on how this is done – it is through belief and invention: 'Belief and invention are the two modes of transcendence' (ES 132). It is precisely through the creativity of invention and belief that the multiplicity of ideas becomes a system: 'The subject invents; it is the maker of artifice. Such is the dual power of subjectivity: to believe and to invent, to assume the secret powers and to presuppose abstract or distinct powers . . . This subject who invents and believes is constituted inside the given in such a way that it makes the given itself a synthesis and a system' (ES 86–7). These powers that constitute the subject within the given, and a subject able to invent and believe, are the principles of human nature. Deleuze is clear on this point:

> The most important point is to be found here. The entire sense of the principles of human nature is to transform the multiplicity of ideas which constitute the mind into a system, that is, a system of knowledge and of its objects . . . [but for this to be possible] we must give the object of the idea an existence which does not depend on the senses. (ES 80)

The way in which the principles do this involves a double process. First, 'within the collection [multiplicity], the principle elects, chooses, designates, and invites certain impressions of sensation among others.' For example, 'the principles of passion are those that choose the impressions of pleasure and pain,' and 'the principles of association . . . choose the perception that must be brought together into a composite.' As for the second process, the principle 'constitutes impressions of reflection in connection with these elected impressions' (ES 113).[8] What does this mean? For Deleuze, what Hume means by this is that 'the principle produces a habit, a strength, and a power to evoke any other idea of the same group; it produces an impression of reflection' (ES 114). This double process, however, mirrors a more profound double process for Hume, namely the processes associated with the passions on the one hand and the principles of association on the other. And Hume, as Deleuze reads him, gives clear primacy to the passions: 'Association gives the subject a possible structure, but only the passions can give it being and existence . . . the principles of the passions are absolutely primary' (ES 120). To restate this using Deleuze's much later terminology of double articulation, the principles of human nature draw the multiplicity of ideas into a 'possible structure' through the association of ideas (first articulation), and the principles of human nature actualize this possible structure by way of the passions (second articulation). By prioritizing the passions, therefore, Hume gives preference to the actual demands and passions, and the creativity of invention and belief are subordinate to these actual demands (hence Hume's famous statement that reason is and ought to be the slave of the passions [T 415]).

We can now also restate, in Deleuze's terms, the process whereby the underdetermination of identity becomes determined, or the process whereby the identity of blue as a simple impression gives rise to a simple idea that copies it. In the first articulation, an unchanging object becomes related, through a fiction or artifice that is nonetheless natural, to a consistent series of others that change in time. In the second articulation, this series is then synthesized or actualized through an impression of reflection whereby what is constituted is the felt identity or belief of an object in time. We can now see why Hume dismisses the case of the missing shade of blue. Put simply, Hume dismisses the case of the missing shade precisely because it is singular; in other words, the idea of the missing shade of blue is subsumed by the felt identity of the synthesis of the resembling shades of blue, and thus the singularity of the missing shade does not derail the established habits associated with 'blue' – that is, it does not call for a new synthesis.[9] In the case of the Laplanders, an example from Hume's first *Enquiry*, they can form no idea of wine because they have not even had the first in a series of wine-impressions, and thus they cannot even begin fictioning or synthesizing the identity associated with wine.

This double process also clarifies another crucial aspect of Hume's work, the relationship between the understanding and society. As Deleuze states it, there are 'two points of view [that] coexist in Hume: the passions and the understanding present themselves, in a way which must be made clear, as two distinct parts. By itself, though, the understanding is only the process of the passions on their way to socialization' (ES 22). We have seen how the multiplicity of ideas is transformed, through a double process, into the impressions of reflection that create beliefs, habits, and tendencies which constitute, within the given, that which transcends it. The same process is at work within socialization, though this time the multiplicity that comes to be transformed into a system or unity are the partialities, passions, and interests of individuals. Again Deleuze is quite clear on this point: 'Partialities or particular interests cannot be naturally totalized, because they are mutually exclusive. One can only invent a whole, since the only invention possible is that of the whole' (ES 40). This leads Hume, according to Deleuze, to an understanding of society not as a law established to escape our state of nature (*à la* Hobbes), but rather as invented institutions, inventions that are themselves indistinguishable from human nature in that they follow from the principles of human nature:

> The main idea is this: the essence of society is not the law but rather the institution . . . institution, unlike the law, is not a limitation [as Hobbes would understand it] but rather a model of actions, a veritable enterprise, an invented system of positive means or a positive invention of indirect means. (ES 45–6)

What such institutions attempt to do, then, is not to function as representatives of a general interest or a general will, but rather to operate so as to make 'the general interest an object of belief' (ES 51). Such an operation, if successful, will 'enter the natural constitution of the mind as a feeling for humanity or as culture' (ES 130). And it is with this constitution, or invention, of social institutions that the multiplicity of partialities and interests comes to be transcended by the feeling for humanity, such that one comes to be socialized and cultured.

With this latter move, we come to a core concern of Hume's – namely, the relationship between society and what he calls, in his essay of the same name, 'the rise and progress of the arts and sciences.' In this essay Hume recognizes that since the geniuses of the arts and sciences are frequently few in number, to discuss the conditions that give rise to them may seem a futile task, but he argues that though they 'be always few in all nations and all ages, it is impossible but a share of the same spirit and genius must be antecedently diffused throughout the people among whom they arise, in order to produce, form, and cultivate, from their earliest infancy, the taste and judgment of those eminent writers' (EMPL 114). This diffusion of 'the same spirit and genius' 'throughout the people' – or what Deleuze might call the drawing of a multiplicity into a plane of consistency – is the condition that allows for the actualization of the great geniuses and hence for the rise and progress of the arts and sciences. Moreover, as Hume makes quite clear, such geniuses were able to create the works for which they are known only when they were able to experiment in a manner such that their works were not predetermined and prejudged by established national models:

> A man's genius is always, in the beginning of life, as much unknown to himself as to others; and it is only after frequent trials, attended with success, that he dares think himself equal to those undertakings, in which those who have succeeded have fixed the admiration of mankind. If his own nation be already possessed of many models of eloquence, he naturally compares his own juvenile exercises with these; and, being sensible of the great disproportion, is discouraged from any further attempts, and never aims at a rivalship with those authors whom he so much admires. (EMPL 135)

With this recognition of the significance of 'frequent trials' whose outcome is not predetermined, we can see once again the convergence of Hume's project with that of Deleuze. For Deleuze, transcendental empiricism is a creative experimental project whose outcome is not predetermined. Deleuze will later refer to this project as pragmatics, intentionally alluding to pragmatism. To further clarify Deleuze's transcendental empiricism, his pragmatics, we shall briefly compare Deleuze's project with the radical empiricism of William James.

III. Radical Empiricism

It might seem ill-advised to bring in James' radical empiricism to bolster Deleuze's Humean transcendental empiricism. Although James finds promise in Hume's analysis of causation as arising from the customary transition we feel as a result of the constant conjunction of two impressions, James ultimately believes that Hume never fully embraced the reality of this conjunction. To the contrary, James claims that Hume, rather than affirm the reality of these conjunctive relationships, follows the 'conceptualist rule' whereby if 'there is a separate name there ought to be a fact as separate,' and consequently Hume is led by 'this rule [to hold that] every conjunction and preposition in human speech is meaningless' (James 1987, 1083–4). In short, by arguing that 'any fact of reality must be separable,' Hume, James contends, is led 'to his preposterous view, that no relation can be real' (ibid. 1084). And this 'preposterous view,' James concludes, is typical of the 'intellectualist method [which] pulverize[s] perception and triumph[s] over life' (ibid.). By reducing causality to a feeling derived from a constant conjunction of distinct and separable impressions, Hume thereby effectively eliminates the possibility for novelty, since to see a novel thing as caused would entail that it already be identified and associated with that which is believed to cause it. 'The effect,' James argues, 'in some way already exists in the cause. If this be so, the effect cannot be absolutely novel, and in no radical sense can pluralism be true' (ibid. 1079).

With respect to this last claim, Hume might very well reply by pointing out that a consequence of asserting that there are no intrinsic relations between a cause and its effect is precisely to assert that a cause does not contain the effect. Nevertheless, if the emergence of novelty involves a causal relationship that is unprecedented, it does appear difficult to see how Hume could affirm and recognize a novel effect as an effect without presupposing prior conjunctions of this effect with a preceding cause. This, however, would rule out the possibility for novelty. Had Hume embraced the reality of conjunctive relations – in short, had he been a pluralist or radical empiricist as James understands it – he would then have both been able to avoid the skepticism regarding causal relations for which he received much criticism, and been able to account adequately for novelty. It would thus seem that James is not the proper place to turn for a clarification of Deleuze's Humean transcendental empiricism. And yet James' criticisms, as with Pears' and Bennett's discussed earlier, assume the already established identities of the simple impressions and ideas, identities that are distinct and separable. However, as will be argued in this and later chapters, the transcendental empiricism Deleuze finds in Hume is not at odds with James' radical empiricism.

This is clearly recognized by Deleuze when he identifies himself as 'an empiricist, that is, a pluralist' (D vii), thereby immediately and self-consciously placing his thought into a context James would likely also recognize as his own. For Deleuze, as we have seen, to be a pluralist entails not using the abstract to explain a state of affairs, but rather beginning with the assumption that the abstract 'must itself be explained,' and explained in a way that enables one to 'find the conditions under which something new is produced (creativeness)' (ibid.). This is the task of empiricism as Deleuze understands it, a task he admits is at odds with the traditional view of empiricism:

> Empiricism is often defined as a doctrine according to which the intelligible 'comes' from the sensible, everything in the understanding comes from the senses. But that is the standpoint of the history of philosophy: they have the gift of stifling all life in seeking and in positing an abstract first principle. (D 55)

The key to the empiricism Deleuze believes does not stifle life, in contrast to the view of empiricism offered by the 'history of philosophy,' is to affirm, as does James, the reality of conjunctive relationships: 'Thinking with AND, instead of thinking IS, instead of thinking for IS: empiricism has never had another secret. Try it, it is a quite extraordinary thought, and yet it is life' (D 57).

With his radical empiricism, James pointedly contrasts his own view of empiricism with what he takes to be the intellectualist version one finds in Hume. 'Ordinary empiricism,' James claims, 'has always shown a tendency to do away with the connections of things, and to insist most on the disjunctions' (James 1987, 1160), whereas an empiricism that is radical takes 'every thing that comes without disfavor, conjunction as well as separation, each at its face value . . . Radical empiricism, as I understand it, does full justice to conjunctive relations' (ibid. 1161).[10] And yet the path that led James to radical empiricism was neither easy nor straightforward. The crucial problem that kept James from readily giving 'full justice to conjunctive relations' was the effort to account for how many consciousnesses 'can be at the same time one consciousness . . . How can one and the same identical fact experience itself so diversely?' (ibid. 723). James found himself unable to address these questions – 'I found myself in an impasse' (ibid.) – until he read Bergson and came to recognize the need to give up the logic of the one and the multiple – the logic that there are either singular, multiple identities that are separable and distinct [i.e., atomism], or there is an absolute one. As Deleuze would also do much later, James garnered from Bergson the concept of multiplicity, whereby a multiplicity is understood to exceed the logic of the one and the multiple. 'Reality, life, experience, concreteness, immediacy,' James argues, 'use what word you will, exceeds our logic [of the one-multiple], overflows and surrounds it' (ibid. 725). James will come to refer to this 'reality, life, experience, concreteness, [and] immediacy' that exceeds the logic of the one and the multiple as 'pure experience':

> My thesis is that if we start with the supposition that there is only one primal stuff or material in the world, a stuff of which everything is composed, and if we call that stuff 'pure experience,' then knowing can easily be explained as a particular sort of relation towards one another into which portions of pure experience may enter. (Ibid. 1142)

This pure experience is not an identifiable one from which the multiple comes about by subtraction; to the contrary, James argues that 'the separation of it [pure experience] into consciousness and content comes, not by way of subtraction, but by way of addition,' and thus he adds that 'a given undivided portion of experience, taken in one context of associates, plays the part of a knower, of a state of mind, of "consciousness"; while in a different context the same undivided bit of experience plays the part of a thing known, of an objective "content"' (ibid.). To clarify this point by way of analogy, James argues that just as one point can be on two lines at the intersection so too can 'the "pure experience" of [a] room [be] a place of intersection of two processes, which connected it with different groups of associates respectively . . .' (ibid. 1146). In and of itself, pure experience is the reality that forever exceeds – by the power of conjunction, the power of

AND – the realities with which it comes to be identified. As James puts it, 'the instant field of the present is at all times what I call the "pure" experience. It is only virtually or potentially either object or subject as yet. For the time being, it is plain, unqualified actuality or existence, a simple that' (ibid. 1151). As virtually object or subject, pure experience does not predetermine its actualization as subject or object; rather, there are always further actualizations, further novelties, for pure experience that exceed the actualizations that have already occurred. It is in this way, then, that pure experience allows James to account for 'the conditions under which something new is produced,' in that pure experience, as the reality of the virtual, does not contain within it the identity of that which comes to be actualized. Rather, pure experience is the reality of conjunctive relations, the power of AND, that exceeds the identities of what IS and allows, by adding to the actuality of what is, for the emergence of new identities. This pure experience, however, is not a reality separate from the reality of the actual; it is not an otherworldly reality. To the contrary, James identifies pure experience with the very concrete immediacy and reality of life itself. With references to examples that will also become prominent in Giorgio Agamben's work, and for much the same reason, James argues that

> 'Pure experience' is the name which I give to the immediate flux of life which furnishes the material to our later reflection with its conceptual categories. Only new-born babes, or men in semi-coma from sleep, drugs, illnesses, or blows, may be assumed to have an experience pure in the literal sense of that which is not yet any definite what, tho ready to be all sorts of what; full both of oneness and of manyness, but in respects that don't appear; changing throughout, yet so confusedly that its phases interpenetrate and no points, either of distinction or of identity, can be caught . . . But the flux of it no sooner comes than it tends to fill itself with emphases, and these salient parts become identified and fixed and abstracted; so that experience now flows as if shot through with adjectives and nouns and prepositions and conjunctions. (Ibid. 782–3)[11]

Pure experience is thus the concept that enabled James to resolve his prior impasse concerning the one and the multiple, and it allowed him to avoid the intellectualist tendency to stifle life – a tendency James found in Hume and which left Hume unable, as we saw James argue, to account for novelty. Before addressing the extent to which we believe James has wrongly placed Hume in the intellectualist camp while Deleuze rightly saw in him an early proponent of the empiricism James, Bergson, and Deleuze himself (among others) will later take up, we will first turn to address Deleuze's understanding of the reality of the virtual. This discussion will not only give further details to James' understanding of pure experience, but will also allow us to address some of the more frequent criticisms that have been directed towards Deleuze's philosophy. With this in hand, we will then be able to return to Hume and see how the transcendental empiricism Deleuze finds in Hume not only avoids the criticisms set forth by Pears, Bennett, and James, but more importantly offers a critique of the very presuppositions that give these criticisms their weight.

IV. Reality of the Virtual

In his book *Deleuze: The Clamor of Being*, Badiou focuses upon the theory of the virtual and directs his harshest criticisms of Deleuze at this theory. Badiou argues that in claiming that the virtual is complete in itself and yet only part of an actual object, the *indiscernible* part, Deleuze stumbles because of his commitment to the univocity of One Being, to affirming 'a single and same voice for the whole thousand-voiced multiple, a single and same Ocean for all the drops, a single clamour of Being for all beings' (DR 304).[12] As Badiou states his criticism:

> when the only way of saving – despite everything – the One, is by resorting to an unthinkable Two, an indiscernibility beyond remedy . . . one says to oneself that, most decidedly, the virtual is no better than the finality of which it is the inversion (it determines the destiny of everything, instead of being that to which everything is destined). Let us be particularly harsh and invoke Spinoza against his major, and indeed sole, truly modern disciple: just like finality, the virtual is *ignorantiae asylum*. (Badiou 2000, 53)

To respond to this criticism we can return to Spinoza himself, and especially to a problem many commentators have had with Spinoza's *Ethics* – namely, the relationship of the attributes to the modes of these attributes. Badiou himself notes this problem, recognizing that 'Although it is on the basis of which the attributive identifications of substance exist, the intellect itself is clearly a mode of the attribute "thought"' (Badiou 2004, 84). Stating the problem baldly, Badiou asks, 'how is it possible to think the being of intellect, the "there is intellect," if rational access to the thought of being or the "there is" itself depends upon the operations of the intellect?' (ibid.) This problem has long been recognized by Spinoza scholars and has received a number of solutions.[13] Badiou's particular solution, however, is quite revealing.

At the basis of Badiou's understanding of the relationship between the infinite intellect, as an infinite mode of the attribute thought, and the attribute thought itself, is the premise that the intellect is distinct from the objects that are objects or 'ideas of' the intellect. For Badiou, then, since 'every idea is an "idea of," it is correlated with an ideatum,' it follows that 'the attributes of God and the modes of these attributes are objects of the infinite intellect' (ibid. 86). With these assumptions in play, Badiou is naturally led to conclude that 'the attribute of thought is not isomorphic with any of the other attributes' (ibid. 88) for the very reason that it is an infinite mode of this attribute that has, as its object, the other attributes, thereby constituting the essence of substance. Add to this claim Badiou's extension of Spinoza's argument – in the Demonstration to 2P21 that 'the mind is united to the body from the fact that the body is the object of the mind' – and it again follows for Badiou that there must then be 'instances of union that straddle the disjunction between attributes. It is this union, the radical singularity proper to the operations of the intellect, which I call coupling' (ibid. 87). In other words, since the infinite intellect, as an infinite mode of thought, is united to the objects that are its ideas – the other attributes – it is 'coupled' to these other attributes, a coupling made possible by the attribute thought that is not 'isomorphic with any of the other attributes.'

These arguments lead Badiou to a surprising conclusion. With the notion of coupling, a notion Badiou admits is not to be found in Spinoza but is necessary to make sense of Spinoza's (supposed) understanding of the relationship between the infinite intellect and the objects that are the distinct objects of this intellect, Badiou claims a further consequence follows: 'As a matter of fact, infinite intellect by itself constitutes an exception to the famous Proposition 7 of Book II: "The order and connection of ideas is the same as the order and connection of things" ' (ibid. 88). Because the intellect is coupled to the other attributes and to their modes, the order of the ideas in the infinite intellect is not the same as the order and connection of things, for the infinite intellect is what makes possible the very actuality of attributes and things, and hence the parallelism between them.[14] Yet it is just this conclusion, that the intellect is an exception to Spinoza's famous parallelism, that Spinoza himself would likely find unrecognizable.

The reason Badiou is led to what we believe is a mistaken conclusion concerning the relationship between the attributes and their modes is that he presupposes the *identity* of both the infinite intellect and the attributes and modes that are the identifiable objects of this intellect. For Deleuze, however, the best way to understand the relationship between the attributes and the infinite intellect is to argue for the primacy of the modes themselves.[15] In other words, there is the necessity for the modification of an attribute – infinite thought – as that which perceives substance and constitutes its identifiable, actualized essence, precisely because the attribute is identifiable as such only as actualized in a mode. The attributes are thus not distinct identities or objects waiting for the infinite intellect to perceive them; rather, it is the very perception of the attributes by the infinite intellect (as infinite mode) that actualizes the identifiable essence of substance itself. Furthermore, if one understands Spinoza's notion of substance as absolutely indeterminate, the attributes can then be understood as the condition for determining the infinite and infinitely determinable essence of substance.[16] This identifiable essence is made possible by the actualization of a mode of an attribute, and substance is therefore identifiable as such only when actualized within a mode – that is, the infinite intellect. Unlike Badiou's, this conclusion is not one Spinoza would find unrecognizable, but instead simply repeats Spinoza's own definition of the attributes: '1D4: By attribute I understand what the intellect perceives of a substance, as constituting its essence.'

It is this relationship between the modes and attributes that is, we argue, extended by Deleuze in his understanding of the relationship between the virtual and the actual. Just as the attributes are the conditions that allow for the possibility of determining, by way of the intellect, absolutely indeterminate substance, so too the virtual is indiscernible from the actual not as a distinct *identity* that is to be contrasted to the *identity* of the actual, but rather as the condition for identity itself. How, then, as Badiou might ask, can we know that the virtual is real, as Deleuze contends,[17] if it is indiscernible? The reason Badiou might ask such a question – why he finds the virtual problematic in its purported resort to an 'unthinkable Two' (Badiou 2000, 53) – is because he subordinates knowing to a conceptual knowing, whereas Deleuze, in good Nietzschean-pragmatist fashion, subordinates knowing to the practical problems that are inseparable – indiscernible – from the actualities that are themselves the identifiable solutions to these problems.[18]

We can turn to an example from a perhaps unexpected source to clarify Deleuze's understanding of the reality of the virtual and the process or problem that is inseparable (indiscernible) from the actualization of this virtual. This is the work by David Sudnow, *Ways of Hand*, a book that describes in minute detail the processes and challenges Sudnow encountered in learning improvisational jazz. After mastering the technical difficulties of moving effortlessly across the keyboard, a more fundamental problem confronted Sudnow as he sat down to play improvisational jazz – where to go? As Sudnow puts it, 'when it came to sitting down at the piano, it was a rhythm of something, an intensity of something, an intonational structure of something, subtleties of something, and the something that first mattered was: these and those particular notes being played . . . but the prime question,' Sudnow adds, in trying 'to make up melodies with the right hand, was, Where?' (Sudnow 1978, 15). In other words, in encountering the virtual reality of the notes, for the notes are indeed real, the problem in making up melodies is precisely in how to actualize these melodies, where to go with the virtual so that it can become an orderly actual, a melody. Sudnow told his teacher, 'tell me where to go,' and though hesitant, the teacher, when pushed, was able to give Sudnow a list of scalar devices (i.e., jazz sounding scales, runs, and so on) that Sudnow then incorporated into an expanding repertoire of skills, of predetermined paths in short.

These scalar devices, however, did not of themselves constitute improvisational jazz. As Sudnow watched his teacher play, for example, 'he was flying over the keyboard, producing the jazz I wanted so much to be doing . . . he was not simply using the few scalar devices that I had been employing for each of the chord types. He was going many more places over the keyboard . . . [and yet he was] "orderly" ' (ibid. 25). The problem for Sudnow, in short, was that he experienced the reality of the virtual – namely, the excessive multiplicity of ways to go – and sought to actualize it as a determinate and orderly sequence of notes rather than the indeterminate and indefinite number he was encountering. Occasionally, while playing improvisational jazz, Sudnow would stumble upon 'good-sounding jazz that would come out in the midst of my improvisations,' but when he tried to 'latch on' to the melody, take charge of it and direct it, 'it would be undermined, as when one first gets the knack of a complex skill, like riding a bicycle or skiing, the attempt to sustain an easeful management undercuts it' (ibid. 83–4). Rather than encountering the multiplicity of melodic paths and actualizing it in a sustained path, Sudnow instead found himself lunging for a melodic path that was prefigured.[19] What he was slowly finding himself doing as he become more adept at improvisational jazz was to affirm the multiplicity, to let it sing in a jazzy way. Sudnow realized 'there is no melody, there is melodying' (ibid. 146). There is no predetermined way to actualize an improvised melody, there is simply the process whereby the jazz phonemes become actualized, or there is melodying. As Sudnow began to play improvisational jazz with more success, he recognized that he no longer needed to lunge but could instead find the notes where his hands were rather than predetermining the path his hands should take. Sudnow is explicit on this point: 'I began to see and then find use for further work in the observation that note choices could be made anywhere, that there was no need to lunge, that usable notes for any chord lay just at hand, that there was no need to find a path, image one up ahead to get ready in advance for a blurting out [i.e. a lunging]' (ibid. 94). In other words, the reality of the virtual is indiscernible from the actual, as Deleuze argues, precisely because the virtual is only identifiable as actualized. Although Sudnow did indeed experience the reality of the virtual as an indeterminate, indefinable multiplicity – much as an infant, for James, can be said to have an indeterminate, indefinable 'pure experience' – this experience is the power of excess, the power of AND, inseparable from that which actualizes it. The reality of the virtual is thus not out of this world, but is rather the life of this world that cannot be reduced to the identities of conceptual analysis, just as improvisational jazz cannot be reduced to a set of scalar devices. Although Hume has been criticized, as we have seen, for reducing experience to the identities of conceptual, intellectual analysis, with his concept of belief, coupled with the fictioning of identity discussed earlier, it will be seen that Hume's philosophy belongs fully within the empiricist tradition, and it is this tradition that Deleuze sought to carry forward.

V. Belief

With Hume's notion of belief, we return to the problems Deleuze associates with transcendental empiricism – namely, how the multiplicity of ideas and impressions that constitute the mind becomes a system, and related to this how a subject comes to be constituted within the given in such a way that it transcends the given. For Deleuze, Hume's understanding of belief is pivotal to his approach to these problems. Deleuze is quite blunt: 'through belief and causality the subject transcends the given,' but 'before there can be belief,' Deleuze adds, 'all three principles of association must organize the given into a system, imposing constancy on the imagination' (ES 24). In short, through belief, and in particular through belief in necessary, causal relationships, the mind transcends the given. On this point, Hume is quite clear as well, arguing that causation is the only 'relation of objects, which can lead us beyond the immediate impressions of our memory and senses' (T 89). This comes about, however, as Deleuze stresses, only after the mind itself has acquired the consistency and systematicity necessary for the belief in causation to occur, and yet this consistency can draw on no resources other than the principles of human nature. As Deleuze puts it, 'the given, the mind, the collection of perceptions cannot call upon anything other than themselves' (ES 89). The problem for transcendental empiricism, therefore, stated in terms Deleuze will later use, is to embrace a philosophy of immanence that can account for transcendence without presupposing the very transcendence to be explained. In the context of Hume, this emerges as the problem of accounting for the transcendence of the given in a way that does not 'call upon anything other than [the given] themselves.'

For Hume the simple answer to how the mind comes to transcend the given is 'by custom.' 'Our idea,' Hume states, 'of necessity and causation arises entirely from the uniformity observable in the operations of nature, where similar objects are constantly conjoined together, and the mind is determined by custom to infer the one from the appearance of the other'. Without this 'constant conjunction of similar objects,' Hume concludes, we would 'have no notion of any necessity or connexion' (EHU 82). The principles of association, therefore, systematize or stage the mind by drawing the impressions and ideas into relations that allow for easier transitions from one idea to another. In the *Treatise* Hume claims that this move towards easy, smooth transitions is the result of 'principles [of human nature] which are permanent, irresistible, and universal; such as the customary transition from causes to effects' (T 225). For Deleuze, the mind has 'become nature' when it 'has acquired a tendency'; or, as he also puts it, 'reason is imagination that has become nature' (ES 25, 65).[20]

Key to the process of acquiring a tendency or nature, Deleuze argues, is the fictioning of identity. What is so crucial for Deleuze about the necessity of fiction – why 'fiction' itself becomes, on Deleuze's reading, 'a principle of human nature' – is that 'for a system to exist, it is not enough to have ideas associated in the mind; it is also necessary that perceptions be regarded as separate from the mind, and that impressions be in some manner torn from the senses' (ES 80). In other words, for a multiplicity of impressions and ideas to become an identifiable system that can then be an object of knowledge and belief, an identity that is irreducible to the impressions must be forged. For Deleuze, this occurs when ' "a seeming interruption" of an appearance to the senses is surpassed "by [the] feigning [of] a continu'd being which may fill those intervals, and preserve a perfect and entire identity to our perceptions" ' (ibid.).[21] By way of this 'feigning' or 'fiction,' Deleuze believes 'the system is completed in the identity between system and world' (ibid.). If left to themselves, the principles of association would simply enable the easy transition from one perception to another, but they would not give us distinct identities that are irreducible to these perceptions. The fiction that feigns continued existence is thus not fictional in the sense that what is fictioned is not real; to the contrary, the very reality of identifiable objects in the world is itself fictioned, and it is this fiction that enables the principles of association, with all their skeptical implications, to function as a corrective to our beliefs in objects and the world. It is in this sense then that Deleuze argues that

> The imagination is opposed, as a principle, that is, as a principle of the world, to the principles which fix it and to the operations which correct it. To the extent that fiction, along with the World, count among the principles, the principles of association encounter fiction, and are opposed to it, without being able to eliminate it. (ES 82)[22]

Our belief in the world of independent objects, therefore, is not a belief that can be derived from any sense impressions, but rather than see this, as Pears, Bennett, and others might, as yet further evidence against Hume's copy principle, on Deleuze's reading our belief in the world is the very principle [fiction as principle] that enables the principles of association to begin their work of associating *identifiable* impressions and ideas.[23] It is for this reason that Deleuze stresses the significance for Hume of 'practice' (ES 84).

In particular, the general rules of practice and ethics function as 'the middle and temperate region, where the contradiction between human nature [and the principles of association] and the [principle of] imagination already exists, and always subsists, but this contradiction is regulated by possible corrections and resolved through practice' (ibid.) Through practice, and the general rules that both guide practice while being derived from it, the excesses of an imagination that can generate fictions that are untethered to perceptions come to be reconciled with the principles of association that do not, of themselves, lead one beyond the perceptions themselves. Delirium and madness, as Deleuze will often say, and as we will explore in later chapters, are inseparable from our belief in the world.

To clarify Deleuze's reading of Hume, it will be helpful at this point to turn to what has come to be called the New Hume debate. The central question of this debate concerns what Hume meant by causal powers. More precisely, how one is to take Hume's statements that appear to affirm the presence of secret, causal powers within the objective, natural world? In his first *Enquiry*, for example, Hume claims that

> It must certainly be allowed, that nature has kept us at a great distance from all her secrets, and has afforded us only the knowledge of a few superficial qualities of objects; while she conceals from us those powers and principles on which the influence of these objects entirely depends. (EHU 33)

For Galen Strawson, who claims to be resurrecting the 'traditional' interpretation of Hume, Hume does indeed believe that there are real causal powers at work in the objective world, though we are unable to know these powers (see Strawson 2002). Thus, Strawson claims, Hume is sincere when he claims that our bodies are indeed actuated by the causal powers of 'muscles and nerves,' and other things besides, even 'though we are ignorant of those powers and forces, on which the regular course and succession of objects totally depends' (EHU 55). In response to the problem Deleuze finds to be the central concern of transcendental empiricism, Strawson thus argues that the systematicity of our perceptions is to be accounted for by the presence of the causal powers upon which this 'regular course and succession of objects totally depends.'

Kenneth Winkler, by contrast, in his essay on the New Hume debate, argues that all Hume means by secret powers is that if 'we were acquainted with these unknown objects and their patterns of behavior, we could predict the future with greater reliability,' and thus for Hume 'To ascribe power to a secret cause is to say something about the expectations we would have were we to experience unseen parts or mechanisms' (Winkler 1991, 577).[24] In other words, for Winkler, all Hume ever intended in his discussions of cause was to refer to the regularities that enable us to even formulate the idea of causation. As cited earlier, for Hume we would 'have no notion of necessity or connexion,' and hence of causation, without 'the uniformity observable in nature' (EHU 82).

We can now restate, with the reading of Hume we have seen Deleuze put forth, the relationship between the 'uniformity' and regularity of perceptions and the idea of causation and necessity, including the idea of secret causes. The principles of association draw the multiplicity of impressions and ideas into a plane of consistency, or into a uniform tendency and regularity; and this consistency is then actualized as the belief in causation and necessity. The belief in causation is inseparable from the impressions themselves – Hume will repeatedly argue that the belief in cause and necessity, as with the beliefs in continued existence, the self, and so on, is not a distinct idea founded upon a distinct impression – and yet the belief is irreducible to the given impressions.[25] To recall Sudnow's efforts, the multiplicity of notes comes to be actualized as improvisational jazz when the virtual multiplicity of notes becomes actualized as 'melodying.' The actual performance of the improvisational jazz, the melodying that actualizes the reality of the virtual, is inseparable from the reality of the virtual (the multiplicity of notes) but irreducible to them. Similarly for Hume, on a Deleuzian reading, the virtual multiplicity of impressions and ideas is actualized, and is only actualized, by way of the beliefs that are inseparable from practical action. More to the point, it is the situated subject engaged in practical action that actualizes the virtual multiplicity of impressions and ideas as beliefs in the world. Thus, as Deleuze addresses the theme that is at the heart of the New Hume debate, he claims that there is a dualism at the heart of empiricism – namely, the dualism between the 'causes of perception and the causes of relations,' or between the 'hidden powers of nature and the principles of human nature' (ES 109). It is to clarify further this dualism at the heart of empiricism that we now turn.

Notes

1. Reid argues that the ideas we acquire of various sensory qualities, such as 'hardness and softness, roughness and smoothness . . . had not the least resemblance to those sensations that correspond to them & by which we are made acquainted with them' (Reid 1997, 259). The idea of softness, in short, does not resemble the impressions from which it is derived. In his letter to Blair, Hume suspects that Reid's theory ultimately 'leads us back to innate ideas,' and it is in this same letter that Hume reaffirms his copy principle and the dependency of all our ideas upon correspondent impressions.
2. Marina Frasca-Spada has made this claim recently, arguing that 'the fact that the missing shade of blue is very "particular and singular" means that the

principle may not be applicable in extreme cases, but does not affect its suitability for ordinary, common situations; and he insinuates that, however weak, such an exception is the strongest possible argument against his position' (Frasca-Spada 1998, 62). Frasca-Spada will show that there are a number of arguments against the common situations we find ourselves in and she claims that this boils down to a fundamental tension between Books I and II of the *Treatise*. Either, she argues, 'consciousness is . . . projected in the isolation of a metaphysical emptiness where nothing can be taken for granted [Book I and skeptical rejection of common situations], or [it is] immersed in the atmosphere of our basic everyday objects, experiences, and familiarities and of our common human conversation' (ibid. 198). This disparity between Books I and II will be addressed in the next chapter.
3. Robert Fogelin will also stress this point (Fogelin 1984), which he believes opens Hume up to the notion that 'every simple idea is derived from a simple impression' *except* 'possibly for those (1) where we are dealing with a quality admitting of degrees, and (2) we have had suitably many impressions of other degrees of that quality' (269–70).
4. This is largely Robert Cummins' argument as well (see Cummins 1978). Cummins focuses on Hume's claim that a blind person cannot have an idea of color because they lack impressions of color while he is yet unbothered by a sighted person who can have the idea of a missing shade of blue without the corresponding impression. The difference, for Cummins, is that the sighted person has a 'recognitional capacity' for such an idea whereas the blind person does not. Interestingly, Cummins must have been unaware of Hume's letters regarding Blacklock, for he says 'a blind person can talk of colour . . . without disclosing his blindness by misuse of language, and Hume must have known that' (552). Clearly, as we will see, Hume did know this.
5. Pears 1990, 20–1: 'So his phenomenological division of ideas follows lines laid down by definitions until it reaches indefinables. That is how Russell too and Wittgenstein in his early period saw the task of logical analysis . . . His [Humes's] concentration on this kind of definition, reinforced by the metaphor [of dividing an apple into parts], drives him to atomism. For it makes him neglect the lateral connections of any thing whose idea is under analysis.'
6. Quine, in his *Pursuit of Truth*, offers the most well-known discussion of underdetermination, which for him means that facts do not adequately determine theories. As he puts it, 'What the empirical underdetermination of global science shows is that there are various defensible ways of conceiving the world' (Quine 1990, 102). Understood in the current context, impressions do not adequately determine the belief in continued existence, and hence these beliefs can assume varied forms, ranging from, as both Deleuze and Hume recognize, the reasonable to the mad and delusional. For a critique of Quine's arguments, see Bergström 1993.
7. See Saul Traiger's essay, 'Impressions, Ideas, and Fictions,' where much the same point is made. As Traiger puts it, for Hume 'Nothing suggests that this fiction itself is false, only that it is improper or inexact. A fiction is an idea applied to something from which it cannot be derived' (Traiger 1987, 386).
8. In support of the constitutive role of impressions of reflection, Deleuze cites the *Treatise* (T 36–7; cited ES 97). The text runs as follows: 'Five notes play'd on a flute give us the impression and idea of time; tho' time be not a sixth

impression, which presents itself to the hearing or any other of the senses. Nor is it a sixth impression, which the mind by reflection finds in itself. These five sounds making their appearance in this particular manner, excite no emotion in the mind, nor produce an affection of any kind, which being observ'd by it can give rise to a new idea. For that is necessary to produce a new idea of reflection, nor can the mind, by revolving over a thousand times all its ideas of sensation, ever extract from them any new original idea, unless nature has so fram'd its faculties, that it feels some new original impression arise from such a contemplation.' Such a new original impression is an impression of reflection, and these impressions are the results of the principles in their constitutive role.

9. Garrett largely echoes our points when he speaks of the idea of the missing shade being based upon a 'set of very closely resembling impressions' (Garrett 1997, 52), a view Garrett expands upon when discussing the formation of abstract ideas. An abstract idea, for Garrett, is one whereby a particular instance, such as blue, a dog, and so on, enables a person, through custom and habit, 'to call up any member of an appropriate set of ideas of particular instances,' what Garrett calls a 'revival set' (ibid. 196).

10. See also James' comment in his *Pluralistic Universe*: 'Intellectualistic critics of sensation insist that sensations are disjoined only. Radical empiricism insists that conjunctions between them are just as immediately given as disjunctions are, and that relations, whether disjunctive or conjunctive, are in their original sensible givenness just as fleeting and momentary, and just as "particular," as terms are' (James 1987, 757).

11. For the similarities with Agamben, see *Infancy and History*, where, for instance, Agamben argues that 'A primary experience, far from being subjective, could then only be what in human beings comes before the subject – that is, before language: a 'wordless' experience in the literal sense of the term, a human *infancy* [*in-fancy*], whose boundary would be marked by language' (Agamben 2007, 54). A few pages later, this point is reiterated: 'In terms of human infancy, experience is the simple difference between the human and the linguistic [or between bare life and the polis as Agamben also discusses this – see Chapter 6 below]. The individual as not already speaking, as having been and still being an infant – this is experience' (ibid. 58).

12. Recently there have been a number of essays defending Deleuze's work against Badiou's criticisms. See especially Todd May, 'Badiou and Deleuze on the One and the Many' (in Hallward 2004, 67–76); and Daniel W. Smith, 'Mathematics and the Theory of Multiplicities: Badiou and Deleuze Revisited' (Smith 2003, 411–50). May argues that if one emphasizes Deleuze's resistance to transcendence and understands the virtual–actual distinction as following from Deleuze's Bergsonian conceptualization of time – in contrast to Badiou who, May points out, 'separates his discussion of time from his discussion of the virtual and the actual' (74) – then most of the difficulties Badiou has with Deleuze would be overcome. For Smith, Badiou fails to appreciate the significance of the mathematical basis for Deleuze's theory of multiplicities. In particular, Smith argues, and quite correctly I believe, that whereas Badiou's ontology understands Being solely in terms of axiomatic set theory, Deleuze recognizes the necessary tension between axiomatics *and* problematics. Interpreted in this way, Smith shows that not only has Badiou failed to grasp the real *differend* between himself and Deleuze (for Badiou it revolved around

the One and the Multiple), but more importantly his neglect of problematics leads to difficulties for his own philosophy. Both arguments are compelling. Where our approach differs is in offering a reading of Spinoza that corrects what we take to be Badiou's misreading of Spinoza, and hence Deleuze's Spinozism as we see it; but it also highlights, with our discussion of Hume, the manner in which an experimental philosophy drawn from problematics was a concern of Deleuze's from early in his career.

13. For a more detailed discussion of this problem and our proposed Deleuzian solution, sketched below, see the second chapter of my book, *Philosophy at the Edge of Chaos: Gilles Deleuze and the Philosophy of Difference* (Bell 2006b).
14. Badiou is quite forthright on this role of the infinite intellect: 'The infinite intellect provides the modal norm for the extent of modal possibility. All the things that it can intellect – "*omnia quae sub intellectum infinitum cadere possunt*" – are held to exist' (2004, 85).
15. Deleuze is quite forthright in his assertion that Spinoza, as he reads him, makes substance turn upon the modes. In correspondence with the translator of the English edition of *Expressionism in Philosophy: Spinoza*, Deleuze sees his original contribution to Spinoza scholarship being precisely his effort in 'making substance turn on finite modes' (Deleuze 1990a, 11).
16. H. F. Hallett has argued that Spinoza understands substance as 'absolutely indeterminate,' and the reading offered here largely echoes Hallett's position (see especially Hallett 1930, 1973). For other, similar interpretations, see Pierre Macherey, *Introduction à l'Éthique de Spinoza: La première partie la nature de choses* (Macherey 1998), and for Macherey's sympathetic reading of Deleuze, 'The Encounter with Spinoza,' in *Deleuze: A Critical Reader* (Patton 1996b), pp. 139–61; Charles Ramond, *Qualité et quantité dans la philosophie de Spinoza* (Ramond 1995); Lorenzo Vinciguerra, *Spinoza* (Vinciguerra 2001); and François Zourabichvili, *Deleuze: une philosophie de l'événement* (Zourabichvili 1994), and in particular Zourabichvili's essay, 'Deleuze et Spinoza,' in *Spinoza Au Xx^e Siècle* (Bloch 1993), pp. 237–46.
17. That the virtual is real is one of Deleuze's central claims and he states it on numerous occasions. See, for instance, DR 208: 'The virtual is opposed not to the real but to the actual. The virtual is fully real in so far as it is virtual.'
18. A preliminary indication that supports this reading of the difference between Deleuze and Badiou can be seen in Badiou's work itself, where, in the introduction to the *Clamor of Being*, Badiou claims that Deleuze did not want to have his correspondence with Badiou published for on rereading it 'he found them too "abstract"' (Badiou 2000, 6). It is also worth noting that the subtitle to Deleuze's second book on Spinoza is 'Practical Philosophy.'
19. As Sudnow describes it, 'The particularly said jazz sayings would be done, and then I would lapse into usual lunge-ful and unsingingly path-following ways' (1978, 86). The reason for this was that in playing he 'always felt required to prefigure the route onto which I would switch when the next chord's arrival was imminent' (92).
20. Edward Craig comes to a similar conclusion by arguing that Hume's primary target was religious belief, and hence 'the question about the genesis of beliefs will weigh heavier than the theory of impressions and ideas' (Craig 2002, 214).
21. Deleuze is citing T 208. Here Hume repeats what he says earlier, and as we cited above, whereby 'a fiction of the imagination . . . the unchangeable object

is suppos'd to participate of the changes of co-existent objects, and in particular of that of our perceptions' (T 200–1).
22. Deleuze is quite adamant that the world is fictioned: 'There is no complete system, synthesis, or cosmology that is not imaginary' (ES 83); or again, 'The world as such is essentially the Unique. It is a fiction of the imagination – never an object of the understanding' (ES 75).
23. This position differs as well from one offered by Donald Baxter, who sees Hume as 'a pyrrhonian skeptic in the tradition of Sextus Empiricus' (Baxter 2006, 115), by which he means that for Hume the fictioning of identity leaves our beliefs without empirical warrant, such that Hume is left to account for them by 'acquiescing to nature's insistence without epistemic warrant' (ibid. 130). On the Deleuzian reading offered here, by contrast, the fictioning of identity does not entail vacating our beliefs in the world but is rather the very principle that enables such beliefs – this, again, is the task of transcendental empiricism, to discern the conditions for the possibility of our actual beliefs in the world.
24. Earlier, Winkler states this same point as his thesis: 'the hidden powers of observable things rest not on unobservable (and unanalyzable) real powers, but on unobservable mechanisms or structures' (1991, 549).
25. As Hume stresses in the *Treatise*, a belief is not a distinct idea; rather, it is 'nothing but vivacity' (T 86) and thus belief adds nothing to an idea but 'only changes our manner of conceiving it' (T 101).

Chapter 2

Becoming Who We Are

In *Empiricism and Subjectivity* Deleuze is, as we have seen, forthright in asserting that 'empiricism will not be correctly defined except by means of dualism' (ES 108). For Hume this consists of the dualism of the causes of perception, the hidden powers of nature, and the causes of relations, or the principles of human nature. Understood in light of the transcendental empiricism Deleuze finds at work in Hume, there is that which is 'given' in experience, the multiplicity of impressions and ideas, but within this 'given' there is 'the subject which transcends experience and the relations which do not depend on ideas [that] are also given' (ibid.). This, as we have already noted, is simply the problem of transcendental empiricism, the problem of determining how the subject is constituted inside the given while not being reducible to the givens of experience. Stated in the terms of the New Hume debate, it is the dualism of an already existent though *hidden* identity upon which the 'regular course and succession of objects totally depends' (EHU 44), and an identity yet to come, the identity that will emerge into the full light of day as we become increasingly acquainted with the 'unseen parts or mechanisms' (Winkler 1991, 577).

On Deleuze's reading of Hume, however, the very notion of identity is itself problematic, whether this is the identity anterior to the systematic regularity it makes possible, or the identity that results when unseen mechanisms become revealed. Identity, as was argued in the previous chapter, is in fact fictioned; consequently, the question ' "how does the subject constitute itself within the given?" ' becomes the question, ' "how does the imagination become a faculty?" ' (ES 110). Stated in other words, how is the imagination able to constitute, fiction, or synthesize an identity without presupposing a predetermining identity to guide the faculty? Kant's solution to this problem was to argue that one *must* presuppose a predetermining identity. As Deleuze notes, for Kant there must be 'something within thought [that] transcends the imagination without being able to do without it' (ES 111). This something is the 'synthetic unity of apperception' which accounts for the unity and identity of the given by relating it to the unity and identity of the subject. Kant's critical philosophy is thus 'not an empiricism' (ibid.) for Deleuze, because 'things [the *identifiable* givens of experience] presuppose a synthesis whose source is the same as the source of relations,' namely they both presuppose the synthetic unity of apperception. Kant thus avoids the dualism that 'correctly defines' empiricism.[1] Hume, by contrast, attempts to account for the relationship between the givens of experience and the faculty of imagination – that is, the synthesizing of identity – while maintaining that 'nothing within thought surpasses the imagination, nothing is transcendental' (ibid.). But this leaves Hume with the question that is at the heart of transcendental empiricism: how do nature, as cause of perceptions, and human nature, as cause of relations, come together in such a way that a subject comes to be constituted that is irreducible to either nature or human nature? For Deleuze it is 'purposiveness' that enables Hume to address this question, that is, as will be argued in this chapter, it is the notion 'that subjectivity is in fact a process' (ES 113), that we are forever becoming who we are, that allows Hume to account for the synthesis and fictioning of identity without presupposing an already constituted identity.

This brings us to an issue that is central to Deleuze's entire philosophic project – namely, his efforts to develop a philosophy of difference, a philosophy, as Deleuze puts it in *Difference and Repetition*, that proposes 'to think difference in itself independently of the forms of representation which reduce it to the Same' (DR xix). It is no wonder then that Deleuze found early on in his career an inspiration in the work of Hume, and why throughout the rest of his career he would repeatedly refer to himself as an empiricist. Moreover, Deleuze's empiricist project fundamentally engages with dualism, as did Hume's. Numerous dualisms appear throughout Deleuze's, and Deleuze and Guattari's, texts – deterritorialization/reterritorialization, molecular/molar, minor/major, virtual/actual, to name but a few. In response to the charge that his philosophy has not escaped dualism, Deleuze counters that

> You only escape dualisms effectively by shifting them like a load, and when you find between the terms, whether they are two or more, a narrow gorge like a border or a frontier which will turn the set into a multiplicity, independently of the number of parts. (D 132)

The same is true for Hume. Between nature and human nature, between the causes of perception and the causes of relations, there is the frontier that is the self, and in particular a self with beliefs that are inseparable from practical engagement with the world. Although Hume's claim that belief is 'a lively idea related to or associated with a present impression' (T 96) has been the source of much debate among commentators, it nonetheless follows from Hume's attempt to steer a path into the 'border' or 'frontier' 'between the terms' of the dualism, and this 'frontier' is nothing less than the multiplicity inseparable from the relationship between nature and human nature. More to the point, Hume's theory of belief enables him to escape the dualism of holding that beliefs are either justified and true if they correspond to an autonomous reality (nature), or they are merely 'lively' sentiments and feelings that are the result of custom, habit, and the association of ideas (human nature), and thus are neither true nor false. For Hume, *the more a belief is constructed* – the more the principles of association and custom produce a lively and forceful sentiment – *the more autonomous and true the reality of that which is believed*. The processual multiplicity in between the dualism of the constitutive process (e.g., human nature) and the autonomous reality that is not constituted (e.g., nature) is what we will refer to as historical ontology.

I. Historical Ontology

To begin clarifying these points, we will first address some frequent criticisms of Hume's theory of belief. Jonathan Bennett, for example, follows through on an objection Hume himself raises against his argument that 'belief is *nothing but a strong and lively idea deriv'd from a present impression related to it*' (T 105). Due to an ambiguity in the use of the 'words strong and lively,' Hume admits that 'not only an impression may give rise to reasoning, but that an idea may also have the same influence,' implying, it appears, that 'strong and lively' can be meant in more than the pictorial sense of strong, lively, and vivid (vivid colors, and so on). 'For suppose,' Hume states, 'I form at present an idea, of which I have forgot the correspondent impression' (T 106). Bennett offers the example of having the 'idea of a certain kind of sound' that one has forgotten. Convinced that all our ideas are copies of impressions, one is then led to believe they 'once had an impression of such a sound, though [they] have no memory of it' (Bennett 2001, 206). 'From whence,' Hume (and Bennett) asks, 'are the qualities of force and vivacity deriv'd, which constitute this belief [that is, the belief that one once had the correspondent impression]?' (T 106). Hume answers this question 'very readily,' claiming the force and vivacity derives 'from the present idea . . . [and that] The idea here supplies the place of an impression, and is entirely the same, so far as regards our present purpose' (ibid.). For Bennett, however, this does not resolve the problem, for how can an idea supply 'the place of an impression' and provide the force and vivacity of an impression when the impression that would otherwise do so is absent?

For Bennett, Hume's difficulty here derives from adhering to the notion that 'ideas are images,' whereas Bennett proposes that we 'regard them only as meanings or concepts,' and thus as ideas that are related to other ideas and ultimately to the world (Bennett 2001, 214). For Bennett, an idea is meaningful not if it is a copy of a correspondent impression, its meaning rather 'consists in how [one] uses it' (Bennett 2002, 103); for Bennett a belief is not, as Hume says, 'a mental content with a certain intrinsic feel,' but is rather a mental state with a certain dynamic role in the producing of action' (Bennett 2001, 239). The belief regarding the absent, forgotten impression, therefore, would be strong and lively, in Bennett's sense, to the extent that it plays a possible dynamic role in producing the actions that would enable the absent color to be selected from a collection of other colors. As Hume characterizes belief, however, Bennett argues that he 'makes us too passive with regard to these matters, too little in control, too much governed by our pasts' (ibid.). As a result of emphasizing the passivity of belief, Bennett claims that Hume is then subsequently led to account for belief in 'independent continuous objects' by 'an identity-concept' (ibid. 304), or the fictioned identity as discussed above. There are, however, as Bennett makes clear, 'no strictly correct uses' for this identity-concept, since the concept and idea of continuous identity is not founded upon any impressions, and thus Bennett wonders why such a theory is necessary 'if tolerable "imperfect" uses involve us in lying to ourselves' (ibid.). Hume would have been better off had he explained the belief in 'independent continuous objects' as being simply the result of the 'dynamic role in the producing of action' these beliefs play in 'help[ing] us to cope with our experience' (ibid.).

In summarizing his overall problem with Hume's theory of belief, Bennett claims that 'The crucial trouble is that Hume's theory is genetic rather than analytic'; that is to say, it is a theory 'about what must occur before there can be understanding, rather than about what understanding is, or about what it is for an expression to have a meaning' (Bennett 2002, 103). By focusing on the genetic interpretation of belief, Hume is unable to resolve problems that could be addressed if belief were interpreted in line with the 'utility-providing account.' In a 'utility-providing account,' ideas are no longer private copies that generate beliefs as the result of a history of which the beliefs are largely passive byproducts; rather, a belief is a means to achieving an end – namely, coping with our experience and engaging successfully with the world. From this perspective, a belief would be seen as fundamentally related to an objective world, and understanding itself would, from the start, be seen as an understanding of the world. As Bennett puts it, 'you cannot know that I understand [an expression] E unless there is something that you and I can both connect with E – that is, something interpersonal and thus objective' (Bennett 2002, 105). In short, rather than accounting for how we come to have a belief in a world of independent objects, Hume ought instead to have presupposed this belief from the start.

From Deleuze's perspective, however, Hume was quite right not to presuppose our belief in the world and to offer a genetic account of this belief. Deleuze is not unique here. Don Garrett, for instance, argues that one can resolve a number of puzzles or 'problems that have long stood in the way of understanding Hume's philosophy' if Hume's conclusions are interpreted as part of a general effort to understand 'the underlying processes of our cognition' (Garrett 1997, 10).[2] To take one such puzzle as an example, and one relevant to our present concerns, commentators have wrangled over precisely how best to interpret Hume's claim in the *Treatise* that repeatedly reflecting upon the fallibility of our reasoning faculty can in the end extinguish belief itself. The key passage is the following:

> Let our first belief be never so strong, it must infallibly perish by passing thro' so many new examinations, of which each diminishes somewhat of its force and vigour. When I reflect on the natural fallibility of my judgment, I have less confidence in my opinions, than when I only consider the objects concerning which I reason; and when I proceed still farther, to turn the scrutiny against every successive estimation I make of my faculties, all the rules of logic require a continual diminution, and at last a total extinction of belief and evidence. (T 182–3)

Interpreted as Bennett would have it, Hume would be arguing that the objective evidence supporting our beliefs comes, through successive reflections upon the fallibility of our faculties, to be doubted, and the belief is finally extinguished due to a lack of evidence. None of our beliefs, then, are epistemically justified. And yet, even if true, even if there is no reason for continuing to believe, or even if our beliefs are not epistemically justified, we nonetheless continue to believe. Why? Hume himself asks this very question: ''Tis therefore demanded, how it happens, that even after all we retain a degree of belief, which is sufficient for our purpose, either in philosophy or common life' (T 185). Garrett's reading of Hume's answer to this question assumes, first, that Hume's conclusion regarding the 'total extinction of belief' is a 'conclusion of cognitive psychology, rather than a conclusion of epistemic evaluation' (Garrett 1997, 227); and second, that belief would only be extinguished if 'reason [were] left to operate alone.' It is only when the 'repeated self-applications of causal and probable reasoning to reasoning itself' are left unchecked that we would then have the total extinction of belief (ibid.). But they are not left unchecked, as Hume notes: 'Where reason is lively, and mixes itself with some propensity, it ought to be assented to. Where it does not, it can never have any title to operate upon us' (T 270). Garrett calls this the 'Title Principle,' and it is Hume's ultimate response to the problem concerning the diminution and extinction of belief. In short, an elaborate chain of reasoning fails to lead to the extinction of belief, for it fails, in the end, to eliminate our propensities – that is, our passions and actions that are engaged within a situation. A belief, on this reading, is inseparable from our propensities and the strong and lively sentiments they entail. As David Owen puts it, largely echoing Garrett's position, 'to believe something is to assent to it as true . . . [and thus] If our assent is weakened, then so is the degree to which we believe something to be true' (Owen 1999, 189).

Returning now to Bennett's difficulties with Hume's theory of belief, we saw that for him Hume would have been better served in understanding belief as providing the means necessary 'to help us cope with our experience' rather than as a 'strong and lively' idea. This is also true, on Bennett's account, for Hume's notion of identity, whereby the 'identity-concept' precedes the belief in independent continuous objects rather than the reverse, as Bennett would have it. As we saw in the previous chapter, however, Hume's understanding of identity emerges as part of an effort to steer between two incompatible alternatives. As Norman Kemp Smith correctly pointed out, identity differs 'both from unity and number' (Kemp Smith 1941, 474), and thus maintains its identity in the midst of change. A single, unchanging impression gives us the idea of unity but not of identity; similarly, a number of distinct impressions in the imagination does not give us the idea of identity but rather that of number. With the fictioning of identity within the imagination what we have then, as Kemp Smith puts it, 'is an idea which is either number or unity according to the view in which we take of it; and it is this idea – a fiction of the imagination – which we call the idea of identity' (ibid. 475). If we imagine an identifiable object at different times, we have number, and if we imagine an identifiable object as unchanging through time, we have unity. What is important to stress here, however, is that the fiction of the imagination that is identity is not to be confused with being either number or unity. What we have, in short, is precisely Deleuze's notion of multiplicity. Even though Deleuze defines a multiplicity as being neither One nor Multiple, with multiple being interpreted as a multiple of units (*unités* in French), a multiplicity is nonetheless inseparable from the actualities of the One and the Multiple.

We can now see why the 'identity-concept' precedes the belief in independent continuous existence. As Kemp Smith states the case, 'the opinion of the continued existence of body is prior to that of its distinct existence and leads on to it; and for the generating of the prior opinion, it is constancy and constancy alone which operates' (ibid. 473). The stress Kemp Smith places on constancy bears a striking resonance with Deleuze's emphasis upon consistency, and for much the same reason. In order for the idea of the continued existence of body to become actualized, the multiplicity of impressions in the imagination needs to be drawn into what could be called, in combining Deleuzian and Humean terminology, a plane of constancy. As Hume argues:

> My bed and table, my books and papers, present themselves in the same uniform manner, and change not upon account of any interruption in my seeing or perceiving them. This is the case with all the impressions, whose objects are suppos'd to have an external existence; and is the case with no other impressions, whether gentle or violent, voluntary or involuntary. (T 195)

It is this constancy of impressions, therefore, that comes, through the fictions of the imagination, to be actualized as the belief in external existence. Moreover, this belief, as Garrett, Owen, and Kemp Smith each point out, is inseparable from a subject with actively engaged propensities, and more precisely inseparable from the propensity towards easy transitions from one idea to another. In the imagination, therefore, Hume will thus distinguish

> betwixt the principles which are permanent, irresistible, and universal; such as the customary transition from causes to effects, and from effects to causes: And the principles, which are changeable, weak, and irregular . . . The former are the foundation of all our thoughts and actions. (T 225)

One could also add, as Kemp Smith does, the belief in external existence, which he claims is one of the two forms 'natural belief' takes, natural belief being, for Kemp Smith, a belief to which 'the mind is committed by Nature,' and which 'operates in and through the imagination, and so by way of "fictions"' (Kemp Smith 1941, 485–6).[3] One thus does not begin with the distinction between a natural world and a subject who reacts to and engages with this natural world; rather, we begin with a propensity, a process, and the distinction between subject and object, self and the world, is an effect of this propensity. In other words, the beliefs we come to hold are inseparable from the imagination, and hence from the 'fictions' that facilitate the propensities to transition more easily from one idea to another. These beliefs, however, are susceptible to being undermined, either by force of an overly vivid imagination or by force of reason. In the case of an overly vivid imagination, the imagination fails to distinguish between that which is constant and regular and that which is changeable and irregular. Such 'a lively imagination very often degenerates into madness or folly,' and as a result our ideas can become strong and lively without 'a present impression and a customary transition [i.e., constancy]' (T 123), and hence one belief can be readily undermined by another. In the case of reason, a belief can become undermined as one acquires greater discernment in relation to matters of fact and to the differences between them. For instance, in the case of prejudice, one may presume, to cite Hume's example, that 'An Irishman cannot have wit, and a Frenchman cannot have solidity' (T 146). 'Human nature,' Hume argues, 'is very subject to errors of this kind,' (T 147) and this is precisely because our beliefs regarding *identifiable* states of affairs are realized through the multiplicity (in Deleuze's sense) of the imagination. And yet the very multiplicity of the imagination that comes to be actualized through the fictions of the imagination as a belief regarding Frenchmen is a belief that can in turn be undermined when the multiplicity inseparable from this belief comes to be further actualized as greater discernment and reflection upon matters of fact. Kemp Smith is thus quite right to argue that reason and imagination are not opposed to one another, and that what we rather have is a conflict 'between two naturally conditioned propensities of the imagination, not between the imagination and a faculty with other and higher claims' (Kemp Smith 1941, 490).

Stated in our terms, the beliefs generated by reason and the imagination are each, as identifiable beliefs, inseparable from the historical ontology of the imagination. Whether they be the beliefs of a madman whose lively imagination gives force to ideas without a corresponding impression, or the reasoned beliefs of a philosopher whose arguments may well undermine the beliefs of the prejudiced and superstitious (as was Hume's hope); all these beliefs are nothing less than the very process whereby a multiplicity in the imagination comes to be systematized (drawn into a plane of consistency/constancy) and actualized as a belief in an identifiable state of affairs. The more systematized and constant the impressions of the imagination become, the more evident the truth and reality of that which comes to be believed. Rephrasing Owen's point that to the extent to which 'assent is weakened, then so is the degree to which we believe something to be true,' we can say that the strength which our assertions and ideas acquire by becoming increasingly drawn into a plane of constancy is itself the strength whereby that which is asserted is taken to be what is. The multiplicity of the imagination is not the cause of the beliefs that would be its effect; to the contrary, the very distinction between an identifiable cause and effect is itself inseparable from an historical ontology that allows for the possibility of identity itself. Bruno Latour, who will be discussed at greater length in subsequent chapters, makes a very similar point when he argues that 'Causality follows the events and does not precede them,' by which he means that an event is not predetermined by a cause that already contained, as a hidden potential, the event within it; rather, cause and effect is itself a constituted relationship that actualizes a process to which it is irreducible (Latour 1999, 152). It is for this reason, finally, that Hume, and subsequently Deleuze, are correct to stress the genetic interpretation of belief instead of the analytic approach favored by Bennett. By presupposing the terms of the relationship as consisting of the relationship between a subject and an objective world, one predetermines the manner in which problems are to be couched and hence solved. Bennett would no doubt find this unobjectionable. Deleuze's Hume, however, along with Latour and others whose thought develops along quite Humean lines, presupposes the multiplicity of impressions in the imagination, a multiplicity which does not resemble or predetermine the identities, and hence the identifiable relationships, that come to be actualized. Put simply, Deleuze's Hume stresses the becoming of the self, the self as process, in order to account both for the emergence of beliefs in the world, and for the intrinsically unpredictable and contingent manner in which these beliefs arise. To clarify this point, we turn now to discuss Hume's arguments concerning personal identity, and then to the problem of the subject as Deleuze finds it at work in Hume's project.

II. Personal Identity

At first it might appear that Deleuze's Hume is actually Deleuze's hijacking of Hume for Deleuze's own purposes. As Kemp Smith argues, beliefs, and especially natural beliefs, do not arise unpredictably but arise quite predictably. As we saw, for Kemp Smith 'the mind is committed by Nature to the belief in continuing, independently existing, bodies.' As natural beliefs, therefore, the belief in external existence and causation do not seem to be beliefs that Hume would see as unpredicted and unpredictable creations. The same predictability would seem to be the case for our ideas and beliefs concerning personal identity. As Hume argues in Book II of the *Treatise*, ''Tis evident, that the idea, or rather impression of ourselves, is *always* intimately present with us,' and thus despite the skepticism in Book I regarding personal identity it is nonetheless a belief we are led to by nature (T 317, emphasis mine). And finally, in discussing the behaviors of individuals, Hume argues that it is

> universally acknowledged that there is a great uniformity among the actions of men, in all nations and ages, and that human nature remains still the same, in its principles and operations. The same motives always produce the same actions: The same events follow from the same causes. (EHU 83)

To the extent, therefore, that Kemp Smith is correct, and that our beliefs follow from our human nature, it would seem that our beliefs do not arise unpredictably. At the same time, however, Hume will equally emphasize human inventiveness and creativity. 'Mankind,' Hume argues, 'is an inventive species' (T 484); and on Deleuze's reading it is precisely this inventiveness of the human species that facilitates the systematization of the multiplicity of impressions. Moreover, this very inventiveness addresses the central concern of transcendental empiricism – namely, the constitution of an identity (for example a subject) that is irreducible to the elements (givens) from which it is constituted. As Deleuze puts it, 'This subject who invents and believes is constituted inside the given in such a way that it makes the given itself a synthesis and a system' (ES 86–7). In short, the question of how the imagination becomes a faculty becomes the question of how the imagination becomes a subject who invents and believes.

In Hume's well-known arguments concerning personal identity, the manner in which the imagination becomes a self is akin to the manner in which a multiplicity of impressions becomes the belief in continued existence. 'The mind,' Hume claims, 'is a kind of theatre, where several perceptions successively make their appearance; pass, re-pass, glide away, and mingle in an infinite variety of postures and situations' (T 253). The self, then, is 'nothing but a bundle or collection of different perceptions' (T 252). These different perceptions, furthermore, are each distinct, and as such each 'is a distinct existence, and is different, and distinguishable, and separable from every other perception, either contemporary or successive' (T 259). Within this bundle of perceptions there is not one continuing, unchanging perception of the self, nor do we perceive 'any real connexion among' the distinct perceptions (T 259). The self, however, as Hume argues, 'is not any one impression, but that to which our several impressions and ideas are suppos'd to have a reference' (T 251). In other words, the identity of the self can neither be explained in terms of a single, unchanging impression, nor can it be accounted for by the perception of a 'real connexion' between perceptions, a connection made possible by the self; rather, the self is the manner in which a bundle of perceptions is related.

It is at this point that Hume's arguments draw on his earlier claims concerning our belief in the continued existence and identity of objects. As we saw, the multiplicity of impressions in the imagination becomes the fiction of a continued existence that is neither unity nor diversity (one or multiple). More precisely, we arrive at this fiction by virtue of our natural propensity to confound similarity with identity. Since there is a strong resemblance between distinct yet interrupted perceptions we 'pass with facility from one to the other,' and tend, Hume argues, to 'fix our thought on any object, and suppose it to continue the same for some time' (T 202, 203). Similarly for personal identity, Hume argues that the principles of association and memory facilitate an easy transition from one distinct idea to another, and yet we then confound this easy transition with the fiction of an identity that remains unchanged. As Hume puts it:

> Identity depends on the relations of ideas; and these relations produce identity, by means of that easy transition they occasion. But as the relations, and the easiness of the transition may diminish by insensible degrees, we have no just standard, by which we can decide any dispute concerning the time, when they acquire or lose a title to the name of identity. (T 262)

Inseparable from identity, therefore, is a 'relation of ideas,' and a process or history whereby 'the easiness of the transition may diminish by insensible degrees.' As with the diminution of belief discussed earlier, so too identity, including personal identity, is nothing less than the strength and liveliness that accompanies the 'easiness of transition' from one idea to the next. 'Had we no memory,' Hume argues, 'we never shou'd have any notion of causation, nor consequently of that chain of causes and effects, which constitute our self or person' (T 261–2). In the case of someone who suffers from Alzheimer's disease, their perceptions – whether of their wife, friends, home, neighborhood, or any other once-familiar object – gradually lose their ability to facilitate the easy transition to the ideas and impressions with which they were once associated. As this process progresses, an Alzheimer's patient loses much more than their memory; from a Humean perspective, they lose their very self.

A problem emerges with this account of Hume's theory of personal identity, and it is a problem Hume himself came to recognize in the *Appendix* to the *Treatise*. There, Hume claims that 'upon a more strict review of the section concerning *personal identity*, I find myself involv'd in such a labyrinth, that, I must confess, I neither know how to correct my former opinions, nor how to render them consistent' (T 633). In particular, Hume now admits that 'there are two principles, which I cannot render consistent; nor is it in my power to renounce either of them, *viz. that all our distinct perceptions are distinct existences*, and *that the mind never perceives any real connexion among distinct existences*' (T 636). What is puzzling, as many have noted, about Hume's second thoughts concerning his section on personal identity is that the fact that Hume could not render the two principles consistent does not lead him to reject his arguments concerning the belief in the continued existence and identity of objects. This belief also occurs despite the fact that one neither perceives a continuing object, nor a 'real connexion,' between distinct impressions. In his summary of some of the varied attempts to explain Hume's misgivings, Garrett argues that most accounts (for example, David Pears' and Robert Fogelin's) fail to explain why Hume's dissatisfaction does not extend to 'his entire account of object identity in general' (Garrett 1997, 176).[4]

On Garrett's account, Barry Stroud was correct to see Hume's difficulties with his theory as being 'related to the possibility of there being more than one bundle' (ibid. 171). When Hume argues that the self is 'nothing but a bundle or collection of different perceptions' (T 252), the difficulty in this account arises when one attempts to locate perceptions that are nowhere – desires, passions, and many sensations 'may exist, and yet be no where' (T 235). In listing some examples of non-localizable perceptions, Hume claims a 'moral reflection cannot be plac'd on the right or on the left hand of a passion, nor can a smell or sound be either of a circular or a square figure' (T 236). Perceptions of objects can be differentiated in such a manner, whereas a vast number (and Hume says the 'greatest part') of the perceptions that constitute the bundle that is the self are nowhere. The problem then, as Garrett understands it, is that if we are given two qualitatively identical, non-localizable perceptions, we could not determine whether a later idea was a memory of one idea or the other.[5] 'We cannot,' Garrett argues, 'say, or even conceive, that one rather than the other has been collected into the same bundle' (Garrett 1997, 183). As Hume notes, 'did our perceptions either inhere in something simple and individual, or did the mind perceive some real connexion among them, there wou'd be no difficulty in the case' (T 636). As argued, however, Garrett claims Hume is unable to 'conceive, or represent to ourselves as a genuine possibility, something that clearly is conceivable – namely, the existence of other perceivers with similar and simultaneous perceptions' (Garrett 1997, 184).

Garrett has indeed correctly highlighted the difficulty – Hume's theory, in short, is unable to demonstrate how we can conceive that which we actually do conceive. Stated differently, the problem or question, as Deleuze understands it, is to account for how a multiplicity of impressions becomes an identifiable system that is distinct from others – 'how does a collection become a system?' (ES 22). For Deleuze, however, it is a mistake to assume that Hume's efforts to resolve this problem ultimately reduce to an account based upon the atomism of impressions and ideas. It was this atomism, as discussed in the previous chapter, that caused problems for Pears, Bennett, and others. For Deleuze, however, 'The essence and the destiny of empiricism are not tied to the atom but rather to the essence of association,' and this, Deleuze concludes, leads empiricism to be concerned precisely with the problem of the subject: 'therefore, empiricism does not raise the problem of the origin of the mind but rather the problem of the constitution of the subject' (ES 31). The task of empiricism is further complicated, according to Deleuze, by its effort to account for the constitution of the subject without presupposing a transcendent identity that would predetermine and guide the constitutive process. In understanding how a multiplicity of impressions becomes a distinct, identifiable subject and self, Deleuze always returns to 'the same conclusion; the given, the mind, the collection of perceptions cannot call upon anything other than themselves' (ES 89). How, then – to restate the problem of transcendental empiricism – can a subject be constituted that is irreducible to the 'collection of perceptions' but which nonetheless calls upon nothing but them in order to be constituted? Kemp Smith saw a very similar question uniquely at work in Hume's philosophy. For Kemp Smith:

> The question which has to be asked is not, therefore, how the natural beliefs can be rationally or empirically justified, but the very different question – a question which, Hume declares, all previous philosophies have ignored – how our perceptions, being what they are, internal and perishing, can yet be adequate to the functions they are called upon to discharge in the generation of belief. (Kemp Smith 1941, 457)

On Deleuze's approach to Hume, the collection of perceptions of the mind is best understood as a multiplicity, or virtual system, that gets drawn by the principles of association into a plane of constancy (that is, into easy transitions) that enables the actualization of the beliefs in the continued existence and identity of objects, selves, and so on. As discussed earlier, the imagination is pivotal in that it allows, by way of a fiction, for the move beyond the given. As Deleuze argues, 'for a system to exist, it is not enough to have ideas associated in the mind; it is also necessary that perceptions be regarded as separate from the mind, and that impressions be in some manner torn from the senses' (ES 80). And it is precisely through a fiction, or 'by feigning a continu'd being' (T 208; cited by Deleuze, ibid.), that 'the system is completed in the identity between system and world' (ES 80). 'From the point of view of philosophy,' Deleuze concludes a few pages later, 'the mind is no longer anything but delirium and madness. There is no complete system, synthesis, or cosmology that is not imaginary' (ES 83).[6]

In a later chapter we will return to this theme of madness, and more precisely to how Hume would have us differentiate between delusional and reasonable beliefs, but for now it is important to stress that it is because these fictions cannot be reduced to the givens of experience that they play such a significant role. Understood in Deleuze's terms, the fictions of the imagination constitute the virtual systems that come to be actualized by the practical behaviors and beliefs of subjects, including delusional beliefs. Admittedly such a reading overlays Hume's philosophy with a virtual/actual distinction he would not recognize; however, for Deleuze this distinction is ultimately the dualism that is inseparable from a 'correctly defined' empiricism, or transcendental empiricism in Deleuze's case. And yet Deleuze, as we hope to show, is not unreasonably stretching Hume's thought in directions unwarranted by the questions at the heart of Hume's project. For instance, in the section on personal identity, Hume already recognizes that there are two selves at issue in his thought: 'we must distinguish betwixt personal identity, as it regards our thought or imagination, and as it regards our passions or the concern we take in ourselves' (T 253). This distinction is critical for Deleuze, and crucial to understanding Deleuze's reading of Hume. Understood from the perspective of thought or imagination, what is important is 'the movement of a subject that transcends the given' (ES 34).

The imagination does this, as we have seen, by way of the principles of association that lead to the easy transitions and hence the fictions that then allow for the possibility of beliefs that cannot be reduced to the givens of the imagination. From the perspective of the passions, what is important is the relevance of the circumstances. As Hume argued (cited by Deleuze [ibid.]): 'We do not infer a character to be virtuous, because it pleases: But in feeling that it pleases after such a particular manner, we in effect feel that it is virtuous' (T 471). On his reading of this quote, Deleuze argues that for Hume 'Ethics admits the idea as a factor only of the relevant circumstances and accepts the association as a constituted element of human nature' (ES 34). In the section on personal identity, therefore, what Hume sought to explicate were the constitutive conditions for the beliefs of a subject, a subject that is actively and practically engaged with the actual circumstances of the constituted world.

We can now return to Hume's difficulties with his arguments concerning personal identity. Put simply, Hume's account of personal identity from the perspective of thought and imagination relies upon the identities of the elements that are then constitutive of the identity that is the self. Deleuze stresses, as we have seen, that the critical question for Hume is that of the subject, and he also notes that this question is situated 'in the following terms: the subject is constituted inside the given'; and 'as for [the] atomism and association' Hume develops, they are, for Deleuze, 'but the implications developed from *this* question' (ES 107). Deleuze is thus critical of the 'classical definition of empiricism' that has its roots in the 'Kantian tradition,' whereby 'empiricism is the theory according to which knowledge not only begins with experience but is derived from it' (ibid.). There are two main reasons why Deleuze finds this definition inadequate. '[F]irst of all,' Deleuze argues, 'because knowledge is not the most important thing for empiricism, but only the means to some practical activity' (ibid.). Second, if experience is identified with 'a collection of distinct perceptions,' the relations between these perceptions that give rise to beliefs and knowledge are not themselves derived from this collection (experience) but rather 'are the effect of the principles of association, namely of the principles of human nature, which, within experience, constitute a subject capable of transcending experience' (ES 108).[7] What the principles of association do, on Deleuze's reading, is draw the collection of perceptions into a plane of constancy of relations – they provide 'the subject with its necessary form' – while the 'principles of the passions provided it [the subject] with its singular content' (ES 104). Deleuze will also refer to this 'singular content' as the 'set of circumstances [that] always individuates a subject,' or that which 'gives the relation its sufficient reason,' for 'each particular relation is not in the least explained by the association' (ES 103). Stated in the terms discussed in the previous chapter, the principles of association draw, in a first articulation, the relations into a plane of consistency (constancy) that is the virtual system (or fiction of the imagination) presupposed by the actualization of this virtual within a particular state of affairs, and more precisely by the beliefs of a subject in a world of self-identical objects. The virtual self, the self from the perspective of thought and imagination, does not explain the actual self, the self from the perspective of the passions, and yet this virtual self is inseparable from the actual self and is presupposed each time there is a creative move beyond the actualities of a given state of affairs. Hume recognized the inseparability of the two selves, but by basing his account of the self upon the *identity* of constitutive elements, he is left unable, as Garrett recognized, to render a coherent account of the self of the passions, the self that readily recognizes other selves (through sympathy). On the Deleuzian reading of Hume offered here, Hume ought to have argued that the constitutive elements, the virtual system, are identifiable only as actualized, only as engaged within the affairs of a practical subject. It is perhaps this very recognition of the priority of the actual subject, the subject of the passions, that led Hume to drop all discussion of personal identity in his first *Enquiry*. This is precisely how Kemp Smith famously reads Hume:

> The only main changes [between the *Treatise* and the *Enquiry*] are the complete omission of his discussions on the immateriality of the soul and on personal identity, and his no longer attempting to account by an associative mechanism for belief in an independently existing world. That belief he now treats as being, like the moral sentiments, in itself an ultimate – a natural belief which as little allows of being evaded in thought as in action. (Kemp Smith 1941, 535)[8]

Yet with Kemp Smith's claim that our natural beliefs in self and world are in effect unable to be 'evaded in thought as in action,' we return to our earlier question: if our beliefs are in the end natural and forced upon us, how then, if at all, are we capable of being 'the inventive species' Hume claims we are? What we shall in turn argue for in the next section is that while Kemp Smith was right to recognize the stress Hume places on the passions of the actual self, it is going too far to argue that the concerns involved in Hume's reflections on the self of thought and imagination (the virtual self) have been and ought to be abandoned.[9] The reason Hume does not abandon these concerns, and the reason Deleuze continues to emphasize the principles of association, is in order to account for the inventiveness and creativity of the human species. It is to clarify the inventiveness and creativity of the subject, and the inseparability of this creativity from the circumstances of a practical subject, that we now turn.

III. Creative Evolution and Pragmatics

Alongside his early and continued interest in Hume, Deleuze was also drawn to the work of Henri Bergson. This might at first glance seem to be a departure for Deleuze, given Bergson's criticism of Hume. In particular, Bergson argues that the 'capital error of associationism is that it substitutes for [the] continuity of becoming, which is the living reality, a discontinuous multiplicity of elements, inert and juxtaposed' (Bergson [1896] 1988, 134). For Bergson, the shattering of 'living continuity' – in James' terms the 'intellectualist method [which] pulverize[s] perception and triumph[s] over life' (James 1987, 1084) – may indeed be something that 'is too convenient for us to do without in ordinary life . . . But when we fancy that the parts thus artificially separated are the genuine threads . . . we unavoidably fall into the mistakes of associationism' (Bergson [1889] 2001, 134). The move to Bergson, therefore, would seem to be a move away from Hume, and it is perhaps this assumption that accounts for the paucity of attention given to Deleuze's work on Hume by Deleuze scholars.[10] And yet Bergson's critique of Hume is not unique to Bergson. In addition to William James, we have also seen David Pears and Jonathan Bennett, each in their own way, criticize Hume largely because of his associationism.

And we have also seen Kemp Smith's approach to these problems. The pulverizing of life and belief that occurs as reason reflectively and progressively decomposes beliefs into 'a discontinuous multiplicity of elements' is only something that happens when reason is 'left to operate on its own,' as Don Garrett puts it.[11] For Kemp Smith, what this means is that of the two selves – the self of thought and imagination and the self of passions – the latter takes clear precedence. Stated in Deleuzian terms, Kemp Smith gives priority to the actual self and largely discounts the significance of the virtual self, and thus has no difficulty in accepting both Hume's later rejection of the *Treatise* and his almost complete neglect of his associationist principles in the *Enquiry*.[12] There is thus among many of Hume's commentators an apparent either/or at play in Hume's thought, and one's eventual interpretation of Hume is largely determined by which side of the divide one emphasizes. Pears and Bennett emphasize the associationism, the self of thought and imagination; Kemp Smith emphasizes the self of the passions; likewise in the New Hume debate there is Strawson, who de-emphasizes the skeptical consequences that arise from decomposing the beliefs in causal powers into their constituent elements, and Winkler who, by contrast, takes Hume to be sincere in his skeptical conclusions.

On Deleuze's reading of Hume, it is not a matter of stressing one side or the other of two possible readings; rather, Deleuze argues that there is a double movement in Hume's thought, a double tendency. There is first the movement of imagination forging beliefs that extend beyond the given, with the attendant risk of delusion and superstition. In the context of Deleuze's project, this would be the movement of the virtual to the actual. Understood in this way, the imagination underdetermines belief, such that, for example, a belief in continued existence (identity) cannot be reduced to the givens that support it. The virtual, the creative, fictioning imagination, is never fully determined by the actuality of beliefs. Second, there is then the movement of reason that progressively checks these beliefs, reducing them to nothing if 'left alone.' This is the movement of the actual to the virtual, the movement whereby reason relates the identity of belief, the identity of that which is believed, to the identities that make this belief possible. Reason thus overdetermines the identity of beliefs with the identities that constitute this belief, but in doing so it undermines the very identity of the beliefs themselves. And it is precisely skepticism that is the result of this move from the actual to the virtual, and to a virtual that cannot be accounted for by the identity of the actual – namely, the identity of the impressions and ideas – for the actual does not exhaust, or is underdetermined by, the virtual. Deleuze, as we will see in the next chapter, refers to this movement as counter-actualization.

At this point we can begin to see that Deleuze's work on Bergson does not signal a departure from the concerns that were at play in his work on Hume. To the contrary, there are some fundamental similarities that run throughout his studies of both thinkers. For example, Deleuze argues that a central problem at issue in both Bergson's and Hume's thought is to determine 'how a pure repetition, a repetition of similar cases which produce nothing new, can nevertheless produce something new in the mind looking on' (DI 46).[13] Bergson's solution to the problem is to stress the double movement of intuition and intellect, whereby in the latter case there is, 'Outside us, mutual externality without succession,' and in the former case, 'within us, succession without mutual externality' (Bergson [1889] 2001, 227). As Deleuze understands Bergson's approach, not only does he pose 'the problem in the same way as Hume,' but he 'resolves it similarly'; namely, 'anything new produced is not in the objects but in the mind' (DI 46). What is in the mind is the intuition of duration, or life, that is nothing less than the creation of novelty. Bergson is clear on this point: 'duration means invention, the creation of forms, the continual elaboration of the absolutely new' (Bergson [1907] 1911, 11). There is then for Bergson, as there was for Hume, a double movement: 'Life, that is to say consciousness launched into matter, fixed its attention either on its own movement or on the matter it was passing through; and it has thus been turned either in the direction of intuition or in that of intellect' (ibid. 182). Moreover, it is this very double movement that, for Bergson, defines metaphysics. As we move towards matter, towards dispersion, then at the limit would be pure homogeneity, that pure repetition by which we define materiality. Advancing in the other direction, we approach a duration which strains, contracts, and intensifies itself more and more; at the limit would be eternity . . . an eternity of life . . . an eternity which would be the concentration of all duration, as materiality is its dispersion. Between these two extreme limits intuition moves, and this movement is the very essence of metaphysics. (Bergson [1903] 1979, 49)[14]

What is important to note here is that Bergson is not prioritizing intuition over intellect, duration over matter; rather, and as with Hume, it is not a matter of an either/or but of a double movement between two extremes. The new, therefore, does not appear from outside the pure repetition of the actual, nor is it a one-way movement away from or beyond the actual; to the contrary, the new emerges when the actual comes to be exceeded by the duration that is inseparable from it, and when this duration in turn comes to be within the actuality of the new. The distinction Bergson will frequently use to discuss this double movement, and a distinction Deleuze will also use, is that between the virtual and the actual.

The first point to stress regarding the virtual/actual distinction is that it is not to be understood as a distinction or difference between two elements. The virtual is not identifiably distinct from the actual. As Deleuze states the point, 'the opposition of two terms is only the actualization of a virtuality that contained them both: this is tantamount to saying that difference is more profound than negation or contradiction' (DI 43). The difference or opposition that virtuality contains, however, is not an identifiable difference, it is what Deleuze calls a 'vital difference,' a difference that is 'indetermination itself' rather than a determinate difference (DI 40). It is this 'indetermination itself' that is the virtual inseparable from the actualities that determine the indeterminate through differentiation. Or, as Deleuze puts it, 'Virtuality exists in such a way that it actualizes itself as it dissociates itself; it must dissociate itself to actualize itself. Differentiation is the movement of a virtuality actualizing itself' (ibid.). The difference between the indeterminate difference and determinate difference, however, is not itself a determinate difference, for the only determinate, identifiable difference is that which is actualized. It is for this reason that Deleuze stresses the point that 'it is the essence of the virtual to be actualized' (DI 28). Although it is the essence of the virtual to be actualized, and although we cannot speak of a determinate, identifiable nature of the virtual – since the virtual is 'indetermination itself' – the virtual is nonetheless real.

We have already addressed the issue of the reality of the virtual, but at the time we had not completely detailed the relationship between the virtual and the actual. With Bergson, this relationship becomes a central concern. Most notably, Bergson, Deleuze claims, argues that 'the virtual must have a consistency, an objective consistency that enables it to differentiate itself' – that is, to create determinate, novel differences (DI 43). In the context of discussing Bergson's *Matter and Memory*, wherein 'pure recollection' is taken to be 'virtual' (B 55) and pure action actual, Deleuze claims that a 'whole level of the past... is actualized at the same time as a particular recollection.'[15] This level is not, Deleuze adds, a pure recollection, 'but is not yet, strictly speaking, an image,' and only when it has become an image can recollection 'be said to be actualized' (B 66). Pure recollection or memory thus comes to be contracted to a state of consistency, a 'whole level of the past.' But what is still 'lacking,' Deleuze notes, 'is the final moment, the final phase: that of action' (B 68). In Deleuze's terminology, there is a first articulation as a pure recollection gets drawn into a plane of consistency, and then the second articulation actualizes this consistency as a determinate actuality (e.g., a particular recollection). As Bergson puts it, 'To obtain this conversion from the virtual to the actual, it would be necessary, not to throw more light on the object, but, on the contrary, to obscure some of its aspects, to diminish it by the greater part of itself, so that the remainder... should detach itself from them as a picture' (Bergson [1896] 1988, 36). The virtuality that is not exhausted by the actual in fact becomes actualized through a filtering of an immanent multiplicity that generates consistency.[16] And it is the demands of the actual, most notably the demands of life, that play the key role in filtering and selecting. The 'double movement of contraction and expansion,' and the extent to which the creativity of the virtual is increased or diminished, 'is the result of the fundamental needs of life...' (ibid. 166).

Central to Bergson's discussion of the role the needs of life play is the concept of indetermination. According to Bergson, 'The impetus of life, of which we are speaking, consists in a need of creation.' And yet this impetus of life, he adds, 'cannot create absolutely, because it is confronted with matter, that is to say with the movement that is the inverse of its own.' What life does, therefore, is to 'seize upon this matter... [and] to introduce into it the largest possible amount of indetermination and liberty' (Bergson [1907] 1911, 251). In particular, what the impetus of life, the *élan vital*, creates is a gap or gorge between objective stimulus and subjective response, and what enters this gap is a multiplicity of virtual responses. What enters the scene, for Bergson, is consciousness; or, as he puts it, the 'more the nervous system develops, the more numerous and precise become the movements among which it can choose, the clearer, also, is the consciousness that accompanies them' (ibid. 110).[17] We can see, then, the manner in which Bergson confronts dualism. As cited earlier, Deleuze argues that one avoids dualism 'when you find between the terms,' – in this case subject and object – 'whether they are two or more, a narrow gorge like a border or a frontier *which will turn the set into a multiplicity*, independently of the number of parts' (D 132, emphasis mine). We thus begin, not with dualism, but with indeterminate multiplicities that come to be actualized by determinate differences, such as the difference between a conscious subject and the something this consciousness is a consciousness of.[18] The same is true for Hume, as Deleuze was quick to recognize. 'The subject,' on Deleuze's reading of Hume, 'is the mind [namely, the mind as a bundle and multiplicity of impressions and ideas] activated by principles [of human nature] . . . [and] To the extent that principles sink their effect into the depths of the mind, the subject, which is this very effect, becomes more and more active and less and less passive' (ES 112). Deleuze then immediately notes the similarity this position bears to Bergson: 'To speak like Bergson, let us say that the subject is an imprint, or an impression, left by principles, that it progressively turns into a machine capable of using this impression' (ibid. 113).

A further similarity between Hume and Bergson that emerges at this point concerns the importance of 'purposiveness.' As was mentioned earlier, purposiveness is what enables Hume, as Deleuze reads him, to account for the transformation of a multiplicity into a whole, into a system. As Deleuze understands the process, the 'Ideas get associated in virtue of a goal, an intention, or a purpose which only the passions can confer upon human activity' (ES 63); and it is the emergence of an increasingly active subject capable of 'pursu[ing] a goal or an intention,' of 'organiz[ing] means in view of an end,' that is the process inseparable from the result whereby 'the collection of perceptions, when organized and bound, becomes a system' (ES 98). Bergson makes a similar point when he states that the 'apparent diminution of memory, as intellect develops, is then due to the growing organization of recollections with acts' (Bergson [1896] 1988, 154). In other words, as memory becomes increasingly actualized within an expanding organization of acts, the memories of the dreamer (as Bergson refers to it), the memories that are not actualized within purposive actions, become overshadowed and hence diminished. It is for this reason Bergson claims that 'conscious memory loses in range what it gains in force of penetration' (ibid.). As conscious memory directed towards the active attainment of purposes increases, the range and breadth of virtual memories becomes increasingly filtered, or diminished. The workaholic businessman seeking to close a deal has little time for nostalgia.

At this point an important question emerges. If the determinate difference between subject and object, means and end, is made possible by the filtering that draws a multiplicity into an objective consistency that enables the actualization of the virtual, and if this filtering itself is subordinate to the actions of a purposive subject, then is not the creativity of duration (or virtuality for Deleuze[19]) – 'the creation of forms, the continual elaboration of the absolutely new' (Bergson [1907] 1911, 11) – being predetermined by the actual needs and demands of a purposive subject? Stating the question slightly differently, is not the subject as an impression that 'progressively turns into a machine capable of using this impression' a process that is itself predetermined by the goals and purposes that actualize the belief in self (a belief Hume, as Kemp Smith and others note, takes for granted in Book II of the *Treatise*)? The answer is yes. This is not, however, because the autonomous reality of actualized actions, subjects, and purposes exists prior to the process that actualizes the virtual. This would be to repeat Kant's move, which we have seen Deleuze was loath to do (as was Bergson[20]). Nor is it the case that the virtual pre-exists the actual as a determinant reality that guides the actualization of the actual.[21] Rather, the autonomous reality of actualized actions, subjects, and purposes are autonomous and predetermining *precisely because of the filtering of the virtual* that enables the actualization of the virtual.

Let us clarify this point. The virtual does not create an actuality or new form that is distinct from the virtual that created it. As Bergson himself argued, 'Everything is obscure in the idea of creation if we think of things which are created and a thing which creates, as we habitually do, as the understanding cannot help doing' (Bergson [1907] 1911, 248). Rather than presuppose the creator–created dualism, Deleuze, following Hume and Bergson, argues for a multiplicity that is the liminal, virtual frontier between creator and created, and a multiplicity that affirms the autonomy of the created – what Deleuze, as we will see in the next chapter, refers to as the autonomy of the effect – that becomes increasingly autonomous as it becomes increasingly constructed (much as, for Hume, the subject becomes increasingly autonomous as it becomes increasingly active and capable of doing more). A determinate subject presupposes an historical ontology in that the more historical it is – the more it is constructed – the more autonomous and ahistorical it becomes. Understood in this way, becoming who we are is not a matter of actualizing a subject that already existed as the possibility that is now actualized, nor is it a matter of becoming the subject that exists as *telos*, as predetermining end and final cause. We become who we are in becoming creative, or, as Bergson would argue, we become who we are through the intuition of the *élan vital* that is inseparable from the life we live and the things we actually do. But this very intuition threatens to overturn the things we do, the lives we lead, and thus one must proceed cautiously and experimentally.

With this last point, we come to Deleuze's use of the term 'pragmatics'. With pragmatics Deleuze signals his continuing adherence to empiricism and, more importantly, to an experimental empiricism. As we have already seen, Bergson argues that a true empiricism is one that seeks 'to get as near to the original itself as possible, to search deeply into its life' (Bergson [1903] 1999, 36–7), and this is done, we now know, by way of intuition, which is just 'the kind of intellectual sympathy by which one places oneself within an object in order to coincide with what is unique in it and consequently inexpressible' (ibid. 23–4). For Bergson, therefore, unlike Kant, the goal of metaphysics is not a matter of moving beyond experience in order to determine the possibilities of all experience, possibilities that are themselves not experienced; instead, it is a matter of moving beyond experience to the concrete conditions of experience, conditions that are experienced in intuition. Deleuze makes this point explicitly: 'We go beyond experience, toward the conditions of experience (but these are not, in the Kantian manner, the conditions of all possible experience: They are the conditions of real experience)' (B 23). Transcendental empiricism, therefore, pursues exactly what its name suggests: rather than deduce the conditions for possible experience, and conditions that are themselves abstracted from actual experience (for example, the abstract, noumenal 'object = x' that is deduced to be the condition for the possibility of actual experiences), transcendental empiricism seeks to arrive at the conditions for real, actual experience, and these conditions are themselves experienced. For Bergson this is the true empiricism, the true metaphysics, and it is nothing less than an intuition and experience that is inseparable from the actualities of experience. If this intuition is not dismissed or filtered away (as is often done) because it is not useful to our actual, practical needs, then it can lead to the transformation of these actualities. For Deleuze, pragmatics is precisely the effort to effect such a transformation, to effect a Bergsonian intuition, through an experimentation that accesses the virtual multiplicity inseparable from the actual. As Deleuze and Guattari suggest,

> Schizoanalysis, or pragmatics, has no other meaning: Make a rhizome [that is, a multiplicity]. But you don't know what you can make a rhizome with, you don't know which subterranean stem is effectively going to make a rhizome, or enter a becoming, people your desert. So experiment. (TP 251)

The objective of pragmatics is thus a matter of experimenting with the actual such that it can 'enter a becoming' that moves it beyond this actuality and forces it to become other. For Bergson the artist is able to do this because they are 'less intent on utilizing [their] perception . . . [and hence they perceive] a greater number of things' (Bergson [1946] 1992, 138).[22] Consequently, for the philosopher to become creative as well, to become who they are, they would be best served by turning their 'attention aside from the part of the universe which interests us from a practical viewpoint and turning it back toward what serves no practical purpose' (ibid.). 'By unmaking that which [the] needs have made,' as Bergson states this point in *Matter and Memory*, 'we may restore to intuition its original purity and so recover contact with the real' (Bergson [1896] 1988, 185). In *Creative Evolution* Bergson speaks of this process as the 'twisting about on itself' of the intellect which is necessary to think, in intuition, 'that creative evolution which is life' (Bergson [1907] 1911, 162). Intuition is thus, as Deleuze puts it, 'an essentially problematizing method' (B 35) in that it problematizes the actualities and determinate identities with which the intellect deals in order, through intuition, to think the 'creative evolution' that may transform these actualities. And with this method we return to Hume, for he too was interested in the abstruse thinker who goes beyond truth, whose thought transforms the accepted actualities of the day. We can thus see that Deleuze's move to Bergson after his work on Hume was not a departure at all, for Hume's concern, in both his philosophical and historical writings, was – as for Bergson (and for Deleuze) – to problematize the actual and thereby allow the creativity and inventiveness of the human species to shine forth.

Notes

1. Deleuze addresses Kant's philosophy most thoroughly in his book, *Kant's Critical Philosophy* (Deleuze 1984). Here, Deleuze will again note Kant's non-dualistic, and hence non-empiricist, approach: 'Hume had clearly seen that knowledge implied subjective principles, by means of which we go beyond the given. But these principles seemed to him merely principles of human nature, psychological principles of association concerning our own representations. Kant transforms the problem: that which is presented to us in such a way as to form a Nature must necessarily obey principles of the same kind (or rather, the same principles) as those which govern the course of our representations' (Deleuze 1984, 12–13).
2. Jerry Fodor has more recently offered a similar defense of Hume, interpreting Hume as attempting to develop an 'empirical psychology' of belief rather than an epistemic account or justification of belief (see Fodor 2003).
3. For the two forms of natural belief, see Kemp Smith 1941, 455: 'Natural belief takes two forms, as belief in continuing and therefore independent existence, and as belief in causal dependence.'
4. In Pears' explanation, Hume's difficulty with his account of personal identity stems from his inability to clarify precisely how perceptions belong to one bundle (self) rather than another (see Pears 1990); and for Fogelin, similarly, the problem is with relating perceptions to a continuing identity or bundle, and furthermore involves the difficulty of accounting for this identity without the local conjunction and contiguity of perceptions (a problem Fogelin believes is unique to personal identity) (see Fogelin 1984).
5. See Justin Broackes (Broackes 2002) who also recognizes this problem.
6. Deleuze cites the following passage as support for this claim: 'Right, cries Philo: this is the topic on which I have long insisted. I have still asserted, that we have

no data to establish any system of cosmogony. Our experience, so imperfect in itself, and so limited both in extent and duration, can afford us no probable conjecture concerning the whole of things' (DNR 177).
7. Martin Bell has stressed this aspect of Deleuze's transcendental empiricism in one of the few essays on the subject. See Bell 2005, 96.
8. This interpretation of why Hume abandoned his work on personal identity and the associative mechanism used to account for it fits well with Kemp Smith's general thesis that Hume's project be seen in light of the influence of Francis Hutcheson. Kemp Smith thus takes quite seriously Hume's famous statement in the *Treatise* that 'Reason is, and ought only to be the slave of the passions, and can never pretend to any other office than to serve and obey them' (T 415). On this reading of Hume, along with other evidence, Kemp Smith argues that 'Books II and III of the Treatise are in date of first composition prior to the working out of the doctrines dealt with in Book I' (Kemp Smith 1941, vi). Consequently, since Hume was more concerned with morals, or with the self of passions, it is easy to see why he would leave the more problematic themes of Book I behind.
9. M. A. Box comes to a similar conclusion when he argues that Hume does not resign himself to having 'no choice left but betwixt a false reason and none at all' (T 268), but comes to a 'practical compromise' whereby '[n]either can be renounced, neither can be chosen to the exclusion of the other. The most that we can do is somehow use them to check and balance each other' (Box 1990, 106). This theme will be discussed more thoroughly in Chapter 4.
10. Constantin Boundas is one of the few who have written on Deleuze's relationship to Hume. See his introduction to *Empiricism and Subjectivity*. See also Buchanan 1997, who argues quite correctly that a Deleuzian cultural studies needs to address the problem of the subject, and hence Deleuze's work on Hume; Martin Bell 2005; Colebrook 2002, for a nice chapter on transcendental empiricism; Martelaere 1984; and Fosl 1993.
11. Garrett 1997, 230. See also Owen 1999, 195, where he reaffirms Garrett's claim that we are ultimately unable to follow completely on reason's natural tendencies, and thus, as Owen puts it, 'Reason's hold on us is limited, and a good thing too.'
12. This position has been given a more recent and even more forceful presentation by Peter Millican (Millican 2002a). It should also be noted that Hume cut much from the section on the association of ideas in what became the posthumous edition of the first *Enquiry*.
13. Bergson states the problem in *Time and Free Will* ([1889] 2001, 105) as follows: 'When the regular oscillations of the pendulum make us sleepy, is it the last sound heard, the last movement perceived, which produces this effect? No, undoubtedly not, for why then should not the first have done the same?'
14. In a letter William James wrote to Bergson after reading Bergson's recently published *Creative Evolution*, James admits to finding this double movement difficult to understand: 'I feel very much in the dark still about the relations of the progressive to the regressive movement . . . after my one reading I don't exactly "catch on" to the way in which the continuum of reality resists itself so as to have to act, etc. etc.' (James 1960, 238).
15. Leonard Lawlor offers a helpful example in his book *The Challenge of Bergsonism* (Lawlor 2003, 51) to illustrate how one places oneself within a

particular level – one's childhood home – and from there is able to recall the particular memory of one's brother 'pasting stamps in an album.'
16. Bergson makes this point explicitly: 'Everything will happen as if we allowed to filter through us that action of external things which is real, in order to arrest and retain that which is virtual: this virtual action of things upon our body and of our body upon things is our perception itself' (ibid. 232).
17. Ansell Pearson has been critical of this aspect of Bergson's philosophy, arguing that there is a 'residual perfectionism and anthropocentrism' in his thought, in that organismic consciousness, and human consciousness in particular, becomes the highest perfection of evolution; and yet 'there are,' Ansell Pearson acknowledges, 'resources in Bergson for a non-organismic mapping of evolution . . .' (Ansell Pearson 1999, 159; see also Ansell Pearson 2002).
18. Here we can see an important difference between Bergson and phenomenology.
19. See DI 28: 'But if differentiation is thus the original and irreducible mode through which a virtuality is actualized, and if *élan vital* is duration differentiated, then duration itself is virtuality.'
20. In speaking of Kant, Bergson argues that 'Experience does not move, to his [Kant's] view, in two different and perhaps opposite ways, the one conformable to the direction of the intellect, the other contrary to it. There is, for him, only one experience, and the intellect covers its whole ground' (Bergson [1907] 1911, 359). Since the intellect, as we have seen, breaks up the continuity of the virtual into determinate, stable elements for the sake of action, experience is thus reducible, on Bergson's reading of Kant, to only that which is determinate and determinable.
21. This is Badiou's interpretation of the virtual, as we have seen.
22. Bergson gives the example of a Beethoven symphony: 'all through the labour of arranging, rearranging, selecting, carried out on the intellectual plane, the composer was turning back to a point situated outside that plane, in search of acceptance or refusal, of a lead, an inspiration; at that point there lurked an indivisible emotion which intelligence doubtless helped to unfold into music, but which was in itself something more than music and more than intelligence' (Bergson [1932] 1954, 252–3).

Chapter 3

The Time of our Life: Historical Ontology and Creative Events

In *What is Philosophy?* Deleuze and Guattari echo Bergson's claim that philosophy ought 'to remount the incline that physics descends' (Bergson [1907] 1911, 208), arguing in this context that to do philosophy 'It would be necessary to go back up the path that science descends, and at the very end of which logic sets up its camp (the same goes for History, where we would have to arrive at the unhistorical vapour that goes beyond the *actual* factors to the advantage of a creation of something new)' (WP 140). This history entails a double reading of events. There is first the effort to read history as accurately as possible, to discern as well as one can what actually happened. Such an approach to history is not unproblematic, even among historians. Deleuze and Guattari, however, will largely leave these debates to historians, and for their part will generally accept and rely upon the findings of historians. The second reading is what we will call the problematizing reading of history. This reading takes the first reading as its starting point but then moves 'back up the path science descends' in an effort to 'arrive at the unhistorical vapour' that will be the condition for the 'creation of something new.' It is this second reading that is the primary concern of Deleuze and Guattari. The point of history for them is not to understand how actualities became actual, but rather how to facilitate a creative move beyond the actualities of the present. This effort was also Hume's primary concern for philosophy in general and history in particular. 'In England,' Hume notes in his *Treatise*, 'many honest gentlemen, who being always employ'd in their domestic affairs, or amusing themselves in common recreations, have carried their thoughts very little beyond those objects, which are every day expos'd to their sense' (T 272). And in his essay, 'Of Commerce,' Hume will refer to such 'honest gentlemen' as 'shallow thinkers', thinkers who 'fall short of the truth'; and such thinkers are to be contrasted with 'abstruse thinkers, who go beyond it [the truth]. The latter class,' Hume concludes, 'are by far the most rare: and I may add, by far the most useful and valuable' (EMPL 253). For Hume, therefore, as for

Deleuze, the goal is not simply to arrive at the truth of history [first reading], but to go beyond this truth, to problematize this truth [second reading] for the sake of going beyond it and creating something new.

I. Problematizing History

Central to Deleuze's account of problematizing history is the concept of 'counter-actualization.' In contrast to a scientific explanation that seeks to explain how a set of causal factors, factors that are themselves actual, gives rise to another actuality, a problematizing history begins with the actual and problematizes it by counter-actualizing the very actuality of the actual itself. But what does it mean to counter-actualize the actuality of the actual itself? In *Logic of Sense*, Deleuze offers the example of an actor playing a role. Although the role is indeed something actual, as is the already written script, and even though the actor does indeed actualize this role on the stage, 'the actor,' Deleuze claims, 'delimits the original [the role], disengages from it an abstract line, and keeps from the event only its contour and its splendor, becoming thereby the actor of one's own events – a *counter-actualization*' (LS 150). When an actor counter-actualizes their role they both embody and actualize this role as an event of the present, and yet, Deleuze argues, there is the

> future and the past of the event considered in itself, sidestepping each present, being free of the limitations of a state of affairs, impersonal and pre-individual, neutral, neither general nor particular . . . It has no other present than that of the mobile instant which represents it, always divided into past-future, and forming what must be called the counter-actualization. (LS, 151)

To counter-actualize the actuality of the actual, therefore, is to access the pre-individual singularities that are inseparable from the individuated actualities.

Counter-actualization also operates, as Deleuze makes clear, as a quasi-cause. This quasi-cause is precisely the paradoxical element, the future-past that sidesteps each present, or 'the aleatory point which circulates throughout singularities,' and which 'does not tolerate the subsistence of God as an original individuality, nor the self as a Person, nor the world as an element of the self and as God's product' (LS 176). What is affirmed, instead, is 'a "chaosmos" and no longer a world; the aleatory point which traverses them [the series of pre-individual singularities] forms a counter-self, and no longer a self' (ibid.). In other words, counter-actualization entails accessing the virtual multiplicity – the 'unhistorical vapour' – that cannot be reduced to the individuated identities and actualities that it nevertheless conditions; and it is in this role as condition that the aleatory point functions as quasi-cause. In *What is Philosophy?* Deleuze and Guattari continue to argue that an event 'is actualized in a state of affairs, in a body, in a lived, but it has a shadowy and secret part that is continually subtracted from or added to its actualization' (WP, 156). This 'shadowy and secret part' is 'the virtual that is distinct from the actual, but a virtual that is no longer chaotic, that has become consistent or real on the plane of immanence that wrests it from the chaos – it is a virtual that is real without being actual, ideal without being abstract' (ibid.). It is precisely this reality of the virtual that then functions as the condition for the actualization of events that are new and cannot be reduced to, or be explained in terms of, any preceding actualities. For the actor to counter-actualize their role, then, is to access the 'virtual that is no longer chaotic,' a 'chaosmos' that then functions as a condition for the transformation of the role itself, a transformation that is in turn susceptible to a further counter-actualization. To counter-actualize is thus to unleash the power of AND.

It is in this sense that one is to understand Deleuze's claims regarding the autonomy of the effect. In *Cinema 1*, Deleuze argues that 'Active causes are determined in the state of things: but the event itself, the affective, the effect, goes beyond its own causes, and only refers to other effects, whilst the causes for their part fall aside' (Deleuze 1986, 106). In other words, as active cause in the state of things, the actor actualizes their role upon the stage. Inseparable from this actualization, however, is the event (the aleatory point, paradoxical element) that draws the chaos into a plane of consistency, a 'virtual that is no longer chaotic', and this event is an effect of the actualization itself – it is, after all, the event of an actual state of affairs (the actor's role) – and yet it is an effect that cannot be reduced to the actuality of the actual. It is in this way, then, that the event is an autonomous effect, for it is irreducible to the actualities it is yet inseparable from, and as effect it 'only refers to other effects' for it is only the virtual as autonomous effect that will condition novel actualities and hence the autonomous effects of these actualities.

To clarify these arguments, we could return to our earlier example of David Sudnow's attempts to learn improvisational jazz, whereby he experienced the virtual multiplicity of 'ways of hand' and actualized this virtual through the melodying of improvisational jazz. However, so as to maintain our focus upon problematizing history, we will turn instead to Max Weber's essay, 'Critical Studies in the Logic of the Cultural Sciences.' Here Weber is confronted with a difficulty similar to Sudnow's – namely, how, with a virtually infinite number of historical circumstances, does one determine which of these are relevant to what actually occurred. Is Bismarck's decision to go to war, to use Weber's example, a sufficient causal explanation of the Franco-Prussian War? In this essay Weber attempts to overcome what he sees as the difficulties in applying the scientific conception of causality to historical events. In science, causal explanations generally take the form of relating an event to the general law of which the event is a particular instance. To explain why a particular levee broke and left an entire city flooded, a scientific explanation would apply the general rules and principles of engineering, soil analysis, and so on, to show that the failure of the levee is a natural consequence of applying these general rules to the particular facts associated with this event. Given the same set of facts and the same general rules, one will and should expect the same results. Weber, however, makes a crucial distinction between facts that are instances of a class-concept (breached levee as an instance of the general laws of engineering) and facts that serve as the concrete link in an historical situation (for example, Bismarck's decision to go to war). For Weber, 'no one will ever succeed in understanding the logical character of history if he is unable to make this distinction in a clear-cut manner' (Weber 1949, 136). Weber makes this point even more clearly in his essay 'Objectivity,' when he states outright that 'We seek knowledge of an historical phenomenon, meaning by historical: significant in its individuality' (Weber 1959, 78); and this significance cannot be determined by way of general, analytical laws:

> The significance of a configuration of cultural phenomena and the basis of this significance cannot however be derived and rendered intelligible by a system of analytical laws, however perfect it may be, since the significance of cultural events presupposes a value-orientation towards these events. The concept of culture is a value concept. (Ibid. 76)

And this value-concept is needed for Weber because, as was the case for Hume as well, the objective facts underdetermine their significance. As Weber expresses the problem: 'The number and type of causes which have influenced any given event are always infinite and there is nothing in themselves to set some of them apart as alone meriting attention' (ibid. 78).

What Weber proposes as a solution to this problem is to offer an explanation of historical events in terms of what has come to be called 'singular causality' (though Weber most often referred to it as particular causality in contrast to the scientific causality of general laws) that thereby enables the historian to determine the causal *significance* of historical events. This approach entails both a value-judgment of general significance, or what will become Weber's theory of types, and a counterfactual analysis. In its most succinct formulation, the approach is as follows:

> The judgment that, if a single historical fact is conceived as absent from or modified in a complex of historical conditions, it would condition a course of historical events in a way which would be different in certain historically important respects, seems to be of considerable value for the determination of the 'historical significance' of those facts. (Weber 1949, 166)

If Bismarck had not decided to go to war, and if the absence of this fact alters the course of historical events – namely, the Franco-Prussian war doesn't happen – then Bismarck's decision becomes 'historically significant.' By contrast, if removing an event from the constellation of historical facts does not alter the expected outcome, then the event is historically insignificant. What is crucial to this approach, for our purposes, is that it relies upon a field of possibilities that are taken, through what Weber refers to as 'imaginative constructs,' to be inseparable from actual events given a 'modification in one or more "conditions" (e.g., Bismarck's decision)' (ibid. 173). Inseparable from the actuality of the Franco-Prussian war, therefore, are the co-determinants of the event; or, as Bergson and Deleuze would say: the past coexists in the present. It is this presence of the past in the present, or the reality of the virtual, that allows for the imaginative construction of alternative historical possibilities, an imaginative construction that in turn allows for a better sense of which events are or are not historically significant.

In anticipation of the criticism that this method opens 'the door wide open to subjective arbitrariness in "historiography"' (ibid. 180) by allowing anyone free range to determine what will or will not count as historically significant, Weber brings in an example of a mother who strikes her child. When the mother tells her husband that she did not really mean it, that it was really an accident, she bases her claim on the fact that her action was anomalous to her general behavioral responses to her child, responses her husband should himself accept based on his own empirical knowledge. As Weber puts it, when the mother

> refers him thereby to his 'empirical knowledge' regarding her 'usual motives,' which in the vast majority of all the generally possible constellations would have led to another, less irrational effect. She claims, in other words, that the blow which she delivered was an 'accidental' and not an 'adequately' caused reaction to the behavior of her child . . . (Ibid. 178)

For Weber, then, although facts underdetermine their significance, it does not mean that the significance or value-judgment we come to hold is arbitrary and relative, or that one value-judgment is as good as any other. The facts, over time, come to be associated with certain general rules, and these rules (that is, Weber's 'types'), insofar as they are associated with empirical facts, set limits to what one can count as significant ('adequate') or insignificant. And yet an anomalous, atypical, unpredicted event may very well transform the subsequent situation. The child's relationship with his mother may well be forever altered as a result of the blow, but to verify this one would have to be able, through Weber's method of imaginative construction, to determine that the actual life and situation of the child would have been different had the blow not occurred, given the general pattern (type) of behaviors that subsequently unfold following the blow. As Weber sums up this approach, 'In order to penetrate the real causal interrelationships, we construct unreal ones' (ibid. 185–6).

Weber's historical approach, however, is not a problematizing history. Although Weber's approach to the significance of historical events does entail an imaginative construction that considers possibilities that are not to be confused with what actually occurs, the goal of this approach is to determine the significance of historical events by ascertaining their causal role within a given constellation of historical facts. From Deleuze's perspective, what is important is that Weber refuses to reduce the historical significance and meaning of events to either their concrete particularity alone or to general analytical rules and laws. Nonetheless, whereas Weber's use of imaginative construction does account for the significance of events by moving beyond the actual to its imagined, counterfactual possibilities, and even though Weber's theory of types is not to be confused with general analytical laws and rules, Weber, in contrast to Deleuze (and Hume), seeks to arrive at the truth of the actual rather than force a creative move beyond the actual. To unleash creative events, to force a move beyond the actual, entails, as we will see in the next section, a fundamental non-relationship with the actuality it makes possible.

II. Creative Events and Counter-causality

To clarify problematizing history further, we can turn to Deleuze's contemporary, Foucault. During a lecture he gave near the end of his life while at Berkeley in 1983, Foucault argues that his work has been an effort do a 'history of thought' rather than a 'history of ideas.' Foucault describes the difference between the two as follows:

> Most of the time a historian of ideas tries to determine when a specific concept appears, and this moment is often identified by the appearance of a new word. But what I am attempting to do as a historian of thought is something different. I am trying to analyze the way institutions, practices, habits, and behavior become a problem for people who behave in specific sorts of ways, who have certain types of habits, who engage in certain kinds of practices, and who put to work specific kinds of institutions. The history of ideas involves the analysis of a notion from its birth, through its development, and in the setting of other ideas which constitute its context. The history of thought is the analysis of the way an unproblematic field of experience, or set of practices, which were accepted without question, which were familiar and 'silent,' out of discussion, becomes a problem, raises discussion and debate, incites new reactions, and induces a crisis in the previously silent behavior, habits, practices, and institutions. (Foucault 2001, 49)

By raising discussion and debate within an 'unproblematic field of experience,' Foucault's 'history of thought,' in effect, problematizes this unproblematic field and thus allows for 'new reactions' other than the already given actualities of the field. From Foucault's early work on madness to his late work, a consistent theme was the analysis of what he took to be the problems inseparable from our current, actual ways of thinking, problems that may lie hidden beneath certain unquestioned assumptions.[1] Jacques Rancière has more recently set forth a similar approach to history:

> An episode from the past interests us only inasmuch as it becomes an episode of the present wherein our thoughts, actions, and strategies are decided . . . What interests us is that ideas be events, that history be at all times a break, a rupture, to be interrogated only from the perspective of the here and now, and only politically. (Rancière 1991, xxi)

For both Foucault and Rancière, then, history ought to force 'a break, a rupture' with the actual, with how things are thought and done. The same is no less true for Deleuze. What we need to clarify, however, is the nature of this break and rupture. What enables, from within and amidst an actual, unproblematic field, the rupture and break that will transform this field? For Deleuze – and this simply follows from his Humean transcendental empiricism – any creative moves beyond the actual, and hence any breaks and ruptures with the actual, are irreducible to anything within the actual itself. The creative, the novel and new, is creative precisely because it accesses a reality (the reality of the virtual) that is irreducible to the actual. It is this move to access a reality irreducible to the actual that is the move of counter-actualization – it is the task of a problematizing history, and it is a task Deleuze shares with Foucault and Rancière, among others.

Among these others is Alain Badiou. Badiou is quite forthright in arguing for the absolute rupture that is the new, and for the irreducibility of the new to anything within the actual, or what he calls the 'situation'. A new truth appears, for Badiou, as a rupture within a situation, a rupture that is unnameable within the situation, or is what he calls the void of the situation. By way of example, Badiou argues that Haydn's music is

> absolutely detached, or unrelated to, all the rules of the situation. Hence the emergence of the classical style, with Haydn . . . concerns the musical situation and no other, a situation then governed by the predominance of the baroque style. It was an event for this situation . . . [an event that] was not comprehensible from within the plentitude achieved by the baroque style; it really was a matter of *something else*. (Badiou 2001, 68)

Badiou's position follows from his anti-Heideggerean ontology. Heidegger's ontological difference, according to Badiou, is a difference subservient to the natural, to the actual; more precisely, Heidegger's philosophy is the philosophy of the naturalization of nature, the actualization of the actual, and of the opening, *phusis* and *aletheia*, that allows for the 'remaining-there-in-itself' that is the realm of being and nature.[2] Badiou, by contrast, understands the event as the anti-natural event that is not the historicization of the natural, as Heidegger would have it, but rather an absolute beginning and separation from the natural, an historical event that can then be naturalized. Haydn's music was therefore an absolute beginning, the void of the baroque situation, and it is only as a result of fidelity to this event that it then became naturalized as the classical style. Despite being naturalized as the classical style, the event that is Haydn is to be subtracted from the series of natural events, and it is this separation that affirms the 'basis of the character of truths as irreducibly original, created, and fortuitious' (Badiou 2000, 75).

In his critique of Deleuze, Badiou argues that Deleuze ultimately failed to understand the creativity of events in a way that did not reduce them to being merely a fold or extension of the natural and actual. Whereas Deleuze affirms the indiscernibility of the virtual from the actual, and from each and every actual, that operates as the condition for creative ruptures with the actual, Badiou, on the other hand, argues that creative events are thoroughly actual though rare, and that 'no count can group the events, no virtual subjects them to the One' (ibid., p. 76). Deleuze, in short, does not, on Badiou's reading, accept the notion of 'absolute beginnings' but holds rather that the 'new is a fold of the past' (Badiou 2004, 91). For Badiou, therefore, Haydn's music was an event for the baroque situation, and only for this situation, but it was its unnameable void. Deleuze, by contrast, with his Humean transcendental empiricism and pragmatics in hand, pursues an experimentation with and within the actual, an experimentation without a predetermining end-in-view, and in doing so he seeks to force the virtualities that are indiscernible from the actual. The important issue for Deleuze, subsequently, is to discern the factors that inhibit the release of virtualities, and to attempt to determine how such inhibiting factors can be challenged and overcome. To take the case of Haydn again, numerous factors come into play. Haydn's musical sensibilities were greatly influenced by Carl Philipp Emanuel Bach, whose six keyboard sonatas Haydn played 'innumerable times' until, as Haydn says, he 'had mastered them all' (Geiringer 1968, 31–2). C. P. E. Bach, the second of five sons of Johann Sebastian Bach, the high baroque composer, is also considered to be one of the founders of the classical style. Haydn was also able to experiment in relative isolation, being under the employ of Nicholas Esterhazy and hence largely removed from the court composers of Vienna. And finally, though not exhaustively, when Haydn left for London after nearly thirty years of service to Prince Esterhazy, he wrote, 'how sweet this bit of freedom really is! I had a kind Prince, but sometimes I was forced to be dependent on base souls. I often sighed for release, and now I have it in some measure' (Landon 1959, 118).

This release, coupled with the novelty of the experience of London itself, led to what many see as the most creative period of Haydn's career.[3] Haydn's creative moves beyond the baroque situation were thus the result of experimentations made possible within the situation, even if the creative results of this experimentation are irreducible to the givens of the situation. It is this creative advance that is just what the experimentalism of transcendental empiricism and pragmatics seeks to accomplish. These experimentations, however, are not guaranteed of success. Rather than transform an actuality through the successful release of virtualities that come then to be actualized in a new idea, concept, belief, invention, or musical style, the efforts may simply come to repeat the same well-worn forms and paths (as the court composers in Vienna were largely doing at the time); or, the existing patterns and paths may become utterly destroyed and nothing coherent results from the experimentation. Whether successful or not, a problematizing history, pragmatics, and so on, will allow for creative moves beyond the actual only by beginning with the actual, by forcing, through experimentation with and within the actual, its problematization. This problematized actual then becomes unproblematic as it becomes transformed into a stable actuality, just as Haydn's problematization of the baroque style becomes the unproblematic classical style.

In his book on Leibniz, Deleuze argues that Leibniz was also concerned with determining the conditions that will allow for the emergence of creativity within the actual. 'For with Leibniz,' Deleuze claims, 'the question surges forth in philosophy that will continue to haunt Whitehead and Bergson: not how to attain eternity, but in what conditions does the objective world allow for a subjective production of novelty, that is, of creation?' (FL 79). In our earlier discussions of Bergson, we saw that creative evolutions do not proceed by subtracting from the situation, or by the rupture of a void within the plentitude of a situation; to the contrary, they emerge when the excesses inseparable from the actual, the power of AND, prompt a contraction that becomes actualized as a new entity. Historical ontology is precisely the processual outside presupposed by any determinate identity. Individuation itself presupposes, Deleuze argues, 'concentration, accumulation, coincidence of a certain number of converging preindividual singularities' (FL 63). 'In this sense,' Deleuze concludes, 'the individual is the actualization of preindividual singularities, and implies no previous determination. The contrary must be noted by observing that determination itself supposes individuation' (FL, 64). It is this accumulation, filtering, and drawing of preindividual singularities that is the historical ontology inseparable from any determinate, individual entity. For Badiou, by contrast, history only begins in the wake of an event, and unfolds only after the event through those who maintain fidelity to the truth of the event. The history of classical music only arose, for example, as a result of the fidelity of musicians to the event that was the truth of Haydn's music. Only as this event became naturalized do we have the history of classical music. Rather than concerning himself with the question of how to unleash creativity within actual historical situations, Badiou is interested in maintaining fidelity to a truth that has no history.

We can gain a clearer sense of the issues at play here by turning to work in science studies. A central claim of science studies, especially in the work of David Bloor, Bruno Latour, and others, is that scientific facts and entities have a history. This, as Latour and Woolgar argue in *Laboratory Life*, contrasts with the traditional notion that scientific facts and entities have a reality independent of the processes that led to their discovery. As Latour and Woolgar put it, 'A fact only becomes such when it loses all temporal qualifications and becomes incorporated into a large body of knowledge drawn upon by others' (Latour and Woolgar 1986, 106). To use an example of Latour's, let us suppose that upon examining the body of Rameses II, as was done in 1976, it is 'discovered' that he died of tuberculosis. For most people, Latour claims, they would assume as a matter of course that the Koch bacillus which causes tuberculosis was the same entity in 1000 BCE as it is now, even though the Koch bacillus wasn't discovered until 1882. By contrast, these same people would likely find it 'impossible . . . to imagine that a machine gun could be transported into the past' (Latour 2000, 250), or that Rameses II could have been killed by machine-gun fire. The difference between the two cases is that while technological objects 'never escape the conditions of their production,' for scientific entities we tend to believe they can and do. In other words, if you take away the technological skills, materials, and resources necessary for the production of a machine gun, then you take away the possibility of there being a machine gun; and yet if you take away the technological skills, materials, and resources necessary to isolate and identify the Koch bacillus you do not, so the usual story goes, take away the Koch bacillus. It was there regardless.

It is this contrast between the ontology of technological objects and those of scientific objects that Latour challenges. Latour argues that facts such as the existence of the Koch bacillus 'cannot escape their networks of production' (ibid.). What Latour proposes is a theory of 'relative existence' that will avoid either the Whiggish or anti-Whiggish positions. The Whiggish position assumes that our current knowledge is what scientific progress has been leading to all along and that it was already at play throughout history and was simply awaiting its inevitable discovery. From the Whiggish perspective, there is no difficulty in extending our knowledge of the Koch bacillus into the past. The anti-Whiggish position, by contrast, holds that it would be anachronistic to extend our contemporary knowledge to the past.

Latour, however, believes that the 'Koch bacillus can be extended into the past to be sure – contrary to the radical anti-whiggish position – but this cannot be done *at no cost*' (ibid. 249). This cost is the recognition that 'none of the elements necessary to prove it [the existence of the Koch bacillus in Rameses II] can themselves be expanded or transported back to three thousand years ago' (ibid.). As Latour will argue at length in *Pandora's Hope*, what needs to be challenged is the assumption that being constructed implies artificiality or lack of reality, when for Latour 'it is because [reality] is constructed that it is so very real, so autonomous, so independent of our own hands' (Latour 1999, 275).

To understand Latour's claim that 'the terms "construction" and autonomous reality are synonyms' (ibid.), we need to return to Hume, and to the underdetermination of theories and beliefs by impressions. In discussing the contrasting theories of Pasteur and Pouchet, the former calling for fermentation and the latter for spontaneous generation, Latour claims that

> Pasteur and Pouchet disagree about the interpretation of facts because, so the historians say, those facts are underdetermined and cannot, contrary to the claims of empiricists, force rational minds into assent. So the first task of social historians and social constructivists, following Hume's line of attack, was to show that we, the humans, faced with dramatically underdetermined matters of fact, have to enroll other resources to reach consensus – our theories, our prejudices, our professional or political loyalties, our bodily skills, our standardizing conventions, etc. (Latour 2000, 263–4)

This Humean line of attack is central to what is called the strong programme in science studies. A guiding thesis of this programme, as spearheaded by David Bloor, is that sociologists ought to 'seek the same kind of causes for both true and false, rational and irrational beliefs' (Bloor 1991, 175). Whereas social causes are often sought to explain why certain false beliefs were once maintained, such causes are not looked for in accounting for why we hold to true beliefs. The assumption Bloor challenges is that true beliefs are not socially caused but are caused by the autonomous reality of the facts themselves. It is at this point that the theory of underdetermination and Hume's line of attack comes in. If facts underdetermine the theories one adheres to, then one must look elsewhere than the facts themselves, and for Bloor and the strong programme we should look for social causes to account for the theories we support. This approach is more generally known as social constructivism, and it has been used to argue for the view that everything from quarks to mental illness is socially constructed.[4]

At first it might appear that Latour's position should be seen as a version of social constructivism. If the Koch bacillus is inseparable from its conditions of production, and if, as we saw, construction and autonomous reality are to be understood as synonymous, then is this not arguing for the social construction of reality? For Latour the answer to this question is a resounding 'No,' and for a very straightforward reason. Social constructivism presupposes, Latour argues, the duality of the human and the nonhuman. It is the nonhuman world that is underdetermined and in need of the human world to come along and speak for it, to provide the determinations the nonhuman world cannot provide itself. Scientific realism adheres to this same view of reality. The entities of science, as we saw above, are commonly taken to be autonomous and independent of the social context within which they may be discussed and disputed. In the case of scientific realism, it is the autonomous reality of a scientific entity that ultimately determines whether the scientific theory we construct is true or not; conversely, social constructivists argue that the truth of a scientific theory is caused, because of the underdetermination of facts, by social factors. Despite their opposing positions, they each base their understanding upon a fundamental dualism – a subject–object, human–nonhuman dualism. 'The acquiescence of the two archenemies, social constructivists and realists, to the very same metaphysics for opposed reasons has,' Latour notes, 'always been for me a source of some merriment' (Latour 2000, 264).

What Latour offers in order to avoid the either/or options of scientific realism/social constructivism, Whiggish/anti-Whiggish, is what he calls 'historical realism.' Key to historical realism is the notion of 'relative existence,' by which Latour means that scientific entities can be said to be 'existing somewhat, having a little reality, occupying a definitive place and time, having predecessors and successors' (ibid. 253); or, as he puts it in *Pandora's Hope*, 'we insist and insist again that there is a social history of things and a "thingy" history of humans' (Latour 1999, 18). What this means is that reality is something that can increase and decline through an increase and decline of heterogeneous associations. It is not all or nothing regarding the existence of entities. 'An entity,' Latour claims 'gains in reality if it is associated with many others that are viewed as collaborating with it. It loses in reality if, on the contrary, it has to shed associates or collaborators (humans and nonhumans)' (Latour 2000, 257). In the case of Pouchet's theory of spontaneous generation, its relative existence in 1864 was high since it was associated with a number of human and nonhuman elements. Latour lists 'commonsense experience, anti-Darwinism, republicanism, Protestant theology, natural history skills in observing egg development, geological theory of multiple creations, Rouen natural museum equipment [the lab where Pouchet worked]' (ibid. 257), as among the associations that were inseparable from the relative existence of spontaneous generation at the time. By 1866, however, Pasteur's theory of fermentation displaced Pouchet's theory by having increased its own heterogeneous array of associations. These associations have continued to increase to this day such that Pasteur's theory has become 'black boxed' (to use Latour's term) by being not only incorporated into textbooks as a largely unquestioned, unproblematic, autonomous fact regarding reality, but also, and more importantly for Latour, it has become black boxed precisely because of the heterogeneous network of human and nonhuman associations. 'I live,' admits Latour, 'inside the Pasteurian network, every time I eat pasteurized yogurt, drink pasteurized milk, or swallow antibiotics' (ibid. 263).

Latour thus argues that the relative existence of entities waxes and wanes relative to the number of human and nonhuman associations it has established within a network. These human and nonhuman associations, moreover, are not held together by society; rather, as Latour and primatologist Shirley Strum argue, 'society is not what holds us together, it is what is held together' (Latour and Strum 1987, 276). And it is held together, they argue, by material (i.e., nonhuman, or non-social) resources. 'As long as it is simply social skills that are brought in,' and brought in to hold together the social group, 'one does not get a society more stable and more technically developed than that of the baboons or the chimpanzees' (ibid. 277).[5] Furthermore, in holding society together one cannot predetermine what will or will not work. Consequently, Latour will understand history in a manner that emphasizes the possibility for novelty. As he puts it.

> If history has no other meaning than to activate potentiality – that is, to turn into effect what was already there, in the cause – then no matter how much juggling of associations takes place, nothing, *no new thing at least, will ever happen*, since the effect was already hidden in its cause, as a potential . . . Causality follows the events and does not precede them. (Latour 1999, 152, emphasis mine)

As with problematizing history, the history Latour seeks to do is similarly interested in moving beyond an analysis of the actual to the conditions that will allow for something new to take place. If the effect is already in the cause as its hidden potential, then the actualization of this potential merely comes to realize what was already *actually* there and hence it is not the upsurge of anything new. This is precisely Deleuze's point and is why he repeatedly argues that the virtual in no way resembles the actual, for only in this way can something truly new come to be.[6] For Latour, then, the effect is not to be understood as the logical, pre-determined result of the cause; to the contrary, 'causality follows the events.' As this is elaborated in *Laboratory Life*, ' "reality" cannot be used to explain why a statement becomes a fact, since it is only after it has become a fact that the effect of reality is obtained' (Latour and Woolgar 1986, 180). We could call this the reality-effect whereby the drawing of a number of associations and links between human and nonhuman elements enables the actualization of the autonomous factual reality that is then taken to be the cause of these relationships. Once actualized as a fact, or black boxed as Latour puts it, the historical processes that draw together a heterogeneous multiplicity of associations come to be eclipsed (black boxed) by the actualized fact. It is only through the counter-actualization of a problematizing history that the hidden reality of the virtual can become tapped, whereby the actual becomes problematized, allowing for its possible transformation. The same is true for Latour's use of history in science studies. Rather than pursue a traditional causal analysis of historical events and attempt to tease out the causal factors in the observed events, science studies seeks to show how the identification of a causal factor is itself inseparable from the relative existence of this factor. Latour thus offers a counter-causal analysis of scientific entities. In the case of the Koch bacillus that 'caused' the death of Rameses II, Latour's counter-causal analysis sees the cause itself as an effect (or quasi-effect) of an actualization of a number of associative relationships. Because of the relative existence of the present network of associations, we can say that Rameses II died of tuberculosis; as the network of associations between humans and nonhumans changes one to two hundred years from now, the relative existence of the Koch bacillus might not be what it is today; in other words, something new and unforeseen might come along to displace it as Pasteur's fermentation displaced Pouchet's spontaneous generation. The same is true, of course, for the counter-causal analysis Latour sets forth. He is not offering a deeper, more thorough causal analysis; to the contrary, his analysis, as he readily admits, is of a piece with scientific analysis to the extent that each attempts to draw order from disorder. As Latour and Woolgar understand it, 'disorder [is to] be considered the rule and order the exception' (Latour and Woolgar 1986, 251), and whereas traditional approaches presuppose a causal order behind every effect that becomes subject to analysis, Latour argues that disorder and chaos is presupposed by every analysis that identifies a causal order, including his own analysis.[7] Latour's theory of relative existence – as with Hume's staging of identity discussed in earlier chapters – thus recognizes the provisional nature of identity, the inseparability of an historical ontology from that which is determinately individuated and known. 'In the metaphysics of history that I want to substitute for the traditional one,' Latour concludes, 'we should be able to talk calmly about relative existence' (ibid. 156).

Returning now to Badiou, we have seen that he does away with the virtual in order to affirm the 'the absolute ontological separation of the event, the fact that it occurs in the situation without being in anyway virtualizable' (Badiou 2000, 75). For Badiou, then, a creative move would not entail an attempt to move beyond the actual, or to virtualize (that is, counter-actualize) the actual. Badiou claims that Deleuze, by making such a move, is simply taking refuge in the ineffability of a 'natural mysticism'

(Badiou 2004, 80), and a mysticism that short-circuits any form of political engagement with the actual before it can even get started.[8] Badiou, as his criticisms of Deleuze belie, seeks an active engagement with the actualities of daily life, and this engagement is best served, he argues, by a thought that maintains fidelity to the event, an event that is the void of the situation. It is in this way that political resistance can become a 'resistance [that] is a rupture with what is' (Badiou 2005a, 7). And the political reality to be resisted is the consensus-driven, popular-opinion dominated ideology 'of contemporary parliamentary States' (ibid., 18). What such States do is 'desingularize' the absolute separability of the event; in short, States rely upon an historicization that identifies the event with a situation (that is, what the public thinks about this, that, or the other situation). This inevitably introduces non-egalitarian statements, policies, and so on, into the political realm, whereas a politics that maintains fidelity to the event 'works,' Badiou argues, 'towards . . . the impossibility, in the situation, of every non-egalitarian statement concerning this situation' (ibid. 93). Resistance, therefore, is best served by those who actually think the truth of a given political situation, and thus for Badiou 'the real situation demands . . . that we pit a few rare political militants against the "democratic" hegemony of the parliamentary State . . .' (ibid. 122).

A crucial difference appears at this point, for while Badiou calls for the 'few rare political militants' whose fidelity to the void of the situation will facilitate the rupture with what is, Deleuze's philosophy has often been interpreted – by Negri, Hardt, and others – as the basis for a philosophy of the multitude, for a radical democratic politics. At the same time, and perhaps inconsistently, Deleuze frequently admits that truly creative work is rare, as are the individuals who do such work. Deleuze ends his essay 'Literature and Life,' for example, with the bald statement that 'there are very few who can call themselves writers' (CC 6). To begin to address these issues, we will turn to Deleuze's final published essay, 'Immanence: a life . . .,' in order to detail further the relationship between creative events and the actual, historical situations within which these events occur. Our guiding example for this discussion will be the life and work of Kafka, for Kafka would indeed be for Deleuze one of the very few who could call himself a writer.

III. Kafka: a Life, an Event . . .

On the night of 22 September 1912, Kafka, as he had done so many times before, sat down at his desk to write. This night, however, Kafka wrote the story 'The Judgment' in one sitting from ten o'clock in the evening until six the next morning. The significance of this night, of this event, was immediately apparent to Kafka and was further validated two days later when, after reading the story aloud to his friends (including Max Brod), Kafka wrote in his diary that 'The indubitability of the story was confirmed' (Kafka 1982, 214). In his biography of Kafka, Reiner Stach claims that the literature we associate with Kafka was born that night:

> Suddenly – without guide or precedent, it seemed – the Kafka cosmos was at hand, fully equipped with the 'Kafkaesque' inventory that now gives his work its distinctive character: the father figure who is both overpowering and dirty, the hollow rationality of the narrator, the juridical structures imposed on life, the dream logic of the plot, and last but not least, the flow of the story perpetually at odds with the hopes and expectations of the hero. (Stach 2005, 115)

We can see how Badiou would interpret this event. On the night of 22 September 1912, the truth we name 'Kafkaesque' was revealed to Kafka, and it is this truth that Kafka remained faithful to throughout the rest of his writings. As the fidelity to the truth of Haydn's music has come to be historicized and named the classical style, the truth revealed to Kafka that night has come to be named Kafkaesque. The truth itself, however, is for Badiou the unnameable void that prompts the efforts to be faithful to it in one's writings, efforts that then come to be named within the situations where these efforts occur. Kafka, for instance, named the point and meaning of his efforts when, in his 'Letter to His Father,' he said, 'My writing was about you'; and the night after he wrote 'The Judgment' he had already begun to identify and attribute various meanings to the story, noting that he had 'thoughts of Freud, of course' (Kafka 1982, 213).

A Badiou-inspired reading of what might be called the 'event' of Kafka's life as a writer, or of his life *per simpliciter*, certainly does seem to be corroborated by Kafka's example. However, what we must not overlook is Kafka's experience of this event as well as the relationship of this experience to Kafka's many abandoned efforts to write an indubitable story. According to Stach, with 'The Judgment,' 'For the first time he [Kafka] had linked theme, imagery, and plot to ignite a spark between literature and life. He called the brightness of this spark "indubitability"' (Stach 2005, 115). Moreover, Kafka's experience of the indubitability of the story is not of an unnameable void that cannot be said and that circulates as an absence within everything that is written and said; to the contrary, as Kafka experienced the writing of the story, he discovered, as he put it, 'How everything can be said, how for everything, for the strangest fancies, there waits a great fire in which they perish and rise up again' (Kafka 1982, 213). Kafka's experience is more akin, then, to a Bergsonian intuition, and thus the indubitability of the story is an experience of the absolute within intuition. 'By intuition,' as Bergson defines it, and as was discussed earlier, 'is meant the kind of intellectual sympathy by which one places oneself within an object in order to coincide with what is unique in it and consequently inexpressible' (Bergson [1903] 1999, 23–4). This inexpressible absolute is not the void for Bergson, but rather the pure duration that cannot be captured by attempts to delineate it within language and analysis. And yet despite its inexpressible nature, this absolute is not a void but is rather capable of being studied, situated, and experienced by what for Bergson would be a true empiricism: 'a true empiricism is that which proposes to get as near to the original itself as possible, to search deeply into its life, and so, by a kind of intellectual auscultation, to feel the throbbings of its soul; and this true empiricism is the true metaphysics (ibid. 36–7).

As we have seen, Deleuze refers to this 'true empiricism' as 'transcendental empiricism', a theme that looms as large in Deleuze's final published piece, 'Immanence: a life . . .,' as it did in his early book on Hume. Deleuze's theory of transcendental empiricism also links to our discussions of Latour, for just as Latour's theory of relative existence and historical realism was part of a general effort to avoid the subject–object metaphysics he saw as prevalent both among scientific realists and social constructivists, so too for Deleuze, 'we will speak of a transcendental empiricism in contrast to everything that makes up the world of the subject and the object' (PI 25). In contrast to Badiou's theory of the void that is absent within the givens of a situation, for Deleuze there are givens to a transcendental experience, such as the 'pure stream of a-subjective consciousness, a pre-reflexive impersonal consciousness, a qualitative duration of consciousness without self' (ibid.). These givens constitute what Deleuze will call the transcendental field, which he proposes to define 'by a pure immediate consciousness with neither object nor self, as a movement that neither begins nor ends'; and yet, as Deleuze clarifies, 'were it not for consciousness, the transcendental field would be defined as a pure plane of immanence, because it eludes all transcendence of the subject and of the object' (ibid. 26). In other words, the transcendental field is expressed, in this instance, as the relationship of subject to object, or, subject and object are the transcendents to the immanence of the transcendental field. However, if the subject or object is taken as the identity to which the immanence of the transcendental field is to be attributed, then the immanence of the transcendental field becomes distorted. As Deleuze puts it:

> When the subject or the object falling outside the plane of immanence is taken as a universal subject or as any object *to which* immanence is attributed, the transcendental is entirely denatured, for it then simply redoubles the empirical (as with Kant), and immanence is distorted, for it then finds itself enclosed in the transcendent. (Ibid. 26–7)

As was discussed earlier, if the virtual is understood in the same sense as the actual, if an actual effect is simply the realization of an already actual potential hidden within a cause, then the creative power of the virtual is distorted ('denatured'). It is for this reason that Deleuze will emphatically argue that 'it is only when immanence is no longer immanence to anything other than itself that we can speak of a plane of immanence' (ibid.). The transcendental field is nevertheless the immanence to the transcendents that actualize and express it – the consciousness, objects, self, and so on that actualize the pre-individual singularities, the 'pre-reflexive impersonal consciousness,' the indefinites, and so on – and thus the immanence of the transcendental field, understood in this way, is an immanence relative to the actualities that express it. 'It,' the transcendental field, 'is expressed in fact, only when it is reflected on a subject that refers it to objects' (ibid. 26). Pure immanence, or absolute immanence, Deleuze defines as A LIFE: 'We will say of pure immanence that it is A LIFE, and nothing else. It is not immanence to life [hence the relative immanence of the transcendental field], but the immanent that is in nothing is itself a life. A life is the immanence of immanence, absolute immanence: it is complete power, complete bliss' (ibid. 27).

Deleuze states the relationship between the transcendental field, plane of immanence, and a life as follows: 'The transcendental field is defined by a plane of immanence, and the plane of immanence by a life' (ibid. 28). The pure or absolute immanence that is immanent to nothing but itself is a life, and the transcendental field is that which allows for the actualization of that which transcends the plane of immanence. 'Transcendence,' Deleuze argues, 'is always a product of immanence' (ibid. 31). Stating this in the manner discussed in earlier chapters, a life is the pure immanence from which is drawn the plane of consistency, a plane of immanence, that defines the transcendental field (first articulation), and this transcendental field then comes to be actualized as a consciousness that is a consciousness of an object (second articulation). Far from beginning, as the phenomenologists do, with the givens of experience being placed in relationship to a consciousness, Deleuze calls for the givens of a transcendental empiricism, and a transcendental experience (*á la* Bergson), of which consciousness itself is the actualized expression.[9]

To clarify what is meant by referring to pure immanence as a life, Deleuze refers to the character from Dickens' story, *Our Mutual Friend*. In the story, a generally despicable and unlikable character is found unconscious, dying. While in this state, Deleuze notes, 'everybody bustles about to save him,' but as 'he comes back to life, his saviors turn colder, and he becomes once again mean and crude' (PI 28). On Deleuze's reading, what Dickens captures in this story is that state 'between his [the character's] life and his death . . . [the] moment that is only that of a life playing with death.' The attributes and characteristics that individuate the character as the 'mean and crude' individual that he is give way, Deleuze claims, 'to an impersonal and yet singular life that releases a pure event freed from the accidents of internal and external life' (ibid.). How are we to interpret this state of being 'freed from the accidents of internal and external life'? It might appear that Deleuze is prioritizing a reality that is outside the world of our daily concerns, the world that includes the despicable man and all that he has done to deserve the ire and contempt of others. As Deleuze would argue, however, following Bergson, what is revealed by Dickens' character is a reality that is inseparable from the dying man, a reality that comes to be expressed and actualized by those traits that individuate the character. For Bergson this reality is the pure duration that can only be experienced by intuition, and for Deleuze this reality is a life, and more importantly it is the indefinite becoming that cannot be reduced to a determinate sequence of moments. It is, in short, the time of our life; not the time that can be dated chronologically – the night of 22 September 1912, for instance – but the time that is the power of becoming, the indefinite power and bliss of being able to say everything. This time of our life, as Deleuze makes clear, is not out of this world but is indeed 'everywhere, in all the moments that a given living subject goes through and that are measured by given lived objects' (ibid. 29). 'The indefinite life,' however, 'does not itself have moments, close as they may be to one another, but only between-times, between moments . . .' (ibid.). Deleuze will frequently use the Greek term *aion* to refer to this time that is not to be confused with the actualities of our life, with the time of chronos that is 'measured by given lived objects'; nonetheless, it is, as Deleuze puts it, a time that can be the subject of visions, not, he points out, as 'interruptions of the process but breaks that form part of it [that is, between-times], like an eternity that can only be revealed in a becoming' (CC 5).

It is critical to understand the importance of the indefinite in Deleuze's discussion. There is our life, *the* life we live as individuals; and then there is *a* life and the pre-individual singularities that are inseparable from the life we live. As Deleuze argues: 'The singularities and the events that constitute a life coexist with the accidents of the life that correspond to it, but they are neither grouped nor divided in the same way' (PI 29–30). There is, for instance, to use Deleuze's example, the transcendental field of pre-individual singularities associated with the child: 'a smile, a gesture, a funny face' (ibid. 30). These singularities are not outside the life of the child, the life of the child who has, Deleuze claims, 'hardly any individuality,' but they are the determinable conditions that allow for the individuation of the child with certain determining characteristics (for example, as a person who is happy, energetic, absent-minded, and so on), characteristics that facilitate the power to say 'I' – I am such-and-such a person. Far from being out of this world, the transcendental field of pre-individual singularities is very much a part of the life of a child. 'The indefinite,' therefore, as Deleuze argues, 'is the mark not of an empirical indetermination but of a determination by immanence or a transcendental determinability. The indefinite article is the indetermination of the person only because it is determination of the singular' (ibid. 30). The gestures, smiles, and so on, of the child are empirically determinable, but they are at the same time indeterminate relative to the individual who will come to actualize these singularities as constitutive elements of their identity.

We can clarify these points further if we return to Kafka. In literature, Deleuze argues, 'writing is a question of becoming . . . it is a process, that is, a passage of Life that traverses both the livable and the lived' (CC 1). And the manner in which writing becomes 'a question of becoming,' according to Deleuze, is to strip the power of the 'the' and inject the indefinite 'a or an': 'the power of the indefinite article is effected only if the term in becoming is stripped of the formal characteristics that make it say *the*' (CC 2). Whereas we may have a tendency to relate the indefinite to an actual individual – such as is exemplified by the tendency to relate Kafka's writing to being about his father, as even Kafka himself did – literature proper, for Deleuze, 'takes the opposite path and exists only when it discovers beneath apparent persons the power of an impersonal – which is not a generality but a singularity at the highest point: a man, a woman, a beast, a stomach, a child' (CC 3). As with problematizing history, a writer writes not in order to actualize thoughts, memories, and so on, or to show how the actual became actual, but rather in order to move beyond the actualities of what is written – the father in 'The Judgment' – to the impersonal, indefinite power of the virtual that made this and indefinite other actualizations possible. As Kafka himself experienced the power of the virtual, it entailed the power to say everything, but he immediately added that 'there waits a great fire in which they [the fancies that are actualized] perish and rise up again' (Kafka 1982, 213). This, for Deleuze, is the power of literature.

This power, moreover, is inseparable from the style in which Kafka writes. To recall Stach's characterization of the Kafkaesque cosmos that was given birth to that September night (a metaphor Kafka himself uses[10]), the indubitable story he wrote included all the motifs that would continue to circulate throughout all his writings from that point forward – the father figure, the 'hollow rationality of the narrator,' and so on. These motifs, however, had been apparent in Kafka's earlier work as well. The difference in this case, as Stach diagnoses the situation, is that he had linked the themes of his previous efforts in such a way that it ignited 'a spark between literature and life' (Stach 2005, 115). Stated in Deleuzian terms, Kafka's many previous efforts – what Stach refers to as 'the interminable sequence of abortive attempts' (Stach 2005, 114) – constitute the transcendental field that is drawn on the pure plane of immanence (first articulation); this transcendental field then constitutes a plane of consistency that is then actualized within 'The Judgment.' The indubitability of this story that Kafka experienced is, on our reading, simply the experience of the inseparability of the plane of immanence, the transcendental field of singularities (motifs, themes, and so on), from what is actually written and then subsequently read aloud to his friends. What is experienced here, for Deleuze (and again following Bergson), is the power of becoming, the intuition of pure duration or the 'eternity that can only be revealed in a becoming'; in short, it is the experience of the time of our life that is the transcendental condition for the creation of something new, and the condition that is inseparable from that which is created. With Bergson understandably in mind, Deleuze thus claims: 'There is no literature without fabulation, but, as Bergson was able to see, fabulation – the fabulating function – does not consist in imagining or projecting an ego. Rather, it attains these visions, it raises itself to these becomings and powers' (CC 3).

A final creative function of literature, and a function with political implications that will be the subject of the next chapter, is the ability of literature, and in particular minor literature, to invent a people and a language within and amidst (that is, inseparably from) the dominant forms of society and language. As Deleuze argues in many places, though most notably in the book he and Guattari wrote on Kafka, a writer such as Kafka is able, through 'the creation of syntax [to bring about] the invention of a new language within language [the maternal or dominant language],' and in doing so exemplify how 'language as a whole can reveal its outside, beyond all syntax' (CC 6). This outside, as should be clear by now, is 'not,' as Deleuze again stresses, 'outside language, but the outside of language' (CC 5). This outside, as Blanchot and others have correctly noted, is inseparable from the work of literature, or it is the outside that problematizes the actual precisely because it is the outside of the actual that is inseparable from it. In thus problematizing the actual, the historian, as with the writer, attempts to unleash the indubitability of the outside of language through language itself, and in the process allow for the creation of something new. Put differently, the power of the outside for literature 'consists in inventing a people who are missing' (CC 4). This power, as Latour recognized, is neither a subjective nor an objective power, neither the power of humans nor the power of nature; it is the power of life and the time of our life to create the very oppositions and actualities that are the actual focus of our daily lives. Problematizing history, as we understand it here, is the attempt to counter-actualize the unquestioned givens and actualities of daily life in order to reveal the transformative powers, the historical ontology, that is inseparable from these actualities. Deleuze will refer to this effort, especially in his later works, as geo-philosophy: 'If the question of geo-philosophy is important, it is because thinking does not occur in the categories of subject and object, but is a variable relation to territory and to the earth' (2RM 379). The political implications of geo-philosophy have been recognized, but we shall now turn to examine the role problematizing history may play in facilitating the counter-actualization of political realities, and what such a counter-actualization might look like or entail.[11] Hume's work will also return to the forefront, for the historical and political writings of Hume are, on our reading, inseparable from the positions set forth in the *Treatise* and the *Enquiries*. To the extent that Deleuze extends Hume's work by developing a transcendental empiricism, we will then not surprisingly begin to see the importance of the historical for Deleuze, or the importance of what we have called historical ontology.

Notes

1. There is voluminous literature on Foucault, but for an excellent place to begin, see Dreyfus and Rabinow 1982, and May 2006.
2. See Badiou 2005a, 179.
3. As Geiringer says in his biography of Haydn, 'it is indeed doubtful that Haydn's genius would ever have unfolded so brilliantly without the stimulus of his English adventures' (Geiringer 1968, 116).
4. The foundational text in this genre is *The Social Construction of Reality* by Peter L. Berger and Thomas Luckman (Berger and Luckman, 1967). For a critical overview, see Hacking's *The Social Construction of What?* (Hacking 1999).
5. Latour has recently focused on these implications of his work in *Reassembling the Social* (Latour 2007). For more, see John Law, who has made similar arguments in his book *Organizing Modernity*, applying it in this case to, among other things, personal identity. As he puts it, 'We are composed of, or constituted by, our props, visible and invisible . . . Each one of us is an arrangement . . . a person is an effect, a fragile process of networking associated elements. It is an unusual theory of agency only to the extent that I want to fold the props – and the interactions with the props – into the person' (Law 1993, 33).
6. In *Bergsonism*, for instance, Deleuze claims states quite bluntly that the actual 'does not resemble the virtual from which it arose' (B 97).
7. In *Laboratory Life* this point is made explicitly: 'Is there any essential distinction between the nature of our own construction and that used by our subjects? Emphatically, the answer must be no. Only by rejecting the possibility of this last distinction can the arguments of this chapter cohere. The notion of creating order from disorder applies as much to the construction of our own account as to that of the laboratory scientist' (Latour and Woolgar 1986, 254).
8. This is ultimately Hallward's critique of Deleuze (Hallward 2006).
9. For more on the contrast between Deleuze's thought and the phenomenological tradition, see my book, *The Problem of Difference: Phenomenology and Poststructuralism* (Bell 1998).

10. 'The story came out of me like a real birth, covered with filth and slime, and only I have the hand that can reach to the body itself and the strength and desire to do so' (Kafka 1982, 214).
11. For work on Deleuze's geo-philosophy, see Protevi and Bonta 2004.

Chapter 4

Becoming Civil: History and the Discipline of Institutions

A number of Hume's commentators criticize Hume's historiography for being more concerned with the ahistorical than the historical.[1] Hume himself seems to encourage this view when, throughout his *Treatise*, he applies the method of 'experimental reasoning' to the study of human nature in order to arrive at certain universal principles that hold at all times and all places. History, it would seem, is simply another opportunity to exercise this method, as the following passage from the first *Enquiry* points out:

> Mankind are so much the same, in all times and places, that history informs us of nothing so new or strange in this particular. Its chief use is only to discover the constant and universal principles of human nature, by showing men in all varieties of circumstances and situations, and furnishing us with materials, from which we may form our observations, and become acquainted with the regular springs of human action and behaviour. These records of wars, intrigues, factions, and revolutions, are so many collections of experiments, by which the politician or moral philosopher fixes the principles of his science. (EHU 150)

It would appear contrary to Hume's true intentions then to argue, as we have in previous chapters, that Hume's experimental reasoning seeks to force a creative move beyond the actual, a move that allows for something new. From the perspective of the ahistorical principles Hume's project aspires to discern, human affairs are 'so much the same, in all times and places,' and thus 'nothing so new or strange' ever really appears.

This ahistorical reading of Hume needs to be balanced, we hope to show, by a reading that gives proper weight to the implications of, and reasons for, Hume's famous disowning of the *Treatise*. There has been a tremendous amount of discussion regarding how seriously we ought to take Hume's rejection of the *Treatise*. Hume had his regrets regarding the *Treatise* from nearly the beginning,[2] and he never revised this work as he obsessively did with all of his other published writings.[3] Hume was also adamant that his posthumous works be prefaced with an advertisement that dissuaded readers from looking to the *Treatise* for his true philosophy. Since the ire of most of Hume's critics were directed at the *Treatise*, Hume emphasizes that since he never owned up to the work it would be beyond common 'prudence and candour' to attack him based on what is said in this work. 'The following pieces,' being the enquiries and his essays, but not the *Treatise*, 'may alone,' Hume argues, 'be regarded as containing his philosophical sentiments and principles' (EHU 83).

What is important to recognize in Hume's rejection of the *Treatise* is his claim that it was a juvenile work; in other words, the arguments were presented with a youthful arrogance and disregard for how they might be perceived by a more cautious if not conservative readership. In the famous conclusion to Book 1 of the *Treatise*, Hume himself recognizes the extreme nature of his conclusions, conclusions that made him feel as if he were left to 'perish on the barren rock' (T 264). As we saw earlier in discussing the New Hume debate, commentators have long discussed how seriously we ought to take these conclusions. Reading them in light of the *Enquiries* and the disavowal of the *Treatise*, it would seem that Hume became aware of the consequences of an unchecked 'abstruse thought,' and thus with the *Enquiries* Hume's approach calls for a balance of abstruse thought and practice. Hume notes this early on in the first *Enquiry*:

> It seems, then that nature has pointed out a mixed kind of life as most suitable to the human race, and secretly admonished them to allow none of these biases to draw too much, so as to incapacitate them for other occupations and entertainments. Indulge your passion for science, says she, but let your science be human, and such as may have a direct reference to action and society. Abstruse thought and profound researches I prohibit, and will severely punish, by the pensive melancholy which they introduce. (EHU 89)

Hume himself had first-hand experience of the consequences of unbalanced 'abstruse thought.' In his famous letter of 1737, Hume diagnosed his own melancholy and inability to engage with life and work to be a consequence of pursuing philosophy without proper attention to a life of action. As Hume put it, he recognized the need to 'Seek out a more active life, and tho' I could not quit my pretensions in Learning, but with my last breath, to lay them aside, in order the more effectually to resume them' (L1 17). What this will mean for Hume is that we are not left to choose between extreme skepticism or irrational superstition – the choice 'betwixt a false reason and none at all' (T 268) as Hume puts it – but rather, as M. A. Box argues:

> There is another choice, and now Hume begins to feel his way toward it. A practical compromise restores him to his usual calm. It emerges that philosophy as well as instinct is natural to man. Neither can be renounced; neither can be chosen to the exclusion of the other. The most that we can do is somehow to use them to check and balance each other. (Box 1990, 106)

Hume's post-*Treatise* philosophy is thus not simply a repackaging of the *Treatise* so as to acquire the fame that eluded him as the *Treatise* '*fell deadborn from the press*' ('My Own Life,' EMPL xxxiv); nor should we completely turn away from the *Treatise*, as Hume suggested, and look to his later works for his true 'philosophical sentiments and principles'; rather, we should read the arguments of the *Treatise* in light of a double movement: there is the philosophical movement of abstruse thought that follows lines of reasoning to their skeptical conclusions, and there is the movement of action, or the pragmatic actualization of philosophy within the concrete circumstances of daily life.

It is at this point that the true significance of history surfaces for Hume. Historical enquiry is precisely the balancing of the abstruse and the practical. As Hume puts it in his essay, 'Of History,'

> When a man of business enters into life and action, he is more apt to consider the characters of men, as they have relation to his interest, than as they stand in themselves; and has his judgment warped on every occasion by the violence of his passion. When a philosopher contemplates characters and manners in his closet, the general abstract view of the objects leaves the mind so cold and unmoved, that the sentiments of nature have no room to play, and he scarce feels the difference between vice and virtue. History keeps in a just medium betwixt these extremes, and places the objects in their true point of view. (EMPL 567–8)

History, therefore, is precisely the double movement that enables the philosopher to extract from history universal, ahistorical principles, and it enables a person engaged in life to become more civil, or to learn from history the practical benefits of virtue and civility.[4] It would be mistaken, then, to argue that Hume's interest in history was solely to ascertain ahistorical principles. This is simply one way in which history, the historical, can be approached, for history can also be turned towards the concrete circumstances of daily life. To be more precise, for Hume history involves a double movement that enables us to place 'objects in their true point of view.'

I. Hume and History

Hume's interest in pursuing historical research was present long before he began to write his *History of England* in 1752. In a 1747 letter to Henry Home, later Lord Kames, Hume confesses that had he 'any fortune which could give [him] a prospect of leisure, and opportunity to prosecute [his] historical projects, nothing could be more useful . . .' (L1 98). When Hume was later appointed keeper of the Advocate's library in Edinburgh, thereby gaining both access to the thirty-thousand volume library and the leisure necessary to pursue his historical projects, he began to 'prosecute' these 'projects.' Furthermore, as Hume pursued his historical enquiries a primary aim was the desire to move beyond – that is, to problematize – a dominant, largely unquestioned issue of the day, namely the factional strife between Whigs and Tories. As Hume wrote in a letter to Adam Smith, concerning the purpose of his historical project, and why he began with the Stuart regimes of James I and Charles I rather than another period:

> I confess, I was once of the same Opinion with you, & thought that the best Period to begin an English History was about Henry the 7th. But you will please to observe, that the Change, which then happen'd in public Affairs, was very insensible, and did not display its Influence till many Years afterwards. Twas under James that the House of Commons began first to raise their Head, & then the Quarrel betwixt Privilege & Prerogative commenc'd. The Government, no longer opprest by the enormous Authority of the Crown, display'd its Genius; and *the Factions, which then arose, having an Influence on our present Affairs, form the most curious, interesting, & instructive Part of our History.* (L1 167–8, emphasis mine)

The factions that then arose, and which had an influence down to Hume's own day, were between the Whigs and Tories. As Hume understands the difference between the two parties, 'A Tory, since the revolution [English Revolution of 1640], may be defined in a few words, to be a lover of monarchy, though without abandoning liberty; and a partisan of the family of Stuart. As a Whig may be defined to be a lover of liberty though without renouncing monarchy; and a friend to the settlement in the Protestant line [i.e., the Hanoverian succession]' (EMPL 71). Stating the debate between the two parties baldly, the Whigs fault the reigns of James I and Charles I for the moves they made to extend the power and prerogative of the monarchy, moves they claim infringed upon the traditional liberties and privileges of the landed gentry; and the Tories, by contrast, argue more generally for the traditional power of the monarch to exercise their prerogative, and more particularly they claim – especially the Jacobins in Scotland – that the Stuart monarchy is legitimate while the Hanoverian succession of Queen Anne was not. What Hume brings to his analysis of the factional debates between these two parties is impartiality, which is a quality sorely lacking, Hume believes, with other historians: 'You know that there is no post of honour in the English Parnassus more vacant than that of History, Style, judgment, impartiality, care – everything is wanting to our historians; and even Rapin, during this latter period, is extremely deficient' (L2 170). And of these qualities, Hume places impartiality at the top: 'The first quality of an Historian is to be true and impartial; the next to be interesting' (L2 209). This impartiality of the historian is of a piece with Hume's call for criticism in general to be free of prejudices,[5] and thus the historical criticism Hume aspires to would portray the realities of the Whigs and Tories in a manner that, not surprisingly, would be different from what one would expect from the proponents of either of the two parties.

The purpose of Hume's *History of England*, however, is not simply to account for how the Whigs and Tories came about, or how they became actualized as the faction they were in Hume's day; more importantly for Hume the hope is that his historical criticism of the Whigs and Tories might have the effect of transforming the deleterious effects of this faction, for 'the influence of faction,' Hume claims, 'is directly contrary to that of laws' (EMPL 55). But understanding the nature of these parties, and thereby allowing for the possibility that their negative effects might be minimized, is no easy task; and yet, as Hume makes quite clear, it is precisely the task for a historian: 'To determine the nature of these parties [Whig and Tory] is, perhaps, one of the most difficult problems that can be met with, and is a proof that history may contain questions, as uncertain as any to be found in the most abstract sciences' (EMPL 69).

In his extended treatment of Hume's efforts to get at the nature of the Whig and Tory faction, Duncan Forbes notes the significance for Hume of institutional factors. In particular, Forbes claims that Hume is right in pointing out that it was precisely the weakness of monarchical governments during the medieval period that led the monarch to justly rely on prerogative powers during times of crisis. As Forbes puts it, 'it was weak, not arbitrary government that led to disorder and therefore the need for prerogative of kings' (Forbes 1975, 286). In contrast to the claims of the Whigs that the king's exercise of prerogative was arbitrary and therefore inconsistent with liberty, Hume argues that the prerogative power of the king was necessary to maintain order during a time when the government was weak, and by maintaining order the king is in this way best able to serve the people. This argument, among others, led many to accuse Hume of being a Tory historian. And yet the Tories would find their own reasons for disliking Hume's book, and this precisely because of the transformations within society that were underway, especially the increase of wealth within England. On Forbes' reading of Hume's history, 'The increase of wealth and luxury weakened the king in relation to his subjects, and made his need for money greater, just when the same cause bred in them a spirit of freedom and independence' (ibid. 289). To maintain the level of power monarchs traditionally had relative to their subjects, they needed to extract significant financial resources. A significant portion of this money was used to fund a standing army which was a highly controversial matter during the eighteenth century, with Andrew Fletcher, among others, leading the charge against what he saw as the corruption of government that resulted from the new use of wealth (the founding of the Bank of England in 1690 was a particularly egregious case in point), especially its use to extend patronage power and to support standing armies.[6] But if the Whigs and others failed to recognize the justifiable need of the monarch for money given the economic transformations underway within England, the monarch likewise failed to recognize that the increased wealth of the people was giving them a greater sense of independence and liberty, and with this an increased impatience with James I's and Charles I's exercise of prerogative power. As Forbes sums up Hume's position:

> This allows one to see the conflict of king and commons as the result of political inexperience and ignorance on both sides: the progress of society created new conditions and new needs and demands, which rendered irregular 'Gothic' governments unworkable, and which at first nobody properly understood. (Ibid. 292)

Central to Hume's interpretation of historical events is the role played by institutions. This position is made quite explicit in his essay, 'Politics as Science,' where Hume argues that how an individual handles political affairs relies more on the institutions through which they act than on their talents: 'And so little dependence has this affair on the humours and education of particular men, that one part of the same republic may be wisely conducted, and another weakly, by the very same men, merely on account of the difference of the forms and institutions, by which these parts are regulated' (EMPL 24). And in his long essay, 'Of the Populousness of Ancient Nations,' Hume sets forth as his guiding premise the claim that 'it seems natural to expect, that, wherever there are most happiness and virtue, and the wisest institutions, there will also be most people' (EMPL 382). Hume then details the institutional advantages modern nations have relative to ancient nations, and with his premise in place summarizes his conclusion as follows:

> Our superior skill in mechanics; the discovery of new worlds, by which commerce has been so much enlarged; the establishment of posts; and the use of bills of exchange: These seem all extremely useful to the encouragement of art, industry, and populousness . . . Thus, upon comparing the whole, it seems impossible to assign any reason, why the world should have been more populous in ancient than in modern times. (EMPL 420)

What history has taught Hume, therefore, is the important role institutions play in determining whether a nation is populous, well governed, virtuous, and civilized. Moreover, as history teaches us how various institutional factors encourage or inhibit certain desirable consequences, the result, Hume hopes, is that his form of historical criticism may encourage the adoption of the successful institutional forms. In discussing commerce, for example, Hume argues that 'If we consult history, we shall find, that, in most nations, foreign trade has preceded any refinement in home manufactures, and given birth to domestic luxury' (EMPL 263). For those, and there were many in Hume's day, who discouraged trade with foreign neighbors out of fear that it would enrich the neighbors at their own expense, Hume calls upon the lessons of history to transform these opinions, and the institutions which realize them in practice. 'In opposition to this narrow and malignant opinion,' regarding the fear of open and free trade with foreign neighbors, Hume 'will venture to assert, that the encrease of riches and commerce in any one nation, instead of hurting, commonly promotes the riches and commerce of all its neighbors' (EMPL 328). As Hume's assertion became increasingly institutionalized, the free market system came to replace the mercantile system.[7]

This is not to say that Hume's historical criticism is responsible for undermining the mercantile system, nor that the historical criticism practiced by intellectuals could bring about such a fundamental change within social institutions. At times Hume does grant individuals tremendous creative potential. In his essay 'Of National Characters,' for example, he argues that 'A few eminent and refined geniuses will communicate their taste and knowledge to a whole people, and produce the greatest improvements; but they fix the tongue by their writings, and prevent, in some degree, its farther changes' (EMPL 209). Couple this statement with the instances where Hume speaks of the passivity of the people and it would seem that for Hume a few 'eminent geniuses' could indeed stamp their views upon the people as a whole, but in doing so they prevent, 'in some degree, its farther changes.' By contrast, in his essay 'Of the Rise of Arts and Sciences,' Hume claims that those 'who cultivate the sciences with such astonishing success, as to attract the admiration of posterity, be always few, in all nations and all ages,' do so because 'it is impossible but a share of the same spirit and genius must be antecedently diffused throughout the people among whom they arise, in order to produce, form, and cultivate, from their earliest infancy, the taste and judgment of those eminent writers' (EMPL 114). How, we might ask, does a creative, eminent genius, bring forth a truly novel innovation if their work was in some way 'antecedently diffused throughout the people'? How, in turn, can a genius stamp their views upon a passive people if the very views the genius is promulgating are themselves derived from the people? With these questions we return to the theme with which we were concerned in the previous chapter – namely, the relationship between creative events and the actual historical conditions within which these events occurred. In the context of Hume, this is now the problem of relating the work of the creative, eminent few to the people, the multitude; and since Hume addresses this theme most thoroughly in his essay on the rise of the arts and sciences, it is to this essay that we now turn.

II. The Rise of Arts and Sciences

Inseparable from Hume's account of the rise of arts and sciences is the notion that inductive generalizations can be applied to populations as a whole. As Hume puts it, 'Those principles or causes, which are fitted to operate on a multitude, are always of a grosser and more stubborn nature, less subject to accidents, and less influenced by whim and private fancy, than those which operate on a few only' (EMPL 112). Hume was not alone, among his Scottish peers, in his efforts to discover those 'principles or causes, which are fitted to operate on a multitude.' Adam Smith, Adam Ferguson, Lord Monboddo, and John Millar, among others, each pursued a similar research trajectory; and it is perhaps this common pursuit that was the most dominant feature of the Scottish Enlightenment, as has been widely noted.[8] It is with this understanding of the predictability of the multitude that the question of the eminent few creative geniuses arises, for the latter seem to appear, as Hume admits, rarely and unpredictably. It is at this point that Hume argues that although creative geniuses arise unpredictably, they do so within a context where the 'same spirit and genius' is 'antecedently diffused throughout the people.' Their occurrence, Hume concludes, must 'therefore be accounted for, in some measure, by general causes and principles' (EMPL 114).

Two further concepts are central to Hume's account: imitation and competition. Imitation is an important component of a number of Hume's arguments. In his essay, 'Of National Characters,' for example, Hume argues that attempts to account for the observed diversity of national characters on the basis of physical causes such as climate and geography ultimately fail to explain why these particular character traits emerged and not some others. Again taking history as his guide, Hume claims that, 'If we run over the globe, or revolve the annals of history, we shall discover every where signs of sympathy or contagion of manners, none of the influence of air or climate' (EMPL 204). Through sympathetic identification we come to imitate the manners and traits of others, and over time these traits become an identifiable national character. Nearly the same process is at work, on Hume's analysis, in the construction of a ship, which by all appearances is the product of great skill and ingenuity. Yet because of imitation, more often than not the opposite is true:

> If we survey a ship, what an exalted idea must we form of the ingenuity of the carpenter, who framed so complicated, useful, and beautiful a machine? And what surprise must we entertain, when we find him a stupid mechanic, who imitated others, and copied an art, which, through a long succession of ages, after multiplied trials, mistakes, corrections, deliberations, and controversies, had been gradually improving ... And a slow, but continued improvement carried on during infinite ages in the art of world-making. (DNR 167)

Such imitating is not, however, simply what the 'stupid mechanic' does, but is what everyone naturally does whenever an improvement is seen, whether this be an improvement in mechanics and ship-building or in the reasonings of science and philosophy. Moreover, such improvements are often initiated by foreigners, and thus through commerce with foreigners we may very well happen upon improvements that we will make our own through imitation. Hume is quite clear on this point: 'Every improvement, which we have since made, has arisen from our imitation of foreigners; and we ought so far to esteem it happy, that they had previously made advances in arts and ingenuity' (EMPL 328).

This leads us to the importance of competition for Hume, for although we may imitate an improvement of a foreigner, we do so only upon a critical examination of the merits of their improvement. For Hume this critical examination is a consequence of competitive jealousy of foreigners, and thus, 'where a number of neighboring states have a great intercourse of arts and commerce, their mutual jealousy keeps them from receiving too lightly the law from each other, in matters of taste and of reasoning, and makes them examine every work of art with the greatest care and accuracy' (EMPL 120). It is this process of imitation and competitive engagement with foreigners, as best exemplified for Hume by commerce, that best promotes the refinement and polished civility of a people. As long as one remains isolated in one's provincial home, seldom if ever having contact with other ways of life, then one is likely to be content with the simple, relatively inactive life of 'rustic hospitality,' as Hume puts it (EMPL 291). Luxuries and refined enjoyments spark a restlessness that draws people out of the lethargy of 'rustic hospitality,' and 'being once roused from their lethargy, and put into a fermentation, turn themselves on all sides, and carry improvements into every art and science' (EMPL 271). Commerce, imitation, and competition are thus inseparably connected to the process of becoming civil, as Hume readily recognizes:

> The more these refined arts advance, the more sociable men become . . . Thus industry, knowledge, and humanity, are linked together by an indissoluble chain, and are found, from experience as well as reason, to be peculiar to the more polished, and, what are commonly denominated, the more luxurious ages. (EMPL 271)

A final premise upon which Hume's account of the rise and progress of arts and sciences is based is the role played by a diverse field (or heterogeneous field as we have referred to it) of interacting agents. It is the diverse field of European states engaged in commercial interactions with one another (and military conflicts[9]) that drives the civilizing process. It is precisely because China lacks this diversity that it has failed, according to Hume, to progress in the arts and sciences in the same way that European states have:

> But China is one vast empire, speaking one language, governed by one law, and sympathizing in the same manners. The authority of any teacher, such as Confucius, was propagated easily from one corner of the empire to the other. None had the courage to resist the torrent of popular opinion . . . This seems to be one natural reason, why the sciences have made so slow a progress in that mighty empire. (EMPL 122)[10]

Had China pursued a commercial path of exchange with foreign neighbors, the natural diversity of resources and talents would have largely guaranteed Chinese progress in the arts and sciences. A diverse, heterogeneous field thus allows for the possibility of becoming civil as the field comes to be drawn into increasingly finer distinctions and habits. Take away these habits and what you will be left with is a blooming, buzzing, senseless diversity. In an example Hume first gave in his *Treatise*, and then repeated in the first *Enquiry*, he argues that 'it 'tis evident, that if a person full grown, and of the same nature with ourselves, were on a sudden transported into our world, he would be very much embarrass'd with every object, and wou'd not readily find what degree of love or hatred, pride or humility, or any other passion he ought to attribute to it' (T 293–4; see also, EHU 120). Most adults have not been suddenly transported into 'our world,' and thus they have long acquired the habitual mode of being in this world, with the various passions, and so on, that are attributed to the objects of this world. And yet, as Hume's thought experiment makes clear, the reality of the world as we experience it is inseparable from the habits themselves.

To recall Latour's argument that construction and autonomous reality ought to be seen as synonymous, we can see now that for Hume as well a customary and habitual construction of reality, or a 'world-making' as Hume put it in an earlier quote, does not imply that the objects of the world are less real. In fact, just as Latour argues that the more constructed a scientific entity is, the more autonomous reality it has, so too for Hume the more habitual and customary our associations, the more real they become. In a different context, Hume says much the same concerning the legitimacy of magistrates, arguing that 'time alone gives solidity to their right; and operating gradually on the minds of men, reconciles them to any authority, and makes it seem just and reasonable' (T 556). The same is also true for Hume's understanding of justice, and in particular the right to property. Justice, Hume claims, arises by convention, but it is not for that reason arbitrary or a result of some 'voluntary choice' (in contrast to social contract theory):

> But if by convention be meant a sense of common interest; which sense each man feels in his own breast, which he remarks in his fellows, and which carries him in concurrence with others, into a general plan or system of actions, which tends to public utility; it must be owned, that, in this sense, justice arises from human conventions. (EPM 306)

This sense of an obligation for the common interest does not arise, as Hume makes clear, from an instinctual love for humanity,[11] but rather arises over time as the process of becoming civil habituates us to the reality of justice. The 'stability of possession . . . arises gradually,' Hume claims, and 'acquires force [i.e., reality] by a slow progression, and by our repeated experience of the inconveniences of transgressing it' (T 490). As Latour set forth a theory of relative existence to avoid the metaphysical dualism of subject–object, it appears Hume offers a similar theory, and for similar reasons – namely, to avoid the instinct–convention dualism. Hume will thus argue that 'we must allow, that the sense of justice and injustice is not deriv'd from nature [i.e. there is no instinctual love for humanity or respect for property], but arises artificially, tho' necessarily from education, and human conventions' (T 483); or again, 'Tho' the rules of justice be artificial, they are not arbitrary' (T 484). Unlike superstition, which is also an unnatural, artificial convention, justice, by contrast, is for Hume 'absolutely requisite to the well-being of mankind and existence of society' (EPM 199). As our instinctual self-interest becomes civilized and virtuous through an increasing historical sense and refinement of our sensibilities, then the interests in justice and property, the interest in the common good, becomes positively reinforced over time – in short, it becomes increasingly real.

We can now begin to address the problem with which this section began – namely, the relationship between the few eminent geniuses who stamp their views upon a passive people and the spirit diffused through this people that provides the fertile soil from which these eminent geniuses arise. As Hume understands the process of becoming civil, it involves a movement of territorialization (to use Deleuze and Guattari's term), whereby the diversity of sentiments, passions, interests, and talents are drawn into an habituated orientation that is then placed under the guidance and direction of the common good. With respect to our individual actions, the intensity and diversity of the passions becomes, through habit, 'a settled principle of action . . . As repeated custom and its own force have made everything yield to it, it directs the actions and conduct without that opposition and emotion, which so naturally attend every momentary gust of passion' (T 418–19). Without the force of custom, without beliefs, we would be left in a state where 'impressions alone influence the will, [and] we should every moment of our lives be subject to the greatest calamities' (T 119); and one such calamity is 'madness or folly' which results when 'a present impression and a customary transition are now no longer necessary to inliven our ideas' (T 123). In other words, if any impression is capable of enlivening our ideas, rather than the beliefs that are the more lively ideas founded upon customary transition and habit, then the result is an uncontrollable furiosity (as madness was frequently referred to in the eighteenth century) whereby one becomes subject to delusional beliefs that 'run wide of common life' (DNR 135). It is as a check on delusional beliefs and superstition that 'abstruse thought' has a positive role to play – a territorializing role. In this context, skepticism will reveal the imperfection of our faculties and thus we 'will never be tempted to go beyond common life, so long as they consider the imperfection of those faculties which they employ, their narrow reach, and their inaccurate operations' (EHU 209).

In contrast to this territorializing movement, there is the deterritorializing movement of abstruse thought that goes beyond truth, beyond the commonly accepted beliefs, in order, as Hume says, that 'they [may] suggest hints, at least, and start difficulties, which they want, perhaps, skill to pursue; but which may produce fine discoveries, when handled by men who have a more just way of thinking' (EMPL 253). Abstruse thinkers who lack a 'more just way of thinking' will present thoughts, problems, hints, and so on, that unsettle the common way of life, and in this sense their thought may indeed be seen by others to be fanciful, false, and possibly even delusional. It is only when these abstruse thoughts become territorialized by those with more skill and ability that they can then be said to be 'fine discoveries' and innovations. The few eminent geniuses, therefore, are able to produce novel innovations only by affirming the double movement of territorialization and deterritorialization. The innovations of the genius become stamped upon the people as the abstruse thoughts become territorialized and become *commonly* perceived as the innovations they are; at the same time, this return of the abstruse thought to the common way of life is made possible by an unsettling and destabilizing of the common from within the common. It is an abstruse thought relative to the territory it deterritorializes, and hence it is from within the spirit of a people that such thoughts acquire their abstruse character. In short, the creative genius initiates a thought at the edge of chaos, a thought that is both destabilizing and chaotic and yet bears enough consistency to become actualized within a transformed common way of life.[12] Hume himself recognizes the necessity of both order and chaos. In *Dialogues Concerning Natural Religion*, for example, he asks and then answers the following question:

> Is there a system, an order, an economy of things, by which matter can preserve that perpetual agitation, which seems essential to it, and yet maintain a constancy in the forms, which it produces? . . . this is actually the case with the present world . . . A defect in any of these particulars destroys the form; and the matter, of which it is composed, is again set loose, and is thrown into irregular motions and fermentations, till it unite itself to some other regular form. (DNR 183)

Deleuze and Guattari, in their two *Capitalism and Schizophrenia* books (*Anti-Oedipus* and *A Thousand Plateaus*), make much the same point. As beliefs and habits are for Hume perpetually haunted by the diversity that makes them possible, and thus are forever susceptible to superstition, delusion, and madness, so too is Capitalism, itself made possible by the chaotic limits it forever attempts to stave off, and subsequently subject to the uncontrolled, undisciplined rupture of chaos, which is precisely how Deleuze and Guattari understand schizophrenia. It is to this comparison that we now turn, and in doing so we shall further clarify the nature of 'abstruse thought' and its role in fostering creative moves beyond the actualities of daily, common life.

III. Commerce and Schizophrenia

In the *Leviathan* (1651) Hobbes claims that for one 'to have stronger and more vehement passions for anything than is ordinarily seen in others is that which men call "madness" ' (Hobbes [1651] 1994, 41). By the middle of the eighteenth century, the Hobbesian view began to show signs of shifting. In his *A Treatise of Madness*, for instance, William Battie, the physician to St. Luke's Hospital outside London, reiterates Hobbes' view that 'too great and too lively a perception of objects that really exist creates an uneasiness not felt by the generality of men,' but he then immediately adds, in a conscious effort to modify the Hobbesian view, that although this 'frequently accompanies madness,' or what was frequently called 'furiosity,' it 'is no more essentially annexed to Madness . . . than Fever, Head-ach, Gout, or Leprosy' (Battie 1758, 4–5). The same is true, Battie adds, for 'idiocy,' where there is 'too little and too languid a perception' (ibid.). It is, Battie argues, a 'deluded imagination, which is not only an indisputable but an essential character of Madness' (ibid. 5–6). It is the 'deluded imagination,' the break with reality – with 'really existent things' as Battie put it – that is the essential characteristic of madness, even though such a break with reality is frequently accompanied by a response to impressions that is beyond the 'common way of life.' This break or withdrawal from reality is integral to the contemporary understanding of madness, and most particularly schizophrenia.[13]

At first it might seem that Hume continues to hold to the Hobbesian view of madness. In his essay 'Of the Delicacy of Taste and Passion,' for example, Hume warns against the dangers of delicacy of passion, which makes people 'extremely sensible to all the accidents of life' (EMPL 3). Consequently, whenever a misfortune occurs, a person with delicacy of passion will feel 'sorrow or resentment [such that it] takes entire possession of him, and deprives him of all relish in the common occurrences of life' (EMPL 4). In the *Treatise* as well, madness, as we saw, was seen to be what occurs when a lively imagination degenerates. Hume then adds, however, that a consequence of this degeneration of the imagination is an inability to distinguish 'betwixt truth and falsehood; but every loose fiction or idea, having the same influence as the impressions of the memory, or the conclusions of judgment, is receiv'd on the same footing, and operates with equal force on the passions' (T 123). While a person who suffers from a delicacy of passion may overreact to a misfortune, the misfortune is nonetheless a real misfortune, whereas the mad will respond to any 'loose fiction or idea' as if it were on 'the same footing' as a real misfortune. As with Battie, therefore, an essential component of madness is its delusional break with reality.

We need to tread carefully here, however, for as Hume makes quite clear, and as was argued earlier, to diagnose madness is not simply to show that one passionately believes something that is false, or that they adhere to an idea that fails to correspond to an objective reality. Such a diagnosis presupposes the vulgar distinction between subjects and objects, when it is precisely this distinction that falls before Hume's skeptical analysis. For Hume, as we have been arguing, reality is not a transcendent entity that is independent of the processes through which this reality comes to be believed in. Echoing Latour's arguments, the habituation of our responses to impressions – the drawing of a diverse, heterogeneous field into a plane of consistent reactions and behaviors – is synonymous to the autonomous reality that comes to be known, and to the true or false statements one can make regarding this reality.

How then are we to understand Hume's comments concerning madness? Put simply, madness is for Hume, as schizophrenia will be for Deleuze and Guattari, the limit that must forever be staved off in order to maintain the common order necessary for the functioning of society. What is the difference between one person who believes they are God, Napoleon, and so on, another who believes that they can take an apple from one tree but not from another a few yards away, and yet another who believes that the bread and wine of communion becomes the body and blood of Christ? In all three cases, there is nothing within the impressions themselves to justify these beliefs. For Hume, however, belief in property rights is 'absolutely requisite to the well-being of mankind and existence of society' (EPM 199). Religious beliefs, as William James argued in *The Varieties of Religious Experience*, may promote an enthusiasm for life that ultimately serves the 'well-being of mankind,' but these beliefs can also serve to prop up dogmatism and intolerance. It was the prevalence of this latter form of religious belief that prompted much of Hume's invective against superstition. Madness, however, breaks with the common way of life by breaking the habits that secure the well-being of society, or it breaks with the reality that is nothing less than the diverse field drawn into a habitual plane of consistency (constancy); and in breaking with this reality madness confronts the common experience of the world with its condition of possibility, a condition inseparable from though not to be confused with this actualization.

At this point we return to our earlier discussions of Deleuze. In an earlier chapter we saw that for Deleuze transcendental empiricism as a philosophical endeavor is to be contrasted with 'everything that makes up the world of the subject and the object' (PI 25). Key to this endeavor is an understanding of a life as the absolute immanence that comes to be drawn into the transcendental fields that are in turn actualized by a consciousness that is a consciousness of an object. In the context of *Anti-Oedipus*, Deleuze and Guattari argue that 'capitalism is indeed the limit of all societies, insofar as it brings about the decoding of the flows that the other social formations coded and overcoded' (AO 245–6). This does not mean, however, that capitalism is itself the limit to be staved off; to the contrary, Deleuze and Guattari quite explicitly argue that 'it would be a serious error to consider the capitalist flows and the schizophrenic flows as identical, under the general theme of a decoding of the flows of desire' (AO 245). The key difference is that capitalist decoding functions by transforming entities into salable commodities, whereas 'schizos,' as they put it, 'are not salable.' Schizophrenia is thus the limit to decoding that capitalism presupposes but must not actualize if it is to continue functioning. As Deleuze and Guattari summarize the point:

> Hence one can say that schizophrenia is the exterior limit of capitalism itself or the conclusion of its deepest tendency, but that capitalism only functions on condition that it inhibit this tendency, or that it push it back or displace this limit, by substituting for it its own immanent relative limits, which it continually reproduces on a widened scale. (AO 246)

The schizoanalysis Deleuze and Guattari propose is an effort then to push capitalism to this limit, to push it to the point where it ceases to be able to function by way of subordinating creativity to a process of universal commodification. Deleuze and Guattari's understanding of pragmatics is similarly motivated, as we saw, in that it strives to push the actualities of life to the point where decoded, pre-individual singularities force a transformation and creative becoming-other of these actualities. For Hume too, abstruse thought deterritorializes and decodes the common conceptions, and when handled by competent hands this abstruse thought can result in an innovative move beyond the actualities of these common conceptions.

For Hume the best way to avoid the dangers of madness that may result if the delicacy of passion degenerates is to become civil, to develop a refined taste: 'nothing is so proper to cure this delicacy of passion, as the cultivating of that higher and more refined taste, which enables us to judge of the characters of men, of compositions of genius, and of the productions of the nobler arts' (EMPL 6). Rather than an undisciplined response to the diversity of phenomena, a refined taste develops a disciplined appreciation of the finer points and distinctions. As Hume puts it in his essay 'Of the Standard of Taste,' this disciplining of sensibilities that produces a person with refined taste entails 'allow[ing] him to acquire experience in those objects, [so that] his feeling becomes more exact and nice: He not only perceives the beauties and defects of each part, but marks the distinguishing species of each quality, and assigns it suitable praise or blame' (EMPL 237). A necessary first step in this process, for Hume, is commerce: 'Laws, order, police, discipline; these can never be carried to any degree of perfection, before human reason has refined itself by exercise, and by an application to the more vulgar arts, at least, of commerce and manufacture' (EMPL 273). In short, the deterritorializing flows of commerce prompt the reterritorializing movement that becomes, in time (historical ontology), the civilities of law and culture. As Deleuze and Guattari put the point, 'Civilization is defined by the decoding and deterritorialization of flows in capitalist production' (AO 244).

For Hume, then, institutions are creative; as Deleuze points out, our natural self-interest 'does not reach its ends except by means of culture, and tendency is not satisfied except through the institution' (ES 44). In short, for Hume, on Deleuze's reading, 'the essence of society is not the law but rather the institution' (ES 45). One becomes who one is, as we saw, through a creative integration of the diversity and multiplicity of impressions in the imagination, and in this way we become the creature of habits we are, with all our partialities. Similarly, society becomes what it is through the creative integration of partialities that then become subordinate to the common good. This integration does not arise instinctually – there is no instinctual love of mankind for Hume – but comes about by way of institutions. As Deleuze reads Hume, the most important of these institutions is the state, which 'is not charged with representing the general interest but rather with making the general interest an object of belief. It succeeds in this by giving the general interest, mostly through the mechanism of its sanctions, the vividness that only particular interests can have for us naturally' (ES 51). The state institution thus provides the discipline necessary to keep the deterritorializing tendencies in check by capturing and reterritorializing them, and when successful in doing so it will 'enter the natural constitution of the mind as a feeling for humanity or as culture' (ES 130).

IV. Institutions, Power, and Culture

In the published conversation, 'Intellectuals and Power,' Deleuze and Foucault address the relationship between theory and practice and the role of the intellectual, if any, in sparking political movements. With the events of May '68 fresh in their memories at the time of their conversation, they draw a straightforward conclusion from these events. As Foucault states it, 'the masses no longer need him [the intellectual] to gain knowledge; they know perfectly well, without illusion; they know far better than he and they are certainly capable of expressing themselves' (Foucault 1977, 207). And yet, despite the fact that the multitude expressed themselves during the events of May '68, the power of the state, and in particular the educational institutions, were not radically transformed. A further lesson Deleuze and Foucault draw from this is just how effective the totalizing power of the state is, and moreover the extent to which we desire our own totalization. For an intellectual to represent the masses, for Deleuze, would then be to play the role of a state functionary who totalizes the interests and desires of the multitude and speaks for them. What then is the role of the intellectual?

The short answer is that theory 'is practice' – 'it is local and regional . . . and not totalizing' (ibid. 208). As Deleuze clarifies the point: 'A theory does not totalize; it is an instrument for multiplication and it also multiplies itself,' and since it 'is in the nature of power to totalize . . . theory is by nature opposed to power' (ibid.). If the role of the state and institutions is to totalize the partialities of the multitude, then theoretical practice, as practice, works at the local level to generate partialities that escape the totalizing nets of power, enabling the power of the multitude to speak for itself. In contrast to a reform movement that changes a totality while maintaining the power of the totalizing form (as happened after the events of May '68), a revolutionary movement arises with an 'action that questions (expressing the full force of its partiality) the totality of power and the hierarchy that maintains it' (ibid. 209). Such a revolutionary practice does not set forth a totalizing view that represents the multitude, nor does it work with power in order to instill the proper sense of humanity, nationalism, and propriety. To the extent that this is Hume's understanding of the role of the intellectual, then Hume is at best a reformer and at worst a mere functionary of state power. Deleuze's Hume, however, provides us with 'a box of tools' (ibid. 208) that can be used to counter-actualize the actualities of state power. In particular, Deleuze's Hume, as an experimental transcendental empiricist, begins with the actualities of this world (the actualities of state power) in order to force into play the partialities that are inseparable from them, partialities that may counter-actualize and transform these actualities. Foucault states this programmatic quite explicitly:

> And when the prisoners began to speak, they possessed an individual theory of prisons, the penal system, and justice. It is this form of discourse which ultimately matters, a discourse against power, the counter-discourse of prisoners and those we call delinquents – and not a theory *about* delinquency. (ibid. 209)

If power totalizes partialities, the counter-discourse of the theoretical practice Deleuze and Foucault pursue is inseparable from the task of labor to express 'the full force of its partiality.' 'Every revolutionary attack or defense,' Deleuze states in the concluding line of the conversation with Foucault, is directed against every effort to totalize the struggle, and only in this way does it become linked to and thus become a part of 'the workers' struggle' (ibid. 217). The workers' struggle is thus not to be understood as a general struggle, a struggle that subsumes all other struggles – for example, the struggle for prison reform, women's rights, same sex marriage, the environment, and so on – but is the struggle of partialities, or what Deleuze and Guattari will also refer to as minorities (in contrast to majorities). These partialities, however, are not to be thought of as partial with respect to a totality that has what the partiality lacks. Nothing is lacking for the partialities themselves. To the contrary, a partiality is what Deleuze and Guattari call a nondenumerable set, a set that 'is neither the set nor its elements; rather, it is the connection, the "and" produced between elements, between sets, and which belongs to neither, which eludes them and constitutes a line of flight' (TP 470). A nondenumerable set is thus the power of AND, the power of multiplicity, or multitude, that 'constitutes a line of flight' and eludes being thought in terms of identifiable sets and elements of sets (as One or Multiple). In mathematics, for example, the set of all real numbers includes the denumerable and nondenumerable (such as *pi*), and since, as mathematicians argue, the nondenumerable far exceeds the denumerable it follows that nondenumerable sets are not lacking what any denumerable set might have; to the contrary, denumerable sets never exhaust and forever underdetermine nondenumerable sets.

Whenever the workers' struggle finds an escape from power and follows a line of flight that decodes and deterritorializes the codes and territories of state power, the predictable response of power is to attempt to reterritorialize these flows. In the 'Apparatus of Capture' chapter from *A Thousand Plateaus*, Deleuze and Guattari analyze in detail the processes associated with the territorializing powers of the state that capture and incorporate these decoded flows. The first form of capture they discuss is the 'imperial or despotic' mode of capture:

> [This] State apparatus is erected upon the primitive agricultural communities, which already have lineal-territorial codes; but it overcodes them, submitting them to the power of a despotic emperor, the sole and transcendent public-property owner, the master of the surplus of the stock, the organizer of large-scale works (surplus labor), the source of public functions and bureaucracy. (TP 427–8)

This capture and overcoding of primitive agricultural communities by imperial states presupposes, as a correlate of this very capturing, the nondenumerable partialities that elude the overcoding. Deleuze and Guattari are clear on this point: 'What counts is that in one way or another the apparatus of overcoding gives rise to flows that are themselves decoded – flows of money, labor, property . . . These flows are the correlate of the apparatus' (TP 449). For example, in the case of property, although the imperial State overcodes the territories in order to constitute the realm of the emperor-despot (what Deleuze and Guattari refer to as 'land' in contrast to 'territory'), a correlate the public realm or land presupposes are the decoded flows that elude capture. The State, Deleuze and Guattari claim, 'does not create a system of public property without a flow of private appropriation growing up beside it, then beginning to pass beyond its grasp' (TP 449). These decoded flows are precisely the power of AND, the power of the multitude, and from the perspective of State power (as totalizing power), it is generally perceived to be a power of uncontrolled chaos, ignorance, and irrationality, and something that needs to be disciplined and controlled by the institutions of the State if the common good is to be realized. Understood in this way, the multitude needs the overcoding, capturing powers of the State in order to maintain the necessary functioning of society. For Deleuze, however, the multitude is the nondenumerable set that is not only inseparable from and presupposed by the capturing powers of the State, but is also in no need of the State.[14] The multitude is lacking in nothing, yet it is precisely the capturing function of the State to instill this lack, and when successful this lack, on Deleuze's reading of Hume again, will 'enter the natural constitution of the mind as a feeling for humanity or as culture' (ES 130). It is this need for humanity or culture that is inseparable from our belief that the institutions of the State will provide for the humanity and culture we otherwise lack. And yet this belief already expresses a capturing and delimiting of the nondenumerable multitude, a multitude that is not, as Foucault realized in the wake of May '68, in need of intellectuals or institutions to tell them what they desire – 'they know perfectly well, without illusion.'

Let us return now to our earlier discussion of the relationship between the few eminent geniuses and the multitude that provides the context from which they arise. First, and most importantly, the creativity of individuals is irreducible to a determinable set of social and cultural preconditions. On this point Badiou was quite correct to argue that the creativity of Haydn, for example, marked the void of the Baroque situation of his day. To reduce the creativity of Haydn to the determinable (denumerable) social and cultural conditions of the time would result, Badiou argues, in a foreclosure of the void, and thus the new would simply be a variation upon the old and would not be truly new. Thus, if the multitude that provides the context from which geniuses arise consists of a denumerable set of relations and conditions, then arguing that this multitude gives rise to the creative individual would indeed be subject to Badiou's criticism. But Deleuze and Guattari do not understand the multitude in this way. Quite to the contrary, the multitude is a nondenumerable set that is irreducible to any (even infinitely many) denumerable sets. What is crucial to the multitude are not the elements that could become part of a denumerable set, but rather the associations and relationships between these elements, or the power of 'and' (TP 470). It is this connective power, the power to draw and redraw associations, that is nondenumerable. This is not to say that these associations are inaccessible, or that they involve processes that are fundamentally *not* of the world of actualities. To the contrary, the connective associations and the power of 'and . . . and . . .' is inseparable from the elements that come to be identified by virtue of their associations.[15]

To clarify the role of the multitude as nondenumerable set, we can contrast it with what Pierre Bourdieu and Fritz Ringer have referred to as the cultural unconscious (or preconscious). Bourdieu, for example, is quite forthright in arguing that an intellectual or artist, in 'his most conscious intellectual and artistic choices [is] always directed by his own culture and taste, which are themselves interiorizations of the objective culture of a particular society, age or class' (Bourdieu 1968, 112). This culture of a particular time 'consists,' Bourdieu adds, of 'credos which are so obvious that they are tacitly assumed rather than explicitly postulated,' and thus the choices of intellectuals and artists are to a large degree 'not properly speaking the object of a conscious choice' to the extent that they continue to adhere to the unquestioned assumptions and credos of the culture. When a creative work appears, Bourdieu argues, its value is nothing less than the position of this work relative to other works, individuals, and institutions within the fields that mediate and determine (overcode) these positions.

Fritz Ringer extends the work of Bourdieu in a manner that has significant parallels to what we take to be Deleuze's Humean approach to intellectual history. In his essay 'The Intellectual Field, intellectual history, and the sociology of knowledge,' Ringer argues that original and coherent thought is to be understood as a 'kind of clarification, an emergence toward clarity' (Ringer 1990, 273), and what is clarified are, following Bourdieu, the 'tacit assumptions of a cultural world,' or what he calls the 'cultural preconscious.' What the creative, original intellectual is able to do, in other words, is to put forth a work that holds together a disparate multiplicity of practices within the intellectual world of the time. This holding together 'clarifies' the work of this field by making explicit what was already implicitly at work in the writings, discussions, and so on, of the intellectuals at the time. The intellectual is not, on this view, the self-caused genius who, like a pied piper, sets the terms that all other intellectuals in the field follow.

Others follow only because they were already implicitly doing what the creative intellectual does, but does more clearly. For an intellectual to become a 'star' or leader they must articulate (first articulation) in a consistent manner the diverse, heterogeneous intellectual field of which they are a part (the cultural preconscious), and as others come increasingly to recognize this clarified field the intellectual comes to be identified as being (second articulation) a canonical figure in that field. This cultural preconscious, however, is on Ringer's view (and the same is true for Bourdieu as well) a field that is an already ordered and consistent field, a denumerable set, and the creative intellectual simply expresses the order of this field to others; they do not, of themselves, problematize by thinking the nondenumerable set, the 'and,' inseparable from it. Thus, from a Deleuzian perspective the intellectual, on Ringer's account, is not truly thinking beyond the intellectual field, beyond what is given. They are not experimenting with the actual relationships that compose the intellectual field – be they textual, interpersonal, and institutional – so as to intensify them and force a reordering of the field, and with it the clarifying work Ringer discusses. The creative intellectual for Ringer simply clarifies to others the givens with which they were already working, but without consciousness (hence the cultural preconscious). But for Deleuze this is not creative thinking, thinking beyond what is actually given; it is an unmasking or revealing of what is already actually given.

There is an additional problem with Ringer's view and others like it that attempt to make society, or social institutions and factors, the already established and constituted element that then prefigures intellectual life. Whether this is an intellectual field, class interest, ideology, and so on, we need to be wary of assuming that society functions as an already constituted causal factor that constitutes the creative individuals who are simply the effects that were already implicated in the cause. Not only does this deny the very novelty of the creative intellectual by treating it as the actualization of what is already there, it also presupposes a subject–object dualism whereby society is the constituting subject and creative intellectuals are the constituted objects. It was precisely to avoid this dualism that Latour refused to categorize himself among the social constructivists, for he does not see society as the subject that constitutes its objects, such as intellectuals or what have you; to the contrary, 'society is more compellingly seen as continually constructed or "performed" by active social beings who violate "levels" in the process of their work' (Latour and Strum 1987, 84). In other words, and as with Hume, the identity of the social, as well as the identity of what it means to be a polished, civil member of society, is inseparable from an historical ontology – that is, inseparable from processes involving the violation of levels Latour and Strum refer to, meaning, on our reading, the processes that test and experiment with actualities in order to force the power of 'and . . . and . . .', and thus enable the possibility of thinking beyond these actualities. This was, recall, what Hume sought to do in his experimental philosophizing, but not what 'honest gentlemen' do who have rarely if ever 'carried their thoughts beyond those objects, which are every day expos'd to their senses.'

Understood in this way, and as we will see in greater detail when we discuss the Scottish Enlightenment in the next chapter, a Deleuzian intellectual history will indeed study the institutional and sociological factors of the time. Deleuze, recall, does not abandon traditional history and in fact frequently relies upon the work of historians. In studying the Scottish Enlightenment in this way, we will look to certain changes in the institutional and social structures of the time as a causal explanation for the rise of creative intellectual work in Scotland in the latter half of the eighteenth century. For Deleuze, however, this would be a standard history, a history that moves from the virtual as a problematized field to the actual solutions and changes that occurred at the time. In moving from the actual to the virtual, however, we will certainly begin with and not ignore the arguments and findings of the traditional histories of the Scottish Enlightenment, including the histories of the intellectual solutions of the literati of the day, but a problematizing history will attempt to force the solutions arrived at by Hume, Smith, Ferguson, and others to express the partiality that is inseparable from them, the nondenumerable sets that can then be actualized by yet other creative solutions. In other words, such an intellectual history will be an attempt to problematize the current intellectual field, the actual field where you, the reader of this book, are situated such that this book was selected to be read based on certain preconceptions of how it might lead you to address issues and problems that are of interest to the current intellectual field. By problematizing this field, the concepts of Hume will come to be seen *not* as tools with a predetermined use and application, but rather as the inventive byproducts of a generative process, an historical ontology that focuses not on what has been thought, but rather on the problems associated with thinking itself, the problems associated with trying to think beyond what has actually been thought, beyond the already actualized intellectual field. Thus, although intellectuals may begin with certain texts and traditions, the very *identity* of what these texts mean needs forever to be reconstituted, and in this process accepted meanings may be violated, or new readings arise that problematize the intellectual field. Approached in this way a study of the Scottish Enlightenment may not satisfy an antiquarian or scholarly interest in what these great thinkers of the past thought, but, hopefully, it may engender creative thinking, a thinking that can open possibilities in today's world that are beyond those already offered, beyond those already tried. It was this type of creative thinking during the Scottish Enlightenment that engendered many of the unquestioned ways we actually think about ourselves and our place in the world today; it will be a similar creative thinking that will bring forth the unquestioned actualities of tomorrow.

Notes

1. One of the more noteworthy of such criticisms is R. G. Collingwood's, who claims that Hume was not historical enough and never showed 'the slightest suspicion that the human nature he is analyzing in his philosophical work is the nature of a western European in the early eighteenth century, and that the very same enterprise if undertaken at a widely different time or place might have yielded widely different results' (Collingwood 1946, 83). For a sympathetic reading, see Schmidt 2003.
2. In a letter to Henry Home, Lord Kames, of 1 June 1739, Hume admits that 'My fondness for what I imagined new discoveries, made me overlook all common rules of prudence' (L1 31).
3. On 12 August 1776, less than two weeks before his death on the 25th, Hume sent his publisher William Strahan corrections to the *Enquiry Concerning the Principle of Morals* (see L2 331).
4. In this same essay, Hume argues that 'The advantages found in history seem to be of three kinds, as it amuses the fancy, as it improves the understanding, and as it strengthens virtue' (EMPL 565). The latter two correspond to the two movements of history, the abstract and philosophical, on the one hand, and the practical on the other. The third will be discussed below as we address the concerns Hume has with an undisciplined sensibility.
5. See EMPL 239: 'But to enable a critic the more fully to execute this undertaking, he must preserve his mind free from all prejudice, and allow nothing to enter into his consideration, but the very object which is submitted to his examination.'
6. There is a tremendous body of literature on this subject. Of note, see Pocock's *The Machiavellian Moment* (Pocock 1975) and *Virtue, Commerce and History* (Pocock 1985). See note 15 below for more on Pocock.
7. At this point there is a convergence between Hume and Adam Smith. There is a large body of literature that explores Adam Smith's position on mercantilism and free market capitalism. For a recent work on the subject, see Evensky 2007.
8. Gladys Bryson, in her book *Man and Society* (1945), was one of the first writers to draw attention to what is now commonly referred to as the Scottish Enlightenment. As the title of her book indicates, with the Scottish Enlightenment the notion developed that society itself can be an object of study. More recently, Christopher Berry has intentionally revisited Bryson's theme in his book *The Social Theory of the Scottish Enlightenment* (Berry 1997). The influence of the Scottish Enlightenment on figures such as Kant is evident in, for example, Kant's essay 'Universal History,' where he echoes Hume's statement regarding the multitude: 'History . . . allows us to hope that if we examine *the play of the human will's freedom in the large*, we can discover its course to

conform to rules as well as to hope that what strikes us as complicated and unpredictable in the single individual may in the history of the entire species be discovered to be the steady progress and slow development of its original capacities' (Kant [1784] 1983, 29).
9. William McNeill has argued that the military competition of European states prompted an arms race that led to a series of commercial and military innovations, and ultimately to the merger of the commercial and military enterprises into the current Military-Industrial complex. See McNeill 1982.
10. John Stuart Mill repeats this same argument in his essay 'On Liberty' (See Mill [1859] 1991, 79–80). More recently, Randall Collins has argued that China failed to maintain the path of innovation it was on during the fourteenth century precisely because it withdrew from commercial interaction with foreign neighbors and moved the capital, out of fear of Mongol invasions, from the coastal town of Shanghai to the interior and more remote northern city of Beijing. See Collins 1990, 130–1.
11. See T 481: 'there is no such passion in human minds as the love of mankind, merely as such, independent of personal qualities, of services, or of relation to ourself.'
12. For more on this, see Bell 2006b.
13. A complicated series of parameters are currently used to define schizophrenia, but a delusional break with reality continues to be one of the dominant symptoms that contributes to a diagnosis of schizophrenia. See the American Psychiatric Association 2000.
14. An important influence on Deleuze and Guattari's work here is Pierre Clastres' *Society Against the State* (Clastres 1987).
15. It could be argued that Pocock's methodological approach to intellectual history is one that attempts to maintain fidelity to these connective associations. For Pocock, '[i]t is a large part of our historian's practice to learn to read and recognize the diverse idioms of political discourse as they were available in the culture and at the time he is studying: to identify them as they appear in the linguistic texture of any one text, and to know what they would ordinarily have enabled the text's author to propound or "say"' (Pocock 1985, 9). In the vein of Foucault, therefore, Pocock's intellectual history seeks to determine the historical *a priori* that functions as the condition for the possibility of what an author actually 'says.' Where a Deleuzian historiography differs is that while what an author says is, on Pocock's view, reducible to the actual associations of the day, for Deleuze (following Hume) when an author says something new it is irreducible to these actual associations and instead draws from the 'unhistorical vapour' (the reality of the virtual) that is inseparable from them.

Chapter 5

Creating Culture: The Case of the Scottish Enlightenment

As Deleuze and Foucault make quite clear, the primary role of the intellectual is not that of representing an already established consensus or intellectual field, but rather one of engaging in a counter-discourse that counter-actualizes the givens of the field. To counter-actualize the unquestioned givens of an intellectual field, or to carry out a problematizing history of this field, is precisely to engage with the reality of the virtual. In *What is Philosophy?* Deleuze and Guattari refer to this engagement as a higher taste, an attunement to the problematic that is inseparable from the actual. And this is the case, they argue, in both science and philosophy, despite the difference they see between the two – namely, whereas science seeks to determine the functions that actualize the virtual (virtual → actual), philosophy strives to move to the virtual and to give 'consistency to the virtual on a plane of immanence' (actual → virtual) (WP 133). Both science and philosophy each engage with 'a *problem*' in a way that

> does not consist in answering a question but in adapting, in co-adapting, with a higher 'taste' as problematic faculty, corresponding elements in the process of being determined (for example, for science, choosing the good independent variables, installing the effective partial observer on a particular route, and constructing the best coordinates of an equation or function). (Ibid.)

It is this higher 'taste' for those 'elements in the process of being determined' that is shared by both science and philosophy. Science, however, as Deleuze and Guattari then argue, will reduce this process to being merely a functional relationship between actualities on a 'plane of reference' (as they call it), while philosophy attempts to draw concepts on a plane of immanence that retains the reality of the virtual and thus engenders the possibility of ' "thinking" in thought' – that is, a creative thought that moves beyond the actual. To state this contrast differently, Deleuze and Guattari's higher 'taste' is to be contrasted with Hume's understanding of taste. For Hume, delicacy of taste is not a matter of heightened sensibility for those 'elements in the process of being determined' that might engender moves beyond the actual, but rather it is precisely a matter of being attuned to the elements that are already actualized. 'Where the organs are so fine,' Hume argues, 'as to allow nothing to escape them; and at the same time so exact as to perceive every ingredient in the composition: *This we call delicacy of taste*, whether we employ these terms in the literal or metaphorical sense' (EMPL 235, emphasis mine). Hume's famous example comes from *Don Quixote*, when Sancho relates how his kinsmen were able to detect the taste of leather and iron in a hogshead. Although laughed at initially, they were vindicated when, upon emptying the hogshead, 'an old key with a leathern thong tied to it' (ibid.) was found. Sancho's kinsmen thus had delicate taste because they were attuned to what was actually there, while the 'bad critic,' Hume claims, is one who 'wants the delicacy, which is requisite to make him sensible of every beauty and every blemish, in any composition or discourse' (EMPL 236).

This contrast between Hume and Deleuze and Guattari in how they understand 'taste' is not, as we will see below, as clear-cut as it might at first appear. To begin to see why, we will turn to discuss the Scottish Enlightenment. In presenting a Deleuzian intellectual history of the Scottish Enlightenment we will argue that the creativity of the period needs to be understood not as the result of intellectuals who were able to clarify the intellectual field or cultural preconscious of their day – that is, intellectuals with good taste; rather, it was precisely an intellectual field in flux, in a liminal, problematized state, that forced a transformative, problematizing rethinking of the field by those with a 'higher taste.' In the case of the Scottish Enlightenment, it will be argued, there was an overdetermination (to use Althusser's term[1]) of structural factors in flux that problematized the intellectual field of eighteenth-century Scotland. It is to a discussion of these factors, and Hume's role among them, his 'higher taste,' that we now turn.

I. Cultural Preconscious

A common tendency among commentators of the Scottish Enlightenment is to pinpoint precisely where the break with the past occurred, a break that marks the beginning of the Enlightenment itself. Among the most frequently cited events is the Union of Parliaments in 1707. With the loss of Parliament in Edinburgh, the Scottish political elite who did not move to London – and they were many since London was prohibitively expensive for all but the wealthiest few – were of necessity largely forced to abandon the traditional language of civic morality, namely, the view that one's virtues were to be derived from civic and political engagement. As Nicholas Phillipson has argued, the post-1707 Scots abandoned the classical republican ideal of participation in parliament or para-parliamentary institutions as a means of releasing their virtue. Rather, they had begun to think of the virtuous citizen as the expert whose skills could be put to public use in an effort to help it towards improvement and happiness. (Phillipson 1981, 38)

Whether we point to the Union of Parliaments or some other event or combination of events as marking the end of the traditional or old and the beginning of the new – the new, in this case, being the works of the literati of the Scottish Enlightenment – others have stressed that the upsurge of intellectual creativity in the latter half of eighteenth-century Scotland was simply an extension of an already strong intellectual tradition. As Alexander Broadie has argued: 'That there was a possibility of something special happening in the eighteenth century is suggested by the impressive level of cultural achievements that existed in the country prior to the union' (Broadie 2001, 8). Scottish intellectuals, in particular, were far from being isolated and provincial; to the contrary, they were frequently educated in Europe and in many cases became significant contributors to European intellectual life. Duns Scotus (1266–1308), for example, was born in Duns, Berwickshire (not far from where Hume was born), was educated at Oxford and the University of Paris, and went on to become one of the most important and influential philosophers of the High Middle Ages. John Maier (1467–1550), from Gleghornie, became a leading professor of theology at the University of Paris. Among his students were Ignatius Loyola, John Calvin, François Rabelais, and George Buchanan (1506–82) – another significant Scottish intellectual, historian, and tutor to James VI/I. 'There was at the time,' Broadie argues concerning Maier, 'no more distinguished academic in Europe' (ibid., 9). This tradition continued into the seventeenth century, with important intellectual contributions being made in diverse disciplines such as medicine (Robert Sibbald [1641–1723]), mathematics (James Gregory [1638–75]), theology (Gilbert Burnet [1643–1715]), and law (James Dalrymple, Viscount Stair [1619–95]). With such a fine intellectual pedigree in Scotland, Broadie concludes: 'It is implausible to suppose that the amazing surge of the human spirit in the eighteenth century would have been so magnificent if the intellectual patrimony of the literati had not itself been so magnificent' (ibid. 13).

To return to the contrast between Hume's good taste and Deleuze and Guattari's call for a higher taste, we need now to note our earlier discussion of Hume's double movement, in particular the movement of deterritorialization – namely, the movement of abstruse thought that leads from the actual to the virtual, to the skeptical undermining of belief – and the movement of reterritorialization – the movement of the passions whereby abstruse thought, in capable hands, becomes identified as an innovation within an already constituted situation, where we have the movement from the virtual to the actual. In this context, the literati of the Scottish Enlightenment both exhibit good taste in that they clarify, following Ringer's argument, the inherited intellectual patrimony that serves as their cultural preconscious, their already constituted situation; and they exhibit the deterritorializing movement of 'abstruse thought' Hume so praised for the role it plays in facilitating innovation. It is precisely this double movement in Hume's work that is a primary focus of the present study, and just as Nietzsche argued that one cannot innovate without tradition – for to turn one's back on tradition is to risk becoming 'a sacrifice to the extraordinary' – so too for Hume abstruse thinking (and higher taste for Deleuze and Guattari) is inseparable from an already constituted tradition.[2]

In the case of the Scottish Enlightenment, Broadie is certainly right to stress the continuity between the intellectual innovations of the eighteenth-century literati and the work of their 'intellectual patrimony.' When, by contrast, the emphasis shifts to what is new in the Scottish Enlightenment, attention is then understandably directed to that which *cannot* be placed into the situation which preceded it. As Badiou would put it, the event that is the Scottish Enlightenment is precisely the *void* of the situation. Rather than being a further elaboration and clarification of the intellectual field of the day, the event that is the Scottish Enlightenment forces that which is said and written by the literati while remaining at the same time irreducible to that which is said and written. To show how the case of the Scottish Enlightenment can help to clarify these issues, let us return to Hume.

In many ways, Hume was fully embedded in the situation of his time.[3] Among the influences that provided the situation from which Hume's philosophy emerged there is Bishop Berkeley. Berkeley is one of the very few philosophers Hume actually acknowledges in his *Treatise*. Moreover, Berkeley's influence was quite widespread at the time, especially in Edinburgh where many of the faculty were members of the Rankenian Club, a society dedicated to the thoughts of Berkeley and of which Berkeley himself gave high praise when he purportedly claimed that 'no persons understood his system better than this set of young gentlemen in North Britain' (Mossner 1954, 48). In addition, Hume also read the 'polite' essays of Addison and Steele in the *Spectator* and the *Tatler*, essays that provided a model for those Hume would later write; and we know Hume acquired, in 1726, a copy of Shaftesbury's three-volume *Characteristicks* (Stewart 2005, 37). Hume's thought would have also been shaped by his encounters with Locke, Samuel Clarke, Bishop Butler, Bernard de Mandeville, and especially, as Kemp Smith has argued, Francis Hutcheson.[4] The writings of these philosophers plus classical texts, most notably Cicero and the Stoics, were what Hume read during college and continued to read, by his own admission, after he graduated. In fact, in 'My Own Life' Hume confesses that while 'they [his family] fancied I was poring over Voet and Vinnius, Cicero and Virgil were the Authors which I was secretly devouring' (EMPL xxxiii). Mossner argues that this self-assessment 'oversimplifies the situation' (Mossner 1954, 52), and that from the time he left Edinburgh University until the spring of 1729, Hume 'studied law and general literature,' and from then on dropped his legal studies to pursue 'an independent programme of philosophical and scholarly research directed towards the formulation of a new system of philosophy and criticism' (ibid.).

What is key here is precisely the event surrounding the spring of 1729, the event that moves Hume beyond the already constituted philosophical situation of his day to the formulation of a new philosophy, or a 'new scene of thought' as Hume puts it. This event marks, as was discussed in Chapter 3, the time of Hume's life, the time that is inseparable from the creative, philosophical path Hume pursued. It is as a consequence of this event that Hume abandoned his legal studies and single-mindedly worked on his *Treatise*; and it is also the event that very nearly pushed Hume to the brink of a mental and physical breakdown. Hume describes the context of this event, as well as its consequences, in his famous 1734 letter to Dr George Cheyne. Because this leads us directly to the question concerning the relationship of Hume's work as an event to the context and situation of his day, it is worth quoting in full:

> You must know then that from my earliest Infancy, I found alwise a strong Inclination to Books & Letters. As our College Education in Scotland, extending little further than the Languages, ends commonly when we are about 14 or 15 Years of Age, I was after that left to my own Choice in my Reading, & found it encline me almost equally to Books of Reasoning & Philosophy, & to Poetry & the polite Authors. Every one, who is acquainted either with the Philosophers or Critics, knows that there is nothing yet establish in either of these two Sciences, & that they contain little more than endless Disputes, even in the most fundamental Articles. Upon Examination of these, I found a certain Boldness of Temper, growing in me, which was not enclin'd to submit to any Authority in these Subjects, but led me to seek out some new Medium, by which Truth might be establisht. After much Study, & Reflection on this, at last, when I was about 18 Years of Age, there seem'd to be open'd up to me a new Scene of Thought, which transported me beyond measure, & made me, with an Ardor natural to young men, throw up every other Pleasure or Business to apply entirely to it. The Law, which was the Business I design'd to follow, appear'd nauseous to me, & I cou'd think of no other way of pushing my Fortune in the world, but that of a Scholar & Philosopher. I was infinitely happy in this Course of Life for some Months; till at last, about the beginning of September 1729, all my Ardor seem'd in a moment to be extinguisht, & cou'd no longer raise my Mind to that pitch which formerly gave me such excessive Pleasure. (L1 13)

It was this extinguishing of his Ardor, and the accompanying physical symptoms, such as 'Scurvy Spots' on his fingers, that Hume self-diagnosed (as discussed in an earlier chapter) as being the result of excessive 'Study & Idleness' – namely, excessive abstruse thinking – and this in turn led to his decision 'to seek out a more active life' so he could 'more effectually' resume his philosophical work (L1 17). On a Badiouian reading of Hume's event, it is precisely the void of the situation, much as the event that was Haydn was the void of the Baroque situation. Hume, however, does not characterize his 'new scene of thought' as Badiou would, namely, as an absolute rupture or break with the past. To the contrary, Hume's 'new scene' is a new scene in a series and tradition of other scenes, such as Locke's, Berkeley's, Shaftesbury's, Hutcheson's, and so on. Stated in Deleuzian terms, Hume's philosophy as an event presupposes a multiplicity of thought elements (or conceptual personae as Deleuze will also refer to them), and yet this event is irreducible to this multiplicity. The event is that which both draws the multiplicity into a plane of consistency and actualizes this consistency as a novel entity, a new scene of thought.

At this point Badiou might argue that our characterization of Hume's event undermines the very possibility that it could indeed be the new scene Hume believed it to be. Is not the event, as Deleuze understands it, simply a folding of what already is, a permutation and reshuffling of a multiplicity that is given while the truly new is just what cannot be reduced to the given, to what is? A multiplicity, however, is not *identifiably* given, for the very givenness of the multiplicity of ideas and impressions, as was argued earlier, presupposes an historical ontology that is inseparable from a self capable of increasingly using and associating ideas and impressions. In the case of Hume, the multiplicity his philosophy actualizes into a new scene of thought is not simply the philosophies of Berkeley, Locke, Hutcheson, and so on, but is rather the problematic inseparable from the philosophical solutions these philosophies offer. Hume thus does not begin from a series of given problems he then appropriates and makes his own, for these problems are only given when they become actualized as the solutions that solve these problems. Hume's philosophy draws from the virtual multiplicity of problems that is inseparable from these actualized problems-solutions, but his philosophy is irreducible to them, or is irreducible to the givens of the situation. The new scene of thought that emerges with Hume is thus not simply a fold of the given but entails a fundamental non-relation to the given in that the virtual can in no way be related to the given in the manner of resemblance or identity, much as Sudnow's improvisational jazz as performed does not resemble the multiplicity of ways of hand, for a relation of resemblance presupposes identity when it is the historical ontology of the virtual that is the condition for identity itself. Consequently, the virtual multiplicity of problems that serves as the condition for Hume's new scene of thought is how we will understand the cultural preconscious.

To restate these arguments with Hume's terminology in mind, we can say that Hume's new scene of thought exemplifies 'abstruse thinking.' This abstruse thought is irreducible to the givens of the situation and it forever risks, when not handled by capable hands, slipping into madness. On our reading, this abstruse thinking problematizes the actual by thinking the virtual problems (cultural preconscious) inseparable from it. Abstruse thought sets the actualities of a given tradition on a line of flight that enables the cultural preconscious (multiplicity) to be drawn by capable hands into a new scene of thought. But this line of flight could just as easily become a line of destruction; or, to put it differently, the cultural preconscious is not guaranteed of being drawn into a new scene of thought by abstruse thinking, for it may indeed fail, and in its failure give rise to nothing but the undisciplined madness that is inseparable from becoming civil. It was precisely to avoid this consequence that Hume claimed abstruse thought must be 'handled by men who have a more just way of thinking' (EMPL 253), a thinking that reterritorializes the deterritorializing tendencies of abstruse thought and allows for the emergence of identifiable, useful innovations. Whether they be the philosophical innovations of Berkeley, Locke, or Hume, such innovations, as identifiable, presuppose an instituting of abstruse thought, an instituting of culture, an historical ontology, that can, in turn, become the basis for a new abstruse thought, for the 'higher' taste, that 'goes beyond' these innovations. It is to clarify this point further that we now turn.

II. Instituting Culture

With Hume's concern that abstruse thought be properly handled in order to draw forth the innovations it makes possible, we return to our earlier theme regarding the schizophrenic limits of capitalism. As was argued earlier, capitalism deterritorializes markets in order to create new opportunities for the flows of capital investment, and yet this deterritorialization forever resists and staves off complete deterritorialization, for then the capitalist system would lack the predictability necessary to continue functioning. This complete or absolute deterritorialization is the schizophrenic limit that capitalism simultaneously presupposes and resists. Similarly for Hume, abstruse thought both deterritorializes truth – it goes beyond truth – and yet to be innovative and useful this thought must become reterritorialized as truth by those with a 'more just way of thinking.' The importance of capitalism here is especially relevant for Hume because it is precisely commerce, as we saw, that creates the conditions that encourage a polite, civil culture, when the deterritorializing moves of commerce become reterritorialized by the 'just way of thinking' that can best handle abstruse thought.

For both Hume and Deleuze (and Deleuze and Guattari), capitalism (commerce) is fundamentally related to the subject. 'Capitalism forms,' Deleuze and Guattari argue, 'when the flow of unqualified wealth encounters the flow of unqualified labor and conjugates with it' (TP 453). In particular, capitalism forms when the flow of labor is no longer 'determined as slavery or serfdom but must become naked and free labor,' and wealth is no longer 'determined as money dealing, merchant's or landed wealth, but must become pure homogeneous and independent capital' (TP 452). The reason capitalism was not realized in 'China, in Rome, in Byzantium, in the Middle Ages,' Deleuze and Guattari argue, is because 'there must be a whole integral of decoded flows, a whole generalized conjunction that overspills and overturns the preceding apparatuses' (ibid.).[5] In Rome and then in the Middle Ages, for instance, property and wealth continued to be determined by concrete actualities – primarily land. With the generalized conjunction of decoded flows, however, we have, Deleuze and Guattari argue (invoking Marx), 'the advent of a single unqualified and global Subjectivity, which capitalizes all of the processes of subjectification, "all activities without distinction": "productive activity in general," "the sole subjective essence of wealth . . ."' (ibid.). And an important consequence of this global Subjectivity is the deterritorializing effects it has on private property. As Deleuze and Guattari put it: 'Private property no longer expresses the bond of personal dependence but the independence of a Subject that now constitutes the sole bond' (TP 453). This in turn marks a significant change in the understanding of the 'rights' associated with private property:

> This makes for an important difference in the evolution of private property: private property in itself relates to rights, instead of the law relating it to the land, things, or people (this raises in particular the famous question of the elimination of ground rent in capitalism). *A new threshold of deterritorialization.* And when capital becomes an active right in this way, the entire figure of the law changes. The law ceases to be the overcoding of customs, as it was in the archaic empire; it is no longer a set of topics, as it was in the evolved States, the autonomous cities, and the feudal systems; it increasingly assumes the direct form and immediate characteristics of an axiomatic, as evidenced in our civil 'code.' (ibid.)

We can clarify these points by turning to the eighteenth-century debate concerning intellectual property, and in particular the role of the Scots in this debate. In 1710 the Statute of Anne initiated the extension of legal protection for intellectual property, granting authors a fourteen-year monopoly to their works. This statute largely adopted the format of an earlier statute for mechanical inventions (1603). The Scots, however, with their tradition of Roman law, generally ignored the Statute of Anne; or, more precisely, they ignored the implied premise that an author had an abstract right to the products of their intellectual labors. As Henry Home, later Lord Kames, put it in an Answer he wrote for *Midwinter v. Booksellers* (1744):

> If a Man composes a Book, the Manuscript is his Property, and the whole Edition is his property, after it is printed. But let us suppose, that this whole Edition is sold off, where is then his Property? Surely none of the Books sold remain his Property. And as Property, by all Lawyers, antient and modern, is defined to be *jus in re*, there can be no property without a subject. The books that remain upon Hand are no Doubt the Property of the Author and his Assigns; but after the whole Edition is disposed of, the Author's Property is at an End. There is no Subject, no Corpus, of which he can said to be Proprietor. (Prestongrange 1744, 2)[6]

Home presented this argument in support of his earlier opinions that intellectual property is only a statutory right; more specifically, the Statute of Anne, on Home's reading, granted property rights only for those who registered their manuscript with the Stationer's Company. In fact, Home specifically distinguishes between those authors 'who write for Fame only' and 'those who write with a View to Profit. The latter sort,' Home claims, 'must enter their books in Stationers Hall' (Prestongrange 1744, 2). Since the booksellers of Edinburgh and Glasgow were selling books that either exceeded the fourteen-year period of monopoly rights as laid down by the Statute of Anne, or they were not recorded in the Stationers Hall as dictated by the statute (as was the case in Midwinter), Home concluded that Midwinter and the other booksellers of London (which included Andrew Millar, David Hume's bookseller), did not have a right to damages. Twenty-five years later, in 'A Letter from a Gentleman in Edinburgh to his friend in London; concerning literary property,' (Donaldson 1769) the author reiterates Home's arguments. The author of this letter acknowledges that the booksellers of London are following a common law interpretation of the Statute of Anne and interpreting it to be a statute that gives 'additional penalties while a book is newly published,' and thus for the time when 'the greatest run may be expected for it,' but at the same time this statute in no way, so their argument goes, 'takes away a right which all authors have in their works, independent of any statute . . . [which] they call a right at common law' (ibid. 10). By contrast, the point of the letter was to reiterate Home's arguments (and Home's Midwinter opinion is explicitly referred to) and set forth the traditional view of Roman law whereby it is understood to be 'a gross absurdity . . . to establish property without a subject or corpus . . . and property, in a strict sense, can no more be conceived without a corpus, than a parent can be supposed without a child' (ibid. 18).

In contrast to the Scottish Roman law tradition concerning intellectual property, the English booksellers by and large – and notably Andrew Millar, a Scotsman, among them – sought to equate intellectual property with traditional attitudes to property. On this view, the product of one's intellectual efforts is distinct from its appearance in published texts, and it is this *abstract entity* over which the author has proprietary rights in perpetuity, much as they would have similar rights over their other forms of property (land, moveable goods, and so on). As this was expressed in a letter to a Member of Parliament, property as

> the Product of the Mind, as in a Book composed . . . is not confined to the Original MS. but extends to the Doctrine contained in it: Which is, indeed, the true and peculiar Property in a Book. The necessary Consequence of which is, that the owner hath an exclusive right of transcribing or printing it for Gain or Profit. (Warburton 1747, 8)

It is because intellectual property is understood in this way that the Statute of Anne comes then to be interpreted as a means for discouraging piracy by punishing those who would publish a book during the period of time it is most likely to have the highest sales. The statute does not create a right to intellectual property – or for that matter, a right created for those who seek to make money by their writing – but rather simply reinforces a right an author already has. The author in the previously cited letter makes this point explicitly, arguing that 'Authors had a right, prior to this Act . . .' (ibid. 18).

Returning to Deleuze and Guattari's arguments concerning the advent of capitalism, and to their point regarding the transformation of law into an abstract axiomatic or code, we can now see that this transformation is reflected in the debates regarding intellectual property. As a consequence of the generalized decoding and conjunction of labor and wealth, property comes to be viewed as an abstract right that decodes or deterritorializes the traditional proprietary relationships regarding property. In the case of intellectual property, the Scots for the most part maintained the traditional Roman view of property, while the English booksellers affirmed a right to intellectual property.[7] Moreover, we also find a deterritorialization of traditional conceptions of the self. With the advent of capitalism, 'private property,' Deleuze and Guattari argue, 'no longer expresses the bond of personal dependence but the independence of a Subject that now constitutes the sole bond' (TP 453). In other words, the traditional manner in which property would determine relationships of dependency between subjects (for example, serf–lord, patron–client, monarch–subjects, and so on) has become simply the relationship of a subject to itself by way of property.

This latter point has been stressed repeatedly. T. M. Devine, for instance, has argued that the eighteenth century witnessed an explosion of what he calls 'competitive display,' whereby 'social status is increasingly defined by material status' (Devine 1999, 143). Instead of social status being defined by where one stands in a relationship of dependency, wherein private property is seen as a natural extension of one's status, status itself comes increasingly to be seen as an extension and effect of the property one has. Furthermore, as new markets and products are introduced into society, the result is a continual process of competitive emulation, a process Neil McKendrick associates with the birth of a consumer society:

> These characteristics – the closely stratified nature of English society, the striving for vertical social mobility, the emulative spending bred by social emulation, the compulsive power of fashion begotten by social competition – combined with the widespread ability to spend (offered by novel levels of prosperity) to produce an unprecedented propensity to consume. (McKendrick et al. 1982, 11)

With the dynamics of market forces providing a continual stream of new fashions, along with the rising sense that one's status derived from one's possessions and fashions, it should not be surprising to find accompanying these deterritorializing transformations efforts to reassert traditional sources of self-validation. Jonathan Swift, for example, in his *Tales of a Tub*, ridicules, in his inimitable way, the developing propensity for and obsession with novelty, and in his essay, 'Battle of the Books,' he sides with his patron Sir William Temple in defense of Ancient learning against modern learning.[8]

Aside from the reaction of intellectuals to the transformations occurring at the beginning of the eighteenth century, we find numerous other instances where the deterritorialization of traditional forms of self-conception comes to be reterritorialized. The emergence and success of the modern novel, for example, has been accounted for in part by the fact that there was little or no temporal separation between the characters of the novel and the time in which the readers themselves were living.[9] The novel thus provided an opportunity for readers to reterritorialize the deterritorializing tendencies of contemporary consumer society upon the characters of the novel. Historical narratives also provided an opportunity for readers to better understand their contemporary situation. Hume, we saw, began his histories with the Stuarts in order to clarify the factions that were dominant in his own day. It must also be stressed that religious writings, and in particular sermons, were by far the most widely read genre during the eighteenth century. Hume himself owned a copy of the perennial best-seller of his day, *The Whole Duty of Man*, which he studied quite closely as a youth (Stewart 2005). These writings offered yet another reterritorializing source of guidance for how one should be in a time when traditional sources of self-conception were being deterritorialized. And finally, though not exhaustively, the sudden emergence of various forms of life-writing, such as diaries and memoirs, also functioned to reterritorialize the self by attempting to provide a narrative unity or structure to a self or life that seemed otherwise to be eluding the traditional means of capture.[10]

This concern for the possibility of a self that eludes capture, a self that may fail to become the civil, polished subject Hume believed should be the natural consequence of a commercial society, is exemplified by eighteenth-century attitudes towards madness. R. A. Houston has shown that from a legal standpoint madness was understood to entail the likelihood that one would fail to maintain possession of one's property.[11] This was how Lord Stair defined madness in his *Institutions*, where he claims that to determine whether someone is mad or not, we must ask, 'is the person disordered in mind, fatuous and naturally an idiot, someone who is in danger of dissipating not only their lands but also their own heritable and moveable goods?' (cited by Houston 2000, 34). Moreover, with the transformation to a consumer society whereby one's self-conception becomes inseparable from one's possessions, the loss and dissipation of one's possessions is thus the loss and dissipation of one's self. Stair's definition of madness is thus not merely a convenient legal definition providing heirs with the legal means to seize property from someone else (typically a parent). Although this was certainly done, as Houston points out, the sense at the time, he argues, was that the number who were mad was on the increase, a fact not surprising given the profound social and economic changes of the time, for madness, as we have argued, is the undisciplined sensibility that hovers inseparably from civil discourse, and from the processes of self-constitution associated with a consumer society. Madness is the schizophrenic limit capitalism must presuppose while forever staving off; in the context of the eighteenth century it is the undisciplined, deterritorialized limit consumer society presupposes but must not completely actualize. The mad are this actualization.

Turning now to discuss the Scottish Enlightenment, we will begin with the 1707 Union of Parliaments, a union the Scots ultimately agreed to so that Scotland could benefit from the economic growth of its neighbor to the south. As a stateless society after 1707, Scotland became what we could call the power of minority, or the power of partiality. It was this power, coupled with other transformations that would overdetermine it, that facilitated the effectiveness of intellectual efforts in Scotland during the latter half of the eighteenth century. The result is what we have come to call the Scottish Enlightenment.

III. Scottish Enlightenment

As mentioned earlier, in his account of the origins of the Scottish Enlightenment, Nicholas Phillipson singles out the Union of Parliaments in 1707 as the decisive factor in bringing about the changes that eventually led to the intellectual outpouring we associate with the Scottish Enlightenment.

Phillipson claims that as a result of the 1707 union Scots were forced to abandon the language of civil morality – that is, the view that their energies ought to be directed towards civic action.[12] Other commentators, however, stress the continuity in Scotland before and after the Union of Parliaments, and they argue that it is precisely what stayed the same that best explains the emergence of the Scottish Enlightenment (recall Broadie's comments, cited earlier). T. M. Devine and others have stressed the 1707 Act of Security that allowed Scotland to maintain the Church of Scotland and their Presbyterian system of government.[13] This coupled with the already established system of education – something again many people credit the Calvinist era of Scotland for initiating (that is, the act of Privy Council in 1616, and later in 1646, requiring each parish to have a school) – meant that Scotland already had a fertile environment in which the Enlightenment might take root.[14]

The institutions of learning, however, were themselves undergoing significant transformations in the early eighteenth century. Anand Chitnis and others have stressed the key role the abandonment of regenting played in allowing for greater flexibility, and for the intellectual experimentation that gave rise to the new disciplines often associated with the Scottish Enlightenment (for example, economics with Adam Smith, geology with James Hutton, sociology with Adam Ferguson, and literary criticism with Hugh Blair, to name but a few). As Chitnis puts it, when the system of regenting ended – the system whereby a single teacher, with a predetermined set of texts, led students through all their coursework – this 'freed teachers from expounding of set books, left them free to speculate and facilitated the original writing of the Scottish Enlightenment' (Chitnis 1976, 132). Charles Camic (1983) has extended this argument and shown that not only did the universities abandon regenting, but many of the young men who attended the universities were themselves socialized in an environment that encouraged bold, innovative thinking. Camic refers to this process as 'microlevel socialization,' which refers to such things as whether or not one had an authoritarian father, the type of education one received, the competitive atmosphere for employment, and so on, as key factors to be considered in understanding how the intellectuals of the Scottish Enlightenment came to be so creative. What Camic concludes from his study is that most of them did not have an authoritarian father, and when they went to the post-regenting university their experience of education entailed a lack of authoritarian control with the result that most intellectuals had a respect for independence and freedom of thought.

Moving from the microsocial to the social level, the most popular context for face-to-face interaction between intellectuals in Scotland (and England) were the philosophical and literary clubs. With the loss of a parliament these social groups became, as Phillipson argued, the focus of redirected energies. The first important club was the Philosophical Society, founded by Colin Maclaurin, mathematics professor at the University of Edinburgh. Maclaurin, fearing that the illness of famed medical professor Alexander Monro might spell the end of Edinburgh's intellectual achievements, established the Philosophical Society in 1737 to 'preserve the university's scientific society from total dissolution' (Shapin 1974, 7). This began a trend, and by 1754 when the Select Society – the most prestigious of the societies during the Enlightenment – was founded, becoming a member of this society became such a mark of social distinction that Hume, in a letter to Allan Ramsay (painter and co-founder of the Select Society with Hume, Adam Smith, and others) observed that 'Young and old, noble and ignoble, witty and dull, all the world are ambitious of a place amongst us, and on each occasion [of election to the Society] we are as much solicited by candidates as if we were to choose a Member of Parliament' (L1 219). In support of Phillipson's thesis, being a member of the Select Society, as Hume acknowledges, had effectively become the replacement for being a Member of Parliament.

With the Select Society, and in particular Hume's prominent role in it, we can begin to clarify the key role of Hume, Smith, and others in motivating the creative endeavors of the Scottish Enlightenment. Phillipson is quite forthright in pinpointing Hume, along with Smith, as the irritants that prompted the creative energies of the Scottish Enlightenment. As he puts it:

> The course that much of Scottish culture took in the second half of the eighteenth century was determined by the anxiety which many intellectuals and members of this newly-emerging elite felt with a culture associated with Hume and his circle, which, through force of historical circumstance had acquired a social and ideological importance of disturbing proportions. (Phillipson 1973, 142–3)

The historical circumstance Phillipson refers to was 'an ideological crisis within the governing class, precipitated by an important change in their expectations of life which was itself the function of rapid economic growth' (ibid. 133). In particular, prior to the 1750s, the governing elite of Scotland were not wealthy enough to consider themselves equal to their London counterparts. As a result, 'the minor nobility and more substantial gentry were content to lead Scottish-oriented lives focused on the familiar, cheerful and economical pleasures of Edinburgh' (ibid. 130). By the 1750s, however, economic growth had raised the possibility that these same elites 'could look forward to a more expansive London-oriented life of the sort that English noblemen and substantial country gentlemen led' (ibid. 138). And yet these very same gentlemen, Phillipson argues, 'needed an ideological formula which would identify them as a legitimate governing elite but which would not identify their fortunes with their country as closely as that of their fathers' (ibid.). The Select Society and the philosophical positions of its most prominent members – namely, Hume and Smith – became this source of ideological legitimation. But this very class of governing elite who sought membership in the Society as if it 'were to choose a Member of Parliament' was at the same time uneasy with the philosophies of Hume and Smith, and Hume's in particular. It was this very anxiety, Phillipson concludes, that prompted the creative energies of the Scottish Enlightenment – much of this energy being directed precisely at Hume's philosophy, such as the Common Sense school of Thomas Reid and his Aberdeen circle of intellectuals. As Phillipson concludes his essay:

> But the most striking characteristic of Edinburgh's cultural life in the 1750s is its sense of urgency and the sense that intellectual inquiry was socially vitally important. That was due, quite simply to the genius of Adam Smith and above all, David Hume. Their analytical brilliance, their rhetorical force and clarity, their ruthless intellectual honesty, made it exceptionally difficult for intellectuals, working in a civilized environment, to produce satisfying means of allaying the anxieties which a deterministic ideology aroused. Given the social importance of polite determinism this was a situation designed to call forth powerful reserves of ambitious, creative energy. The intellectual power of Scotland's determinists set in a distinctive and complex social environment was the trigger which detonated those social and cultural forces which turned Edinburgh into the Athens of Britain. (Ibid. 147)

Much as Socrates saw himself as the gadfly who stirred the city of Athens from its sluggish dogmatism, so too, on Phillipson's account, did the genius of Hume (and Smith) arouse the creative energies of those who sought to allay the anxieties brought on by Hume's philosophy. Coupled to this gadfly-effect are the social, economic, and political changes that were transforming the landscape within which Scottish intellectuals worked in the latter half of the eighteenth century. More to the point, the combined overdetermination of these transformations was to allow for the power of minority, the power of a nondenumerable multitude, to exert itself.

From a Deleuzian perspective, Scotland's relationship to England allows for the power of minority when the minor deterritorializes the major, thereby creating a foreign element inseparable from the major.[15] As Alexander Carlyle, a key figure in the Scottish Enlightenment, puts it in his autobiography, for 'every man bred in Scotland the English language was in some respects a foreign tongue.'[16] Hume and many others were aware of this predicament. Hume, for example, contributed a list of scotticisms to *Scots Magazine*, with the hope thereby of 'improving the language of North Britain.'[17] Despite their successes in eliminating scotticisms, however, the fact that the Scots were, as a minority in Deleuze's sense, improper relative to the proper language, placed them in a relationship to English that more easily facilitated their ability to utilize the 'higher' taste for the improper inseparable from the proper, for the problematic reality of the virtual inseparable from the actual; and in doing this, the Scots were able to engender creativity (or alternative forms of ordering) into the actualities of English thought and language.

To restate Phillipson's argument, then – that Hume's genius coupled with 'a distinctive and complex social environment was the trigger which detonated' the creative outbursts we now identify with the Scottish Enlightenment – we can say that at several different levels, or plateaus (following Deleuze and Guattari), traditional apparatuses of capture were being deterritorialized, and their subsequent reterritorialization led to the creation of alternative forms of social, cultural, and intellectual ordering. The loss of parliament in 1707 deterritorialized a traditional apparatus of capture for passions and interests in the form civic engagement, passions that were in turn reterritorialized by way of the societies for improvement, most notably the Select Society. The rise of capitalism and a consumer society deterritorialized the traditional relationships to property, relationships that came to be reterritorialized upon a globalized subject. Traditional forms of writing were deterritorialized by the upsurge of facts and novelties (that is, news) associated with newspapers, pamphlets, and other forms of writing that were accessed by increasing numbers of people, and these deterritorializing tendencies were in turn reterritorialized by novels, diaries, and by the protections afforded by intellectual property.[18] The end of regenting in Scottish Universities deterritorialized traditional forms of education, a deterritorialization that came to be reterritorialized by way of new disciplines (geology, sociology, economics, and so on). And finally, though probably not exhaustively, the lack of authority figures at the microsocial level deterritorialized the traditional loyalties and commitments of would-be intellectuals, loyalties that were then reterritorialized by the newly created avenues for intellectual pursuit. These multiple processes of deterritorialization–reterritorialization are precisely how we read 'the complex social environment' that triggered the creative energies and output we associate with the Scottish Enlightenment.

To restate our argument yet again, we could say, following Althusser, that the Scottish Enlightenment was made possible by an overdetermination of deterritorialization. When Althusser used the term overdetermination in his essay, 'Contradiction and Overdetermination' he did so in part to account for why the communist revolution occurred in Russia. It is not sufficient, Althusser argues, to claim the revolution occurred because of the 'contradiction between the forces of production and the relations of production' (Althusser 1969, 99), or between the capitalists and the proletariat. Although it is certainly present, 'If this contradiction is to become "active" in the strongest sense,' Althusser claims, it 'must become a ruptural principle, there must be an accumulation of "circumstances" and "currents" so that whatever their origin and sense . . . they "fuse" into a *ruptural unity*' (ibid.). In the case of Russia, it was precisely this 'accumulation and exacerbation of all the historical contradictions' (ibid. 95) that 'fused' into the ruptural unity necessary to bring about the Russian revolution. Althusser uses the term 'overdetermination' (ibid. 101) to refer to the fusion of diverse, often heterogeneous concrete contradictions, and he contrasts it with what he takes to be the Hegelian view of contradiction whereby the Hegelian contradiction and dialectic fuses by way of an internal principle that has already predetermined the unity that will result from this fusion.

By arguing, then, that the Scottish Enlightenment arose as a result of an overdetermination of deterritorialization, we too are arguing, as did Althusser, that it is not sufficient to argue for a deterritorialization of a traditional apparatus of capture. For a deterritorialization to be effective, there must be an accumulation and synthesis of heterogeneous deterritorializations, or an *overdetermination* of deterritorialization. In the case of the Scottish Enlightenment, as we have seen, there was indeed an accumulation of currents of change and deterritorialization, and as these imperceptibly emerged into a ruptural unity or rogue wave of deterritorialization, this deterritorializing *event* then came to be reterritorialized as the cultural canon we now identify with the Scottish enlightenment.[19]

IV. From Culture to Canon

We are now in a better position to understand the role of Hume in the Scottish Enlightenment. With Foucault, we can say that Hume is not an intellectual who represents the work and concerns of a denumerable set of intellectuals; nor does he represent a denumerable set of problems and concerns other intellectuals will then further develop. Nor, in contrast to Ringer's position, do we see Hume as one who is clarifying the cultural preconscious of his day, if by cultural preconscious we understand an already identified and identifiable set of beliefs (that is, a denumerable set). Rather, Hume had a 'higher' taste for the reality of the virtual, for the nondenumerable set inseparable from the identifiable concepts and issues of his day. As discussed in an earlier chapter, Hume confronted the problem of how a multiplicity of elements could become an identifiable, unified system without presupposing the identity such a multiplicity will become, and without presupposing a transcendent principle that would serve as unifier. By boldly presenting and addressing this problem, Hume's 'higher' taste instilled, as Phillipson argued, an anxiety or hesitation within the intellectual community of his day, and it is this hesitation that prompted the reworkings of the problematic laid out by Hume.[20]

To bring in perhaps the most prominent example of the creative energies that were directed against Hume's problematic, we can turn to Reid. Reid was acutely aware of the consequences of Hume's problematic, in particular of rejecting a unifying source distinct from what is unified, and thereby losing the ability to assert whether or not a particular unity is indeed true or correct, or even if it is truly unified. One ends up, in short, with skepticism. In his *Essays on the Intellectual Powers of Man*, Reid claims that the problem he sees in the philosophies of his contemporaries (most notably Hume's) is their 'proneness to resolve everything into feelings and sensations,' and they do this, he argues, out of a desire to avoid 'an opposite extreme' that was 'common in the ancient philosophy' (Reid 1969, 768). The mistake of the ancients, according to Reid, is that they 'give all their attention to things external,' and consequently for them 'an external existence is ascribed to things which are only conceptions or feelings of the mind' (ibid.). With Descartes, however, 'philosophy took a contrary turn,' when that 'great man . . . discovered, that many things supposed to have an external existence, were only conceptions or feelings of the mind' (ibid. 769). Yet Descartes' famous universal doubt did not come to the final conclusion that all was simply 'conceptions or feelings of the mind.' In his version of the ontological argument, Descartes claimed that there are some ideas in the mind that cannot have come from the mind – namely, the idea of God. Thus, to avoid the problem of unity, Descartes posits a unifying source – God – that is distinct from that which is unified. For Reid, however, Descartes' 'track has been pursued by his successors to such an extreme as to resolve every thing into sensations, feelings, and ideas in the mind, and to leave nothing external at all' (ibid.). Locke, for instance, will transform the external, material world into a world of 'phenomenon only,' and a world that 'has no existence but in our mind' (ibid.). As Reid summarizes Locke's mistake, he 'made heat and cold to signify only the sensations we feel, and not the qualities which are the cause of them' (ibid. 782–3). That is, the phenomena of heat and cold are not, for Locke, as they are for Reid, effects of qualities that are distinct from the feelings and sensations. The extreme and inevitable consequence of the contrary turn in philosophy initiated by Descartes is Hume's skepticism. As Reid puts it, one 'can easily trace the doctrine of feelings from Descartes down to Mr. Hume, who put the finishing stroke to it, by making truth and error to be feelings of the mind, and belief to be an operation of the sensitive part of our nature' (ibid. 769).

This concern with Hume was to be the foundation of Reid's philosophical project, a foundation he laid down some twenty years prior to publishing his *Essays*. In an exchange of letters he had with Hume at the time Reid was working on his *Inquiry*, he acknowledged that if Hume were right that all our ideas are merely copies of sense impressions, then 'I must be an absolute sceptic' (Reid [1764] 1997, 257). For Reid, however, if Hume is right, and 'If what we call Extension, Figure, Motion, Hardness or Softness, Roughness or Smoothness have any Resemblance to the Sensations that correspond to them, then I must subscribe to Mr Hume's Creed and cannot avoid it. But if there is no such resemblance then his system falls to pieces' (ibid. 260). And this is just what Reid claims to have discovered: 'After taking much pains to attend to my Sensations and to form clear and distinct conceptions of them, it appears to me as clear and as certain that they are not like to sensible qualities' (ibid.), and it is this distinction between sensations and the qualities of which these sensations are understood to be natural signs or effects that is the basis of Reid's system: 'This dissimilitude betwixt our Sensations and the sensible qualities known to us by their means, is the Foundation of my System, as their Similitude is the Foundation of all the Systems that went before [for example, Hume's]' (ibid.).

We could multiply the example of Reid many times.[21] As we have argued earlier, the reality of the virtual is inseparable from a multiplicity of actualizations, and in fact it is the multiplicity of encounters with Hume's problematic that contributes to the overdetermination of deterritorialization that leads to what comes to be identified as the Scottish Enlightenment. Cultural creativity, in short, is inseparable from a multiplicity of actualizations, actualizations that then come to be selected for and against in the process of canon formation. Restating Latour's point concerning relative existence, the more a heterogeneous network of deterritorializing, experimental tendencies is overdetermined and drawn together, the more cultural creativity there will be. To clarify by way of example, Jane Jacobs has shown that innovation and creativity within cities presupposes a multiplicity of cities and innovators. Detroit, for instance, had a multiplicity of heterogeneous skills that enabled the type of experimentation crucial for the emergence of the automobile industry, but then the very flourishing of the automobile industry ultimately harmed the city as the heterogeneous multiplicity of talent became subsumed by the interests of the automobile industry alone, largely stifling the creative energies of the city as a result.[22]

Crucial to the creative process in cultural formation, therefore, is the presence of a heterogeneous pool of experimental activity. For this reason Jacobs argues that for cities to be economically valuable they need to be inefficient. She is quite forthright on this point: 'I do not mean that cities are economically valuable in spite of their inefficiency and impracticality but rather because they are inefficient and impractical' (Jacobs 1969, 86). The reason for this, she adds, is that the process of trial and error, of experimenting and trying things out, while not in itself very productive or efficient – it is in fact quite inefficient in that many experiments hit dead ends – is nonetheless just what makes possible the creativity that can transform a city into an economically vibrant place. Which experiments will work is not predetermined, but discouraging experimentation altogether (because it is inefficient, for example) is bound to lead to the economic ruin of a city. It is this multiplicity of experimental actualizations – actualizations that are themselves inseparable from the reality of the virtual in that they have no predetermined end – that is essential to creating culture.

This was already Hume's position. Recognizing the fact that he was a member of a flourishing intellectual period, Hume observes, in reference to the intellectual flourishing of Ancient Greece, that 'Europe is at present a copy, at large, of what Greece was formerly a pattern in miniature' (EMPL 121). In other words, intellectuals in Greece were in competition with one another, and a philosopher whose intellectual experiments were unwelcome in one place could go elsewhere (as, for example, did Pythagoras, Aristotle, and Anaxagoras). This gave greater freedom to intellectuals to pursue their work. As the multiplicity of experimental actualizations comes to be selected and reified as the predetermining models subsequent generations are expected to follow, the result is a stifling of cultural creativity. As Hume puts it, once a culture has enjoyed a period where its arts and sciences have thrived they will 'seldom or never revive in that nation where they formerly flourished' (EMPL 135). Hume's argument for this point is rather straightforward. As was cited earlier, Hume argues that the genius of an intellectual is imperceptible in the beginning, but if experimentation and 'frequent trials' are possible, and are not forced to become the means to realize predetermining expectations, then the intellectual may become the model future intellectuals feel obligated to emulate, thus stifling their incipient creativity. Furthermore, the experimentations of an intellectual are empowered by a network of other intellectuals who are themselves engaging in 'frequent trials' that both contribute to and draw from the endeavors of others. The significance of Hume's philosophy, or Hume's philosophy as event, was thus in the beginning 'as much unknown to himself as to others,' and the emergence of his philosophy as significant occurs inseparably from the developing interactions of a multiplicity of others. As the deterritorializing, experimental trajectories of these *actual* interactions becomes overdetermined, in what Deleuze calls a first articulation, it then makes possible the actualization, in a second articulation, of an established model that will subsequently predetermine the work of intellectuals – discouraging, as Hume argued, future intellectual flourishing. On this interpretation, then, Hume's thought is not the event that is the void of the situation, in Badiou's sense, that causes the Scottish Enlightenment, but is rather that which exceeds the actualities of these situations, forcing them to stutter and hesitate, and it is precisely in this stuttering hesitation or inefficiency that the thinking of others may be led beyond the actualities of their own thought. This beyond, however, is not the void that cannot be thought or said in any situation; it is, as Kafka experienced it (see Chapter 3), the reality whereby everything can be said, the reality of the virtual that is the excess or chaos inseparable from the actualities of thought (that is, the *identifiable* beliefs, doctrines, concepts of the time). Rather than initiating the void that cannot be thought, Hume's thought is inseparable from a thinking that is at the edge of chaos, a thought that is thinking, and only thinking, when it is creating. It is this thinking that begins imperceptibly and only later comes to be *identified* as the creative efforts of Hume and his peers.

We have referred to this thinking at the edge of chaos by various terms – power of minority, immanence, multiplicity, nondenumerable sets, the reality of the virtual, creative evolution, and culture – but our use of the term power needs to be clarified. The power of the nondenumerable multitude, for instance, the power Foucault recognized to be in no need of a representative intellectual to enlighten it regarding the power it has, is a power that undermines hierarchical relationships. This power is thus to be contrasted with the totalizing, hierarchical power Deleuze refers to: 'Since it is in the nature of power to totalize . . . theory is by nature opposed to power' (Foucault 1977, 208). Similarly, to the extent that creating culture involves, as we have been arguing, the non-totalizing, non-hierarchical power of multiplicity and nondenumerable sets – the reality of the virtual – it too will be opposed to power. Culture, on this view, is opposed to power, which is precisely what Nietzsche argued: 'All great ages of culture are ages of political decline: what is great culturally has always been unpolitical, even antipolitical' (Nietzsche 1968, 509).[23] When we refer to the power of the multitude, therefore, we understand the term in Spinoza's sense, as *multitudinis potentia*, and follow Spinoza in contrasting *potentia* with *potestas*. For Spinoza, *multitudinis potentia*, translated as the power of the multitude, is the non-hierarchical power or force of the commonwealth that may, through the social contract, transfer some of this *potentia* to an authority who then acquires hierarchical power over the commonwealth, or *potestas*; but this same commonwealth can, at any time, undermine this *potestas* and reassert its *multitudinis potentia*.[24]

If culture is the power of the multitude, *multitudinis potentia*, it will thus be opposed to hierarchical forms of power, to *potestas*. As *multitudinis potentia*, however, the *potentia* of culture can be transferred to *potestas* – culture can become political. Within a capitalist, consumer economy, this is precisely what occurs; and it is this tendency that Deleuze resists through his efforts to develop a transcendental empiricism and pragmatics, and . . . and . . . In particular, Deleuze's philosophical project resists the tendency for culture's deterritorializing power (*potentia*) to be reterritorialized by the axiomatics of capitalist power (*potestas*), an axiomatics that attempts to reduce the unpredictable nature of creativity to a formulaic process whereby one can acquire predictable returns on one's investments. As Deleuze describes this process with respect to literary creativity, and to what he calls 'a crisis in contemporary literature' (that is, literary *culture*), it is dominated by

> The system of bestsellers [which] is a system of rapid turnover. Many bookshops are already becoming like the record shops that only stock things listed in a top ten or hit parade . . . Fast turnover necessarily means selling people what they expect: even what's 'daring,' 'scandalous,' strange and so on falls into the market's predictable forms. The conditions for literary creation, which emerge only unpredictably, with a slow turnover and progressive recognition, are fragile. Future Becketts or Kafkas, who will, of course, be unlike Beckett or Kafka, may well not find a publisher, and if they don't nobody will notice. (DI, 287)

When cultural products become part of a hierarchical system – a 'system of bestsellers' for instance – and a system that seeks to generate a fast turnover of products in accordance with the 'market's predictable forms,' then culture has become political. Pierre Bourdieu, for instance, in his book *Distinction*, has detailed the extent to which a wide range of judgments and activities related to culture, such as whether one drinks beer or wine, goes to the symphony, and so on, comes to constitute a general pattern of behavior – what he calls habitus – that serves to reproduce the political, social, and economic inequalities of society.[25] Stated in our terms, what occurs when culture becomes political is that its power as a nondenumerable reality of the virtual (*potentia*) becomes confused with the denumerable actualizations that then come to be selected and hierarchically ranked. As nondenumerable, however, culture is not to be confused with its enumerated ranking, even if Kafka's *Castle*, for example, were to make the top ten list of books one should read before one dies.[26] When this confusion occurs, what results is an unbridgeable gap between nondenumerable culture and its hierarchical actualization. This is the gap Sudnow encountered when he attempted to learn improvisational jazz by memorizing the already actualized jazz scales, runs, and so on (see Chapter 1). No matter how proficient Sudnow became at playing in accordance with these scales and runs, his playing always seemed predictable and not truly improvisational. Similarly, when culture is confused with its hierarchical actualizations, the result is the mindless and endless pursuit of 'culture,' culture being in this case the products of culture one seeks to amass in an effort to be 'cultured.' What Sudnow came to recognize was that the reality of the virtual could be actualized without prefiguring this actualization; he could begin where his hands were and play improvisational jazz. The same is true for the 'higher' taste Deleuze encourages as essential to creativity, and thus to creating culture. As long as one fails to appreciate the inseparability of the problematic, nondenumerable culture from its hierarchical actualizations, while at the same time appreciating that the problematic is not to be confused with these actualizations, then one becomes much like the honest gentleman Hume refers to – the one who pursues, and perhaps pursues successfully and passionately, the attainment of an ever-increasing collection of actualities; and yet whose thought is never led beyond the actual. Their thoughts, as we shall see, are never led beyond belief.

Notes

1. For Althusser, see his essay 'Overdetermination and Contradiction' (Althusser 1969). See also note 19 below.
2. See, for instance, *Human, All Too Human*, 'He who strays from tradition becomes a sacrifice to the extraordinary; he who remains in tradition is its slave. Destruction follows in any case' (Nietzsche 1984, 283).
3. For an account of Hume's formative context, see Mossner's biography (Mossner 1980), and more recently M. A. Stewart's excellent essay, 'Hume's Intellectual Development, 1711–1752' (Stewart 2005).
4. See Kemp Smith 1947.
5. Jay Lampert has recently addressed this theme in his book, *Deleuze and Guattari's Philosophy of History* (Lampert 2006).
6. The Scots were also at the center of the most important intellectual property case of the eighteenth century, *Donaldson v. Becket* (1774), where the Scottish booksellers successfully challenged the London booksellers claims for rights in perpetuity. For a detailed discussion, see Rose 1995.
7. It is perhaps no coincidence that at the time England was the most advanced capitalist and consumer society.
8. See Swift [1704] 1970, and 'Upon antient and modern learning,' in Temple 1690, and Wotton 1694.
9. Among the voluminous literature on the rise of the novel, see, in particular, Lennard Davis's *Factual Fictions* (Davis 1996), and J. Paul Hunter's 'Protesting Fiction' (Hunter 1997). Both Davis and Hunter stress the near or actual contemporaneity of events in the novel with the readers themselves, a contemporaneity that left the distinction between factual news stories and fictional accounts ambiguous (an ambiguity that was a central component of the reader's experience of the early novel). These arguments largely extend, with important variations, Ian Watt's classic study, *The Rise of the Novel* (Watt 1957).
10. For work on life-writing, see Horner 1996 and Graham et al. 1989.
11. See Houston 2000.
12. In his *History of the Scottish People: 1580–1830*, T. Christopher Smout offers a similar argument emphasizing the economic changes that occurred in Scotland, seeing them primarily, as did Phillipson, as a redirection of energies. The '"Calvinist" qualities' of seventeenth-century Scotland, and in particular the sense that 'life was a serious pilgrimage from the wicked ignorance in which they had been born to the perfect knowledge of God in which they ought to

die . . . could now [in the eighteenth century] be switched to a purely materialistic end' (Smout 1969, 97–8), including the improvement societies, and the philosophical and literary societies which took very seriously the pursuit of knowledge for the sake of improving one's self. For a study of the aristocratic Scots, the Duke of Argyll in particular, who supported and patronized the literati of the Scottish Enlightenment, see Rendall 1978.
13. See Devine 1999, 12. See also Neil MacCormick, 'Law and Enlightenment,' in *The Origins and nature of the Scottish Enlightenment* (MacCormick 1982). MacCormick argues that the roots of the Enlightenment can be found well into the seventeenth century in the historical and legal writings of the period, in particular the work of Lord Stair. As MacCormick puts it: 'A central question in the Scottish moral philosophy of the eighteenth century is none other than the one raised by Stair,' namely, is it the case that reason 'reveals or contains principles of right conduct?' (155).
14. For more on the important role educational institutions played in the Scottish Enlightenment, see Ronald Cant, 'Origins of the Enlightenment in Scotland: the Universities,' in Campbell and Skinner 1982. See also Richard Sher, *The Church and University in the Scottish Enlightenment* (Sher 1985).
15. See Craig 1996, where a similar argument is made. See also McCrone 2001 and Pittock 1991.
16. Quoted by Sher 1985, 108.
17. *Scots Magazine*, Vol. XXIII (April, 1764), 187. James Beattie, a vocal critic of Hume, and member of the Aberdeen Philosophical Society, agreed with Hume on the importance of this issue and even published a book titled, *Scotticisms*, that sought to provide an exhaustive list of Scottish 'improprieties.'
18. See Hunter 1997, where this case is convincingly made. See also Benedict Anderson's influential work, *Imagined Communities*, where he argues for the influence of newspapers on the emergence of nationalism as a belief (Anderson 1991). Stated in our terms, nationalism reterritorializes the deterritorializing tendencies of newspapers; or, as Hume understands it, it reterritorializes the deterritorializing tendencies of our partialities by instilling a love for one's country and fellow-countrymen.
19. We can now clarify the contrast between the understanding of intellectual history offered here and the influential arguments of Bourdieu (1968) in his essay "Intellectual Field and Creative Project." Whereas Bourdieu argues that a creative project draws from an already constituted field of positions – what he calls the cultural unconscious – for Deleuze it is precisely an overdetermination of already constituted positions that have become problematized that then gives rise to creative changes.
20. The same could be argued for Smith, as Phillipson notes. Moreover, as Hume calls for the emergence of good taste without calling upon a transcendent standard, so too for Smith, as Hont and Ignatieff show, allowing for the free, unregulated exchange and accumulation of goods would not result in a further impoverishing of the poor. Even Bernard de Mandeville, who held the controversial view that private vices produced public virtues, nonetheless believed, Hont and Ignatieff point out, that there needed to be a 'statesman at the helm constantly regulating the circulation of private interest' (Hont and Ignatieff 1983, 11; see Mandeville 1732, 36–7). For more on the influence of Mandeville on Francis Hutcheson and Adam Smith, see Hundert 1994.

21. One obvious example would be Alexander Gerard. In his *Essay on Taste* ([1759] 1963) he criticizes Hume precisely for claiming that there is nothing outside the sensibilities themselves, no unifying standard of taste other than what can be derived from the senses alone. 'Sentiment, it is said,' Gerard argues, 'has not, like judgment, a reference to anything beyond itself, nor represents any quality inherent in the external object . . . and consequently the sentiment cannot be false or wrong' (212).
22. See Jacobs' *The Economy of Cities* (Jacobs 1969). As Detroit suffered from the loss of a heterogeneous multiplicity of talent, so did Rochester, New York, as Kodak redirected the heterogeneous array of talent towards a specific, predetermined purpose.
23. The same is true in the case of Scotland, as McCrone has argued. The effort to discern a distinctive Scottish culture, McCrone claims, 'is likely to degenerate into a pessimistic conclusion' (McCrone 2001, 145); but such identifiably distinct cultures do arise for political ends: 'the important point to make is that nationalism does not derive from a distinctive culture. Rather, it seeks to manufacture and make such a distinctive culture for political ends' (ibid. 191). A voluminous body of literature explores the issue of nationalism. See especially Anderson 1991.
24. For Spinoza's contrast, see *Tractatus Politicus* where he claims 'the right of the commonwealth is determined by the common power of the multitude (*multitudinis potentia*)' (Spinoza [1677] 1951, 305), and 'every commonwealth,' he later adds, 'has the right to break its [social] contract, whenever it chooses, and cannot be said to act treacherously or perfidiously in breaking its word, as soon as the motive of hope or fear is removed' (ibid. 307). By contrast, when speaking of those who, by the social contract, have power or authority over the citizens, Spinoza uses the term *potestas* – for example, in Chapter VII, sec. 14, referring to the authority of a king, Spinoza uses the term *potestas*, and he consistently uses this term when referring to a hierarchical form of power, or the power of one *over* another. For commentators who have recognized the significance of this distinction, see Martial Gueroult (1968/1974), and Negri's *The Savage Anomaly* (Negri 1991).
25. See Bourdieu 1984.
26. Popular books one will often find in bookstores, record stores, and video stores includes: *1001 Books You Must Read Before You Die, 1001 Albums You Must Listen to Before You Die, 101 Things to Buy Before You Die, 1,000 Places to See Before You Die*, and so on . . .

Chapter 6

Beyond Belief: Deleuze's Hume and the Fear of Politics

As we have been arguing throughout this book, Deleuze's interest in Hume derived largely from the manner in which Hume sought to understand the inventiveness and creativity of human nature. While relying solely on the given, this human creativity was able to constitute identities that are irreducible to the given. For Deleuze, this given is the virtual multiplicity of pre-individual singularities, and the activation and actualization of this multiplicity is the condition for the emergence of the novel and the new. As Badiou makes clear on numerous occasions, Deleuze was quite right to develop philosophical concepts that entail 'an embrace of singularities,' and more precisely singularities that are inseparable from what he calls an 'evental advent' of the new, an evental rupturing with what is (Badiou 2004, 67). In the end, however, Badiou believes that 'Deleuze has no way of thinking singularity'; or, to put it differently, Deleuze's thought is incapable of rupturing with what is, but is rather a continual and monotonous folding and refolding of what is.[1] That Deleuze has 'no way of thinking singularity' is evidenced, for Badiou, by Deleuze's continued adherence to empiricism, even his Humean transcendental empiricism. For Badiou, by contrast, we need to set 'aside every kind of speculative empiricism' and move instead to Badiou's own 'theory of the pure multiple' if we are to think singularities and the evental rupture with what is (ibid. 77).

In this final chapter, we will return to our earlier discussion of Badiou's misunderstanding of Deleuze's theory of the virtual (from Chapter 1) and show that Badiou's alternative approach – his theory of the pure multiple – sets forth an understanding of 'events' that Deleuze rejects, and rejects precisely because it forecloses upon the possibility of a thought of singularities that moves beyond the actualities of 'what is.' In the first section we will revisit Deleuze's theory of multiplicity, stressing in this context how Badiou's critique ultimately relies upon an historical/ahistorical dichotomy that Deleuze rejects. To clarify this point further we turn again to Bruno Latour, who explicitly rejects the historical/ahistorical dichotomy, and does so by way of arguments and concepts that are also at work in Deleuze's thought. In the next section we will show that understanding Deleuze's philosophy in light of Latour's own project, as has been done in part throughout this work, enables us to better situate Deleuze's political philosophy. More precisely, in relation to Deleuze's concept of a social multiplicity, or the power of the multitude as discussed in the previous chapter, it will be argued that Deleuze provides us with a concept that can engage fruitfully with the work of Michel Foucault and Giorgio Agamben. Finally, we will see how for Deleuze 'becoming-imperceptible' is indispensable to 'becoming-revolutionary,' and with this latter concept we will find that Deleuze's Humean project is indeed able to provide an understanding of philosophy that involves a thinking that facilitates a 'rupture with what is.'

I. Speech and Event

Deleuze offers as an example of a virtual that is 'fully real,' though not actual, the 'linguistic multiplicity, regarded as a virtual system of reciprocal connections between "phonemes" which is incarnated [i.e., actualized] in the actual terms and relations of diverse languages' (DR 208). The phonemes that come to be actualized within the terms of various languages are not to be confused with the actual, meaningful terms, although the phonemes are no less real than these terms.

As Deleuze makes clear, the linguistic multiplicity 'renders possible speech as a faculty as well as the transcendent object of that speech, that "metalanguage" which cannot be spoken in the empirical usage of a given language, but must be spoken and can be spoken only in the poetic usage of speech coextensive with virtuality' (ibid.). Through the poetic usage of the faculty of speech, however, this equilibrium state can be sent into a stuttering, far from equilibrium state, and it is here that the virtuality of the multiplicity allows for new uses of language that were unpredicted and unpredictable.[2] What the poetic usage of language 'which cannot be spoken in the empirical usage of a given language' attempts to express is what Deleuze refers to as 'the transcendent object,' or the 'metalanguage.' By referring to the sense expressed by the poetic usage as the 'transcendent object,' Deleuze does not thereby endorse a philosophy of transcendence. One of Deleuze's constant themes was to develop a philosophy of immanence that rejects any vestiges of transcendence. It was precisely on this point, as we have seen, that Deleuze found a kindred spirit in the work of Hume (among others, of course, such as Spinoza, Bergson, and so on). And on this point as well Badiou agrees, acknowledging Deleuze's efforts to critique 'the thornier forms of transcendence' (Badiou 2004, 67). Ultimately, however, Badiou believes Deleuze's attempt to 'subvert' what he calls 'the "vertical" transcendence of the One' by way of 'the play of the closed and the open, which deploys multiplicity in the mobile interval between a set (inertia) and an effective multiplicity (line of flight), produces . . . 'a "horizontal or virtual transcendence"' (ibid. 79). What is needed, Badiou believes, is 'a form of writing subtracted from the poetics of natural language' (ibid. 80). Rather than a virtual multiplicity that constitutes the 'transcendent object' that is 'horizontally' or 'virtually' transcendent to the empirical usage of a language, but which manifests itself in the poetic usage of this language, Badiou proposes a form of writing – namely, a mathematical, logical form – that is wholly actual and without transcendence, or what he will call 'the multiple-without-oneness' (ibid.).

At the core of Badiou's criticism is the claim that Deleuze remains committed to a dialectic of the open and the closed. As Badiou puts it, 'in [Deleuze's] thinking the open is always open to something other than its own effectiveness, namely to the inorganic power of which it is a mobile actualization' (ibid. 72). On Badiou's interpretation, then, the poetic usage of speech is the active, mobile faculty and power that is an opening only by virtue of its relation to the closed, equilibrium state of established, empirical usage. The problem with Deleuze's vitalist Bergsonian approach, according to Badiou, is that no matter how closed a multiplicity may be or become, a 'vitalist multiplicity is obliged to signal equivocally toward the opening of which it is a mode' (ibid. 73). In other words, as an opening relative to the habitual, empirical usage of speech, the poetic usage is nonetheless closed to the extent that it draws the multiplicity into a plane of consistency. Badiou argues that, as a dutiful student of his master Spinoza, Deleuze in the end subordinates the thinking of singularities, the thinking that entails a rupture with what is, to the horizontally transcendent One of which these singularities are modes. Badiou is straightforward on this point: 'Deleuze has no way of thinking singularity other than by classifying the different ways in which singularity is not ontologically singular; in other words, by classifying the different modes of actualization' (ibid. 79).

To begin to assess Badiou's criticisms of Deleuze's project, it will be helpful to examine how Badiou believes Deleuze should have proceeded in his efforts to be done with transcendence and think singularities. As has already been indicated, the solution is to be found in mathematics, and more precisely Cantorian set theory. Crucial to Cantor's theory, at least as it pertains to Badiou's own work, is the distinction between belonging and inclusion. To be brief, according to Cantor there is a difference between the elements of a set and the set of all the subsets of this set, what Cantor calls the power set. For Cantor, the power set is greater than the set itself, for not only does it include all the elements of the subsets of the set, it also includes the null set, or the subset that does not include any of the elements of the set. As Badiou defines belonging and inclusion in *Being and Event*, an element *belongs* to a set 'if it is presented and counted as one by that situation,' or by that set (Badiou 2005a, 501). An element is *'included* in a situation if it is a sub-multiple or a part of the latter. It is thus counted as one by the state of the situation' (ibid. 511). An example Badiou offers to clarify this distinction is 'The "voter," ' who is 'not the subject John Doe, [but] is rather the part that the separated structure of the State re-presents, according to its own one; that is, it is the set whose sole element is John Doe and not the multiple whose immediate-one is "John Doe" ' (ibid. 107). If this subject were to escape being identified and re-presented by the State, then although they would belong they would not be included, and yet inclusion itself presupposes the void, the null set that cannot be counted as an element the State re-presents. The function of the State, as Badiou understands it, is to resist the void that is inseparable from the power set. 'The State,' Badiou claims, 'is not founded upon the social bond [i.e., belonging], which it would express, but rather upon un-binding, which it prohibits' (ibid. 109). The State's task, therefore, in prohibiting this un-binding, is 'the re-securing of the one over the multiple of parts (or parties)' (ibid. 110), or it seeks to prohibit the errancy of the void and the rupture with what is that can occur when the void belongs to an eventual site and cannot be counted as an element that is included in the situation.

When Badiou criticizes Deleuze for thinking singularities only insofar as they are modes of the One (that is, virtual openness), he in effect accuses Deleuze of re-securing, in his own way, the primacy 'of the one over the multiple of parts.' With Badiou's theory of the pure multiple, however, the pure multiple cannot be conceived of as parts of a larger whole or one, nor can it be subdivided into parts that are included in this multiple, for beneath the pure multiple is the void, or a pure multiple-without-oneness. The implications of this theory become clear as Badiou analyzes the historicity of events. In opposition to the 'natural or stable or normal multiplicities,' Badiou claims there are the 'abnormal, the instable, the antinatural' multiplicities, and he will 'term historical what is thus determined as the opposite of nature.' In other words, a natural, normal multiplicity consists of elements that are always present in each situation; an abnormal multiple, an 'eventual site,' is 'such that none of its elements are presented in the situation' (ibid. 175). As Badiou reiterates this point, he claims that 'it is enough for us to distinguish between situations in which there are eventual sites and those in which there are not. For example, in a natural situation there is no such site' (ibid. 177).

Earlier we discussed the example of Haydn as an eventual site for the emergence of the classical style in music. Nothing in the situation of the Baroque could count Haydn's music as part of its own project. Haydn's music was thus the void of this situation, or an evental site whose elements were not presented in the Baroque situation. An evental site, however, can become naturalized, and when this occurred in the case of Haydn his music came to be presented as an element within the Classical style. As Badiou notes, 'any evental site can, in the end, undergo a state of normalization' (ibid. 176). When this happens an event comes to be seen as a mode or fold of an already existent One (Nature) that counts these events as parts of its all-inclusive situation. And it is on this point, precisely, that Badiou disagrees most with Deleuze. Whereas Deleuze, on Badiou's reading, understands each event as a mode of the virtual One, Badiou, by contrast, argues for 'the absolute ontological separation of the event, the fact that it occurs in the situation without being in anyway virtualizable,' and 'no count,' Badiou adds, 'can group the events, no virtual subjects them to the One' (Badiou 2000, 75, 76).

Deleuze, in the end, is too loyal to Spinoza, and in particular to what Badiou sees as Spinoza's 'most radical attempt ever in ontology . . . to indistinguish belonging and inclusion' (Badiou 2005a, 113). By failing to think the difference between that which can be presented in a situation and the void (or null set) that leads to the excess of re-presentation (that is, inclusion of the power set) over presentation, Deleuze ultimately naturalizes the historicity and singularity of creative events. Since all events, on Badiou's reading of Deleuze, are simply formally distinct modes of the virtuality of the One, the count of the one is thus secured and there is subsequently no place in Deleuze's thought for historical, evental sites whereby elements are presented in a situation that can in no way be counted as part of the situation. Deleuze, in short, fails to distinguish between the historical (antinatural) and the ahistorical (natural). And yet, we shall argue, this is not a failure on Deleuze's part, but rather a move that leaves Deleuze better able to address key political and philosophical issues, including issues that are central concerns of Badiou.

II. Beyond Belief

In *Politics of Nature* Bruno Latour notes that today we no longer see the Pope in opposition to other leaders; or, to state it differently, we generally come to see the Papal power as just another form of secular power. Similarly, Latour adopts as an hypothesis the view that 'we have not yet secularized the two conjoined powers of nature and politics,' and much of what he does in this work is an attempt to secularize the 'conjoined powers of nature and politics' (Latour 2004, 31). Central to this project is the rejection of the very assumptions that formed the basis of Badiou's critique of Deleuze – namely, the opposition between the natural that is ahistorical and the historical, which includes the political as well as the aesthetic (among others) for Badiou. A guiding tenet of Latour's work, as we have seen throughout this study, is that there is not an ahistorical, autonomous, independent reality that is unconstructed and merely awaiting discovery, on the one hand, and an historical set of human practices that continually constructs, deconstructs, and reconstructs the beliefs regarding the nature of this ahistorical reality on the other. The terms 'construction' and 'autonomous reality,' Latour claims, 'are synonyms' (ibid. 275).

Among the terms Latour uses to express the synonymous nature of 'construction' and 'autonomous reality' are 'relative existence,' as we have seen, and 'factish,' the latter term being a combination of fact and fetish. A fact, traditionally understood, is autonomous and unconstructed. When Pasteur discovered the role micro-organisms play in the process of fermentation he simply, on this view, came to recognize an autonomous fact that was already there and independent of the historical events involved in Pasteur's efforts to locate these micro-organisms. A fetish, by contrast, involves the projection of beliefs upon a mute, passive object. In both cases, according to Latour, what is maintained is the subject–object dichotomy. In the case of facts, objects are ultimately responsible for the success of Pasteur's experiments; and in the case of fetishes, subjects are the ones responsible for projecting beliefs onto objects. A factish, for Latour, is a type of action that does 'not fall into the comminatory choice between fact and belief' (ibid. 306). Rather, a factish entails events; or, as Latour puts it, 'I never act; I am always slightly surprised by what I do. That which acts through me is also surprised by what I do, by the chance to mutate, to change, and to bifurcate' (ibid. 281). In a nod to Deleuze, Latour claims that factishes are 'rhizomelike,' and 'one should always be aware of factishes . . . [because] their consequences are unforeseen, the moral order fragile, the social one unstable' (ibid. 288).

A factish is thus neither an independent reality that comes to be discovered after a successful scientific experiment, nor merely the projection of human beliefs onto an inert object. A factish involves both human and non-human actors, and scientific experiments, as events, involve relations between a multiplicity of actors that return more than anything the actors contributed singly. It is for this reason that Latour claims 'an experiment is an event which offers slightly more than its inputs . . . no one, and nothing at all, is in command, not even an anonymous field of force' (ibid. 298). Latour acknowledges the influence of Whitehead when he uses the term event, most notably the use Whitehead makes of the term to replace 'the notion of discovery' and its attendant assumption concerning the ahistorical nature of objects and the historicity of human endeavors. When

Latour defines an experiment as an event, therefore, he intends precisely to argue that this 'event has consequences for the historicity of all the ingredients, including nonhumans, that are the circumstances of that experiment' (ibid. 306). The similarities with Deleuze on this point are profound, as we have seen in earlier chapters, but before we address them further it is important first to recall our earlier discussion (Chapter 3) regarding Latour's claim that he is not engaging in postmodernism and/or social construction, focusing here upon the role of belief.

Despite all the apparent differences between modernism and postmodernism, Latour argues that they have each 'left belief, the untouchable center of their courageous enterprises, untouched' (ibid. 275). In particular, the modernists, on Latour's reading, felt the task of philosophy and science was to determine which of our beliefs are justified true beliefs. To this end, science arrives armed with facts to hammer away at any beliefs that are not in line with the facts. With postmodernism, on the other hand, science itself comes to be seen as nothing but a set of beliefs that construct a reality, on the assumption that 'construction and reality are the same thing; everything is just so much illusion, storytelling, and make believe' (ibid.). And what we have then, 'when science itself is transformed into a belief,' is 'postmodern virtuality – the nadir, the absolute zero of politics, aesthetics, and metaphysics.' 'Virtuality,' in short, is for Latour 'what everything else turns into when belief in belief has run amok' (ibid. 287). When Latour argues that it is because factishes are constructed that they are so very real he is, therefore, saying something quite different from the postmodernist who claims that 'construction and reality are the same thing.' The difference has to do with who or what is acting. In the case of factishes, there is a 'rhizomelike' network of both human and nonhuman actors, and no one actor is in command, 'not even an anonymous field of force.' For the postmoderns, it is the power of belief that is in command, or the virtuality of the One as Badiou interprets Deleuze, and the autonomous nature of reality is nothing but a mode of belief or virtuality.

If Badiou's critique of Deleuze is correct, then it would seem that Latour would echo Badiou's criticisms, at least on this point. As we unpack precisely what Latour is arguing for when he claims that it is 'because [a factish] is constructed that it is so very real,' we will find that it bears much in common with Deleuze's project, as Latour himself recognizes, and thus Badiou's criticisms are directed at a 'postmodern' Deleuze that never was.[3] Key to understanding how 'construction' and 'autonomous reality' are synonymous is the notion, discussed in Chapter 3, of what Latour calls 'historical realism,' whereby the reality of what is is inseparable from processes that increase or diminish the number of associations that are accumulated over time. It is not all or nothing regarding the existence of entities; we ought rather to speak of 'relative existence.' As Latour puts it: 'An entity gains in reality if it is associated with many others that are viewed as collaborating with it. It loses in reality if, on the contrary, it has to shed associates or collaborators (humans and nonhumans)' (ibid. 257). For Deleuze, the heterogeneous network of human and nonhuman associations that constitutes the relative existence of an entity is just what he calls a multiplicity, and this is the historical ontology, the double articulation and movement, that is inseparable from the reality of entities. Moreover, we could say that the reality of entities is a reality-effect of historical ontology, though an autonomous effect whereby historical ontology is a quasi-cause (see our earlier discussion in Chapter 3). Using Deleuze's terminology, the reality of an entity is inseparable from a double articulation, with the first articulation drawing a number of associations and links between human and nonhuman elements into a plane of consistency, and the second articulation actualizing this plane of consistency as a real, autonomous entity. As Latour and Woolgar state it in *Laboratory Life*, ' "reality" cannot be used to explain why a statement becomes a fact, since it is only after it has become a fact that the effect of reality is obtained' (Latour and Woolgar 1986, 180). For Deleuze, and Deleuze's Hume, the multiplicity is the reality of the virtual that is the quasi-cause inseparable from the reality of entities that are its autonomous effects. A further and related concern of Deleuze and Hume, on our reading, is what Deleuze calls counter-actualization, and what we have referred to as problematizing history, whereby the virtual as quasi-cause becomes tapped, thereby problematizing the actual so as to allow for its possible transformation. Latour's use of history in science studies shares a similar concern. In particular, by problematizing traditional understandings of science and the presuppositions it entails concerning the relation between belief and objects, it could be argued that Latour is attempting to move beyond belief. Rather than attempt to justify beliefs through scientific facts or unmask beliefs as mere fancy and fetish, Latour sees 'the role of the intellectual' as that of 'protect[ing] the diversity of ontological status against the threat of its transformation into facts and fetishes, beliefs and things' (Latour 1999, 291). In short, Latour, as with Deleuze, sees the role of the intellectual as one of affirming multiplicity in order to counter the identification of multiplicity with the one or multiple of beliefs and things.

Having compared Deleuze's Humean project with Latour's, we can begin to see that Deleuze is not to be categorized among the postmodernists, at least as Latour defines them. Badiou explicitly identifies Deleuze as what Latour would call a postmodernist when he asserts that the virtual, for Deleuze, 'is no better than the finality of which it is the inversion (it determines the destiny of everything, instead of being that to which everything is destined)' (Badiou 2000, 53). The virtuality of the One, in short, is in command, determining 'the destiny of everything.' In place of a subject–object dualism, Deleuze adopts, according to Badiou, the virtual–actual dualism with the virtual, instead of the subject, being in command; and yet, as we have seen, this dualism is inseparable from a multiplicity, from a frontier between the two terms, that cannot be thought in terms of the one or the multiple (or the double). Deleuze's theory, therefore, calls for an ontological diversity and historicity that is inseparable from the actualities and realities of this world, much as for Latour there is a relative existence that is nothing less than an accumulation of human and nonhuman associations inseparable from a black boxed fact. With these concepts in hand, Deleuze is able to think singularities in a way that results in creative engagements with the actualities of daily life. To support this claim we will turn to discuss the political implications of Deleuze's thought, beginning with his comments regarding the social multiplicity.

III. Speaking for the Multitude

Deleuze introduces the example of the social multiplicity in the same passage where he discusses the linguistic multiplicity. Here is what he says:

> Take the social multiplicity: it determines sociability as a faculty, but also the transcendent object of sociability which cannot be lived within actual societies in which the multiplicity is incarnated, but must be and can be lived only in the element of social upheaval (in other words, freedom, which is always hidden among the remains of an old order and the first fruits of a new). (DR 193)

Much as the transcendent object of speech as a faculty 'can be spoken only in the poetic usage of speech coextensive with virtuality,' so too the transcendent object of sociability (freedom) 'can be lived only in the element of social upheaval.' The use of the term 'transcendent object' in this context may again appear to support Badiou's charge that the virtual 'plays the role of transcendence' in Deleuze's thought (Badiou 2004, 79). The added fact that this transcendent object 'cannot be lived within actual societies' would seem to reinforce this view. However, when Deleuze says this transcendent object 'cannot be lived within actual societies,' this is not to imply that revolutions are successful only when they turn away from the actual. To the contrary, the transcendent object is precisely the problematic multiplicity that is inseparable from, while not to be confused with, the actual, and yet it is what is presupposed when the actual becomes identified as problematic, and hence becomes a transformed or problematized actual.

At this point Deleuze's project converges with Foucault's. In describing his own project as one of doing a 'history of thought,' Foucault argues, as we saw earlier, that the primary objective of this project is to conduct an analysis of the way an unproblematic field of experience, or set of practices, which were accepted without question, which were familiar and 'silent,' out of discussion, becomes a problem, raises discussion and debate, incites new reactions, and induces a crisis in the previously silent behavior, habits, practices, and institutions. (Foucault 2001, 74)

Foucault will later argue that such problematizations constitute 'an "answer" to a concrete situation which is real,' and yet, he stresses, 'a given problematization is not an effect of an historical context or situation, but is an answer given by definite individuals' (ibid. 172). Understood in this way, therefore, a given problematization is a transcendent object not because it is a pre-established identity that transcends and predetermines the transformations of the actual, but rather because the problematization cannot be reduced to the actual, to the given. As Foucault puts it: 'A problematization is always a kind of creation; but a creation in the sense that, given a certain situation, you cannot infer that this kind of problematization will follow' (ibid. 172–3).

As an example of such a problematization, Foucault cites, in his book *Fearless Speech*, the problematization of *parrhesia* (generally translated as 'free speech') that attended the rise of democratic institutions in Ancient Greece. Foucault quotes a passage from Isocrates' essay 'On the Peace,' where Isocrates complains that 'there exists no "freedom of speech" except that which is enjoyed in this Assembly by the most reckless orators, who care nothing for your welfare, and in the theatre by the comic poets' (ibid. 82). Isocrates' complaint, for Foucault, is that 'real parrhesia, parrhesia in its positive, critical sense, does not exist where democracy exists' (ibid. 83). In other words, rather than provide critical feedback to the people, to the *demos*, the 'reckless orators' merely parrot the will of the *demos* back to them and are not 'courageous enough,' Foucault claims, 'to oppose the *demos*' (ibid. 82).

What underlies Isocrates' criticism of the 'reckless orators,' as well as Pseudo-Xenophon's concerns regarding democracy (which Foucault also cites), is a general 'distrust of the *demos*' feelings, opinions, and desires' (ibid. 83). As Foucault then turns to Plato's references to *parrhesia*, he shows that what most concerned Plato was not the fact that the *demos* will be poorly governed because 'reckless orators' will dare not offer the critical feedback they require; instead, Foucault argues that for Plato the 'primary danger of liberty and free speech in democracy is what results when everyone has his own manner of life, his own style of life, or what Plato calls "καταδκενε του βιου." For then there can be no common logos, no possible unity, for the city' (ibid. 84). And without a common logos, there will be chaos and disorder, and thus a fear of chaos that prompts Plato's moves to ground the 'manner of life' one leads upon transcendent truths that forbid the dangerous consequences of 'liberty and free speech in democracy.' Latour will also stress this point when in his discussion of Plato's *Gorgias* he argues that both 'Socrates and Callicles have a common enemy: the people of Athens' (Latour 1999, 219). Despite the differences between rhetoric and philosophy as represented by Callicles and Socrates in the dialogue, they both, out of a fear of the *demos* that they see as 'a barbaric population of unintelligent, spoiled, and sickly slaves and children,' (ibid. 243) remove from the *demos* the means of being political. In short, for Latour, 'deciding what is right and wrong, what is good and bad' (ibid.), does not require an expert, but by placing such decisions in the hands of experts, Latour believes that both Socrates and Callicles destroy the very means of practicing politics. A further consequence of this move, according to Latour, is the establishment (or reinforcement) of the long-standing 'habit of thinking that the demos lacks morality as totally as it lacks epistemic knowledge' (ibid. 255). And on this final point Deleuze and Foucault, in their published conversation, 'Intellectuals and Power,' could not agree more. As Foucault expresses it, 'the masses no longer need him [the intellectual, or the expert] to gain knowledge; they know perfectly well, without illusion; they know far better than he and they are certainly capable of expressing themselves' (Foucault 1977, 207). If politics entails allowing for the social multiplicity to become effective in 'expressing themselves,' as we believe Deleuze, in agreement with Latour and Foucault, argues, then one way to understand the political project of Deleuze is to see it as counter to the dominant 'habit of thinking' which presupposes a fear of politics. Before turning to discuss Deleuze's project, it will help if we first address the manner in which the fear of politics is addressed by Latour, Badiou, and Agamben, for in doing so we will gain a better perspective upon where Deleuze's thought might be placed relative to a number of important debates.

As just noted, Latour believes that it was due to their respective fear of politics that Socrates and Callicles called upon experts to decide in matters that should belong with the *demos*. If only experts are to speak for the multitude, then it should be no wonder, Latour states, that the *demos* does not 'understand the causes of what it does, [for] he [Socrates] severs all the feedback loops that would make this knowledge of the cause practical' (Latour 1999, 244). As a consequence of the fear of politics, a fear of the *demos*, the social multiplicity comes to be identified with two transcendences rather than being affirmed as a collective that is forever in the process of 'establishing provisional cohesion that will have to be started all over again every single day' (Latour 2004, 147). These two transcendences are Reason and Populism. In the one we have the claims of experts who speak for the *demos*, and on the other 'the whole [the *demos*]' is obliged 'to deal with itself without the benefit of guaranteed information.' Since the *demos* is 'deprived of knowledge and morality,' as the long-standing habit assures us, they are subsequently thought to be in need of outside help, the help of those who claim to represent the truth or the people (or both).[4] The help the *demos* needs, however, is not of this type, Latour claims; rather:

> The specific transcendence it [the *demos*] needs to bootstrap itself is not that of a lever coming from the outside, but much more like the kneading of a dough – except that the demos is at once the flour, the water, the baker, the leavening ferment, and the very act of kneading. Yes, a fermentation, the sort of turmoil that has always seemed so terrible to the powerful, and that has nonetheless always been transcendent enough to make the people move and be represented. (Latour 1999, 252)

In what Latour will refer to as the social world as association, there is no outside factor drawing together the human and nonhuman associations, and politics ought not to see the 'social world as prison,' as something to transcend. Politics is instead to be 'conceived as the progressive composition of the common world' (Latour 2004, 18) which as 'a fermentation,' a 'sort of turmoil,' is not strictly identifiable. As the transcendent object of speech is transcendent for Deleuze in the sense that it cannot be reduced to the actual empirical language from which it is inseparable, so too the fermentation of politics is inseparable from the 'multiplicity of associations of humans and non-humans that the collective is precisely charged with collecting' (ibid. 42). But this collecting, and the provisional unity that comes to be identifiable as a result, is irreducible to the 'multiplicity of associations,' or to the social multiplicity. What is needed so that the collective can grow, Latour argues, are 'two functions, dispersed everywhere; one allows it to catch hold of the multitudes without crushing them, and the other allows it to get them to speak in a single voice without scattering' (ibid. 150). The difficulty, however, is that the multiplicity of associations tends – as a result of the fear of politics, the fear of dispersion and scattering – to speak in a single voice only when the effectiveness of the social multiplicity *as multiplicity* has been crushed. To put it differently, the social multiplicity has a tendency to come to be identified with the voices that would speak for it, a move that is itself inseparable from the social multiplicity, and thus only constitutes a provisional unity.

At this point in our argument Badiou may very well protest against Latour's conception of the collective. Is not Latour, Badiou might ask, simply reducing politics to a process of establishing public opinion and consensus? What would it mean to get the multitude 'to speak in a single voice without scattering' if it is not an attempt to develop a politics of consensus? If it is such an attempt, then Badiou could not disagree more. What such a politics entails, for Badiou, is a 'concession to the One [that] undoes the radicality of the multiple [multiple-without-oneness] . . . It opens the way for a doctrine of consensus, which is in effect the dominant ideology of contemporary parliamentary States' (Badiou 2005b, 18). Badiou would no doubt also break with the historicism of Latour's project – or with what he would perceive as the failure to distinguish between belonging (natural, ahistorical) and inclusion (anti-natural, historical) – for such historicism subordinates the real, for Badiou, to being 'a composite or complex unity' (ibid. 42). Put in other words, for Badiou it is the fear of the radicality of the multiple-without-oneness that is the fear of politics which prompts the re-securing of the count, and hence the historicism that forecloses the void that circulates throughout the presentation of the multiple by assuring that each thing that is presented is included within the unity of an historical situation. And this is just what Badiou admits is 'the central idea of my ontology, i.e. that what the State strives to foreclose through its power of counting is the void of the situation, while the event always reveals it . . .' (ibid. 119).

On Badiou's reading, then, Latour has simply repeated Deleuze's mistake – he has not thought the singularity necessary for the creativity of events to become effective, despite the stated moves to do just this. And yet Badiou is in other ways quite close to Latour in identifying politics proper with the multitude (social multiplicity). 'The mass movement,' Badiou states, 'being presented but not re-presentable (by the State), verifies that the void roams around in presentation,' and it is 'politics [that] deals with the masses, because politics is unbound from the State, and diagonal to its parts' (ibid. 73). For Badiou, 'the word "democracy," taken in the philosophical sense, thinks a politics to the extent that, in the effectiveness of its emancipatory process, what it works towards is the impossibility, in the situation, of every non-egalitarian statement concerning this situation' (ibid. 93). Politics as thought, or democracy 'taken in the philosophical sense,' is a thought of the singularity that cannot be included within a situation. In this case, the thought of an emancipatory equality as a pure multiple-without-oneness (social multiplicity) that is presented but not included in the situation, and this thought evades the re-securing count of the State. Moreover, for those subjects who become subjected to the event of the truth of political equality, the result is a militant resistance to the inequalities of the situation. As Aristotle recognized, 'Everywhere, those who seek equality revolt.'[5] Such revolt is not, for Badiou, a mere reform of the situation, a transformation of what is; rather, it is 'another politics,' a politics that breaks with the politics that is.[6] Badiou refers to this as 'the political event . . . [which] prescribes that all are virtual militants of the thought that proceeds on the basis of the event.' We are, in short, each 'virtual militants,' or subjects who may become subject to the Truth of the political event that renders impossible the thoughts of inequality in the situation.

In the current situation, Badiou argues that 'the egalitarian maxim is effectively incompatible with the errancy of statist excess,' and 'the matrix of inequality consists precisely in the impossibility of measuring the superpower of the State' (ibid. 149). More precisely, it is the 'blind power of unfettered Capital,' Badiou argues, that 'cannot be either measured or fixed at any point. All we know is that it prevails absolutely over the subjective fate of collectives, regardless of who they are' (ibid.). Speaking in favor of capitalist States, traditional liberalism remains convinced of the power of Capital as such, but such confidence is marked by a 'total indecision about its consequences for people's lives and the universal affirmation of collectives' (ibid.). What is required of the militants subjected to the truth of the political event is to challenge this very indecision, to bring into clarity the 'measurelessness in which this power is enveloped,' and most especially the inequalities this power produces. In the tradition of Marx, Badiou thus calls for a militant politics that will set out 'To produce the same, to count each one universally as one . . . [and] to work locally, in the gap opened up between politics and the State' (ibid. 150). Rather than succumbing to the measureless power of Capital and its tendency towards inequality, or the tendency of Capital 'to accumulate in fewer and fewer hands' as Marx puts it,[7] a radical, militant subject injects the thought of universal equality into the inequalities of the situation and thereby thinks the singularity that ruptures with 'that which is.' Deleuze, as we will see, is likewise concerned with the 'insertion of art into everyday life' so as to facilitate a rupture with what is, and most especially the dominance of Capital. There is a crucial difference between the two, however, that becomes clear when we bring in the thought of Agamben.

The relevance of Agamben here becomes most apparent upon examining the various trajectories Badiou, Agamben, and Deleuze have each taken vis à vis Foucault. Badiou, for example, is critical of Foucault for failing to 'think his own thought' (Badiou 2005a, 46). In particular, Foucault's discussions and detailed analyses of the various historical configurations he will call *episteme*, 'remain,' according to Badiou, 'composite, lacking an identification of the prescriptive kernel that lies at their heart' (ibid.). In other words, Foucault lacks a theory of the subject, a subject for whom the truth of the event becomes 'the prescriptive kernel' that can then unleash the transformative effects that attend the thought of singularities. Agamben has a similar difficulty with Foucault's project. As he sees it, there are 'two distinct directives for research' at work in Foucault's thought: there is 'the study of the political techniques (such as the science of the police) with which the State assumes and integrates the care of the natural life of individuals into its very center,' and there is 'the examination of the technologies of the self by which the processes of subjectivization bring the individual to bind himself to his own identity and consciousness and, at the same time, to an external power' (Agamben 1998, 5). It would appear, then, that Foucault does have a theory of the subject, and perhaps a theory that could counter Badiou's criticisms, and yet, Agamben argues, there is a 'blind spot' in Foucault's work, a 'hidden point of intersection between the juridico-institutional and the biopolitical models of power' (ibid. 6). Analogous to Badiou's criticism that Foucault failed to develop a theory of a subject whose thought is the 'prescriptive kernel' that would transform juridico-institutional forms of power, Agamben likewise, although more sympathetically, finds a possible point of convergence between the biopolitical model of the subject and the juridico-institutional model; this is, however, a point Foucault's thought only moves 'toward without reaching' (ibid.). For Agamben the point of convergence lies in what he calls 'bare life,' which he claims constitutes 'the original – if concealed – nucleus of sovereign power' (ibid.).

The manner in which bare life constitutes sovereign power is through its very exclusion. Agamben is clear on this point: 'In western politics, bare life has the peculiar privilege of being that whose exclusion founds the city of men' (ibid. 7).[8] In particular, bare life founds the power of the sovereign decision to declare a state of exception. Agamben offers as an example the military order issued by George W. Bush on 13 November 2001, 'which authorized the "indefinite detention" and trial by "military commissions" of noncitizens suspected of involvement in terrorist activities' (Agamben 2005, 3). For Agamben the military order is not to be confused with the prerogative power of a president to suspend normal juridical procedures in order to achieve the end of securing life and liberty for American citizens. Although this is indeed the stated objective of the decisions regarding the state of exception, what interests Agamben is precisely the fact that these decisions simultaneously exclude the very life that constitutes their power. In the case of the enemy combatants who are held in indefinite detention at Guantanamo, they are neither 'prisoners nor persons accused, but simply "detainees," they are the object of a pure de facto rule . . . entirely removed from the law and from judicial oversight' (ibid. 3–4). It is this removal from the law that interests Agamben. Drawing on Walter Benjamin, Agamben notes that Benjamin was correct to claim that 'in deciding on the state of exception, the sovereign must not in some way include it in the juridical order; he must, on the contrary, exclude it, leave it outside of the juridical order' (ibid. 55). In other words, the power of the sovereign to be a force-of-law, a force that acts within the limitations of law (or constituted power), becomes, in the state of exception, a mere force-of, a force that excludes the law for the sake of securing life while at the same time as mere force-of it excludes human actions from a law that would protect them. As Agamben puts it, 'in the urgency of the state of exception "in which we live" [there is a] fiction that governs this Arcanum imperii [secret power] par excellence of our time,' and this secret power is 'essentially an empty space, in which a human action with no relation to law stands before a norm with no relation to life' (ibid. 86).

In response to the state of exception, Agamben does not call for a return to a sovereign power and force (violence) that is to be exercised only within the limits of the law, nor does he call for a return to the law that truly serves to secure the interests of human life. The reason Foucault's thought ultimately failed to complete the move towards the point where juridico-institutional and biopolitical models of power meet, is because, as Agamben says, the state of exception 'that must ultimately articulate and hold together the[se] two aspects,' is a 'fiction,' and 'between violence and law, between life and norm, there is no substantial articulation' (ibid. 87). Moreover, as one attempts to think the relationship between the two models of power, or between bios and polis, one inevitably confronts the antinomy of constitutive-constituted power. As Agamben shows, it is difficult to detail the constitutive powers of a sovereign to establish by force a set of laws without presupposing certain legal principles;[9] on the other hand, it is equally difficult to conceptualize a set of laws as constituted power without presupposing a force of change to re-negotiate and re-create these laws. This aporia will remain unavoidable, Agamben argues, 'Until a new and coherent ontology of potentiality has replaced the ontology founded on the primacy of actuality and its relation to potentiality' (Agamben 1998, 44). In particular, 'one must think the existence of potentiality without any relation to Being in the form of actuality . . . This, however, implies nothing less than thinking ontology and politics beyond every figure of relation, beyond even the limit relation that is the sovereign ban' (ibid. 47). In other words, rather than attempt to think violence in relation to the law, constitutive power in relation to constituted power, or life (bios) in relation to norms (polis) – which, after all, will lead to the aporia for there is no 'substantial articulation' between them – we ought, says Agamben (who is in turn following Benjamin), to develop an ontology of potentiality that can enable pure violence and pure communication. As Agamben puts it,

> In the [Benjamin's] essay on language, pure language is that which is not an instrument for the purpose of communication, but communicates itself immediately, that is, a pure and simple communicability; likewise, pure violence is that which does not stand in a relation of means toward an end, but holds itself in relation to its own mediality. (Ibid. 62)[10]

At this point we can return to Deleuze, for Deleuze's theory of virtuality offers precisely the ontology Agamben believes is necessary. One of the significant implications of Deleuze's claim that the virtual is real is that, as

Agamben claims was needed, it is a potentiality that 'has its own consistency and [will] not always disappear immediately into actuality' (ibid. 45). Understood in this way, we can also see that Deleuze's thought is not subservient to the dialectic of open and closed, wherein the virtual as open is placed in relation to the actual as the closed. For Deleuze, as for Agamben, the ontology of pure violence, pure communication, or virtuality involves a potentiality 'which does not stand in a relation of means toward an end,' whether that be to open that which is closed or close that which is opened.

For Deleuze, the social multiplicity and its transcendent object that is lived only during times of social upheaval is neither a means to open a closed, stratified space, nor is it the means whereby territorializing forces capture and re-secure the count; quite the contrary, the social upheaval is precisely the power of the multitude that forces a stuttering, stupefying gap and rupture that undermines any attempted reduction to a dialectical relationship between the open and closed. As with Agamben's understanding of pure violence, so too for Deleuze the transcendent object 'is that which does not stand in a relation of means toward an end, but holds itself in relation to its own mediality.' As Deleuze will say of works of genius, they are complete in themselves and not by virtue of their relation to a transcendent standard nor as the result of traversing the path from means (potentiality) to end (actuality). And as Deleuze and Guattari put it in *Anti-Oedipus*: 'from the moment there is genius, there is something that belongs to no school, no period, something that achieves a breakthrough – art as a process without goal, *but that attains completion as such*' (AO 370, emphasis mine). This is also why Deleuze will claim that 'the work of art has nothing to do with communication'; that is, it is in no way a means to relate an identifiable sense or point to an audience whose task it is to decipher this sense. As art has become commoditized, however, it has increasingly become a means to prescribed ends. These ends, Deleuze argues, entail 'Fast turnover [which] necessarily means selling people what they expect' (N 128). The creations of genius, however, emerge imperceptibly, and it is at this point that Deleuze's understanding of aesthetics merges with his concepts of becoming-imperceptible and, more importantly, becoming-revolutionary. It is to this subject that we now turn.

IV. Becoming-imperceptible

In his short essay, 'Mediators,' Deleuze argues that we face a choice 'between creative forces and forces of domestication,' with the latter, as Deleuze makes quite clear, being firmly in control of capitalist markets: 'Creative possibilities may be very different in different modes of expression, but they're related to the extent that they must counter the introduction of a cultural space of markets and conformity – that is, a space of "producing for the market" – together' (N 131). With capitalism, creative forces are no longer forces that are complete in themselves without a purpose or means–end relation; instead, they have increasingly become creative *for the purpose of* 'producing for the market.' In calling for the need to counter the 'cultural space of markets and conformity,' Deleuze is thus calling for a countering move to capitalism, or a revolutionary movement, as we will see.

As for capitalism itself, Deleuze claims it functions as a system of immanent causation, meaning it does not rely upon an outside force to establish its ordered ends and purposes. These arise immanently, much as the provisional order of the collective, for Latour, arose without the need for 'a lever coming from the outside' (Latour 1999, 252). Whenever a new market is discovered or opened, it becomes incorporated into the capitalist system itself, though a now expanded system.[11] These same points apply to Deleuze's notion of the social multiplicity. As a multiplicity, a social multiplicity is 'an affirmation that is irreducible to any sort of unity,' and yet as an immanent, virtual system it is inseparable from the identifiable limits that are the immanent effects of the social multiplicity, much as the limits of capitalism are the immanent effects of capitalism itself. Social multiplicities thus entail assemblages, assemblages with identifiable limits and thresholds that constitute what Badiou would call being included as a part of the social, and they entail those processes that cannot be included, or 'cannot,' as Deleuze puts it, 'be lived within actual societies in which the multiplicity is incarnated' (DR 193). An assemblage, for Deleuze, is precisely the double movement of territorialization–deterritorialization, or what for Hume was the movement of constituting identity (underdetermination)/already constituted identity (overdetermination). As an assemblage, desire, for example, entails a double movement that entails both the production of identity (as immanent cause) and desiring productions, or 'lines of flight,' that elude and transgress the immanent limits and identities set forth by an assemblage.[12] The difference, therefore, between Deleuze and Badiou is that while Badiou calls for the 'absolute ontological separation of the event' (Badiou 2001, 75) from the situation and the state of the situation, or for the separation of the historical event from natural, ahistorical situations, Deleuze claims there is no such gap or separation but rather social assemblages that entail both that which can and cannot be included. From the perspective of politics, therefore, it is not a matter, as it is for Badiou, of waiting upon militants who become subjected to the rare historical Truth and event that prescribes a course of action that founds 'another politics.' By affirming the historical/ahistorical split, Badiou ultimately separates political agency from the truth this agency later naturalizes. For Deleuze and Guattari, to the contrary, 'politics precedes being' (TP 203), 'every politics is simultaneously a macropolitics and a micropolitics' (TP 213), and thus politics presupposes a multiplicity that cannot be understood on the basis of the identity of society or the individual, including the individual or subject as 'fidelity operator.'[13] Deleuze and Guattari are clear on this point:

> in the end, the difference is not at all between the social and the individual (or interindividual), but between the molar realm of representations, individual or collective, and the molecular realm of beliefs and desires in which the distinction between the social and the individual loses all meaning since flows are neither attributable to individuals nor overcodable by collective signifiers. (Ibid. 219)

This statement follows from the claim that

> Desire is never separable from complex assemblages that necessarily tie into molecular levels, from microformations already shaping postures, attitudes, perceptions, expectations, semiotic systems, etc. Desire is never an undifferentiated instinctual energy. (Ibid. 215)

Desire is an assemblage. As such the products and identities that are inseparable from desire are forever subject to the undermining effects of nomadic flows – lines of flight – that transgress these identities and transform the assemblages. This is the creativity of desire, the potential it has to rupture with what is. This creativity, however, runs the risk of fascism, and for a very simple reason. Since the molar, rigid segments maintain the identity of our desires and keep them in check, they thus prevent desire from exploding into chaos and disorder. As a result we all have a potential molecular desire for fascism: 'Our security, the great molar organization that sustains us, the arborescences we cling to, the binary machines that give us a well-defined status, the resonances we enter into, the system of overcoding that dominates us – we desire all that' (ibid. 219). The subject, therefore, as was the case for Hume, is an assemblage – a virtual–practical subject.

The relationship between the subject as virtual–practical assemblage and politics becomes especially clear in Deleuze's (and Deleuze and Guattari's) discussions concerning the 'steamroller' of capitalism (Guattari 1995, 123–4). In order to guarantee a return on an investment a capitalist investor must predict the desires and choices of individuals, but if the system of capitalism can itself produce individuals with a homogenized set of predictable desires, choices, and beliefs, then the capitalist reduces their risk. The ideally constituted and assembled individual will be one who keeps coming back for more of the same. This gets to the heart of Deleuze and Guattari's aesthetic critique of capitalism and their call to inject art into everyday life. In *Difference and Repetition*, for example, Deleuze argues that

> there is no other aesthetic problem than that of the insertion of art into everyday life. The more our daily life appears standardized, stereotyped and subject to an

accelerated reproduction of objects of consumption, the more art must be injected into it in order to extract that little difference which plays simultaneously between other levels of repetition, and even in order to make the two extremes resonate – namely, the habitual series of consumption and the instinctual series of destruction and death. (DR 293)

This injection of art into everyday life counters the tendency of capitalism to create a 'steamrolled' individual, an individual with homogenized, predictably segmented desires, and it does this by making 'the two extremes resonate.' These extremes are the two sides of any and every assemblage – on the one side is the identifiable and predictable, the repetition of the same; on the other is the chaos and unpredictability that results in destruction and death. The creative revolt against this situation as the insertion of art will bring these two sides together in such a way that they are able to resonate within an assemblage.

This aesthetic countermove to capitalism is not a reformation of capitalism. As Deleuze makes clear, a reformer calls for change but does not challenge the existing unities that are to be changed, whereas a revolutionary calls for a destructive break with the existing unities. A conservative or reactionary reformer, for example, calls for a return to a past unity that has been lost – for example, a return to the nuclear family, to traditional values, to a true religious faith and practice, and so on. A liberal and perhaps radical reformer calls for the realization of a future condition and unity that will be more true and pure (or fair) than the present state of affairs. Would the same be true of Marx and Marxism? An argument could be made that Marx too was a reformer, albeit a radical one, insofar as he called for the realization of a communism that would resolve and surpass the contradictions and alienation of the present capitalist system. Would Deleuze then, to the extent that he follows Marx, be a reformer rather than a revolutionary? The answer is a resounding 'No.' From Deleuze's perspective, capitalism, by continually creating and encouraging a multiplicity of desires – carving out niches that target individual consumers, encouraging them to differentiate themselves from other consumers with their purchases – forever pushes the envelope in its ability to produce a predictable consumer who continually returns to buy more of the same.[14] Capitalism risks unleashing desire as multiplicity, a revolutionary desire that will undermine and transform the immanent system of capitalism itself. In *Anti-Oedipus* this unleashed desire, this multiplicity that cannot be normalized, homogenized, and reduced to a commodity to be bought and sold, is referred to as schizophrenia; thus Deleuze and Guattari state, in terms that echo Marx's revolutionary thought: 'The schizophrenic deliberately seeks out the very limit of capitalism: he is its inherent tendency brought to fulfillment, its surplus product, its proletariat, and its exterminating angel' (AO 35).[15]

Coupled to the capitalist tendency to forever expand the limits of what is produced 'for the market' is the emergence of what Deleuze will call the society of control. A society of control, in contrast to the disciplinary societies analyzed in many of Foucault's works, no longer functions 'by enclosure but by continuous control and instantaneous communication' (N 174). Disciplinary societies operate on the principle of molds and enclosures, such as schools, factories, and barracks where a set model is imposed (molded) upon those who are enclosed within the system. This molding requires the disciplinary techniques of institutions, including methods of observation. A society of control, by contrast, operates by the principle of 'constant modulation, like a casting that self-deforms and changes continuously, from one instant to another, or like a sieve where the mesh changes from one point to another' (ibid. 178–9, translation modified). In particular, the society of control operates through constantly testing and comparing information, and it uses this information both in setting targets and goals for employees and for the continuous monitoring of the progress they make towards these goals. This set-up Deleuze refers to as a 'corporation,' which, he points out, 'never ceases to introduce an inexpiable rivalry as healthy emulation, as an excellent motivational force that opposes individuals to one another and which traverses the individuals, dividing them in themselves' (ibid. 179). The popularity of game shows and reality TV programs only goes to show how widespread this desire for 'inexpiable rivalry' has become, along with the belief that this competitive field is reality, a reality that is good and desirable because it brings the creative best out of people!

For Deleuze, however, the societies of control seek to ward off the creativity of multiplicities by putting such energies in the service of 'producing for the market,' such that it is this that we come to desire. Put in other terms, the society of control is an assemblage resisting the tendencies that could become revolutionary by constituting, at the molecular level, the very desires and beliefs that perpetuate the assemblage. We can now see the profound reason for Deleuze's linkage of becoming-revolutionary with becoming-imperceptible. As Deleuze might put it, the societies of control do allow for creativity, but only of a very limited kind. It is true that individuals and corporations in competition with one another will create and innovate in order to increase efficiency, productivity, and hence profits; and that the individuals who implement such processes are paid according to their 'individual' efficiency, determined on the basis of a continuous analysis of information (for example, the 'merit-based' pay system). Efficiency, productivity, and speed then become not only what we are judged on and paid for, but also what we desire. Moreover, with the constant return of information we are also continuously presented with our next target, our next aspiration, and with luck or another burst of 'creativity' we can achieve these goals. In short, the societies of control utilize constant and rapid communications (memos, emails, advertisements, and so on) to inform people where they stand in the constantly shifting field of interpersonal relations, a field wherein there is 'inexpiable rivalry' and competition. If someone does not continuously work and express themselves in such a field of interpersonal relations, they will escape being monitored and become an unknown variable; they will, as we are told, fall behind. The net result is that we come to desire the very systems that control and monitor us. We don't want to be left behind.[16]

We are now in a position to understand some of the claims Deleuze makes that bear upon the practical issues involved with becoming-revolutionary. First and most importantly, Deleuze argues in typical Nietzschean fashion that creativity occurs away from the marketplace, thus reiterating the view, cited earlier, that our creative efforts ought to counter the 'cultural space of markets and conformity.'[17] Thus, in reference to the continuous communication and flow of information within societies of control, Deleuze argues that

> Perhaps speech, communication, are rotten. They are already penetrated by money . . . A turning away from speech is necessary. To create has always been something other than communicating. What is important would perhaps be to create voids of non-communication, interruptions, in order to escape the control. (N 175)

This same thought is expressed in an earlier essay:

> So the problem is no longer getting people to express themselves, but providing little gaps of solitude and silence in which they might eventually find something to say. Repressive forces don't stop people from expressing themselves, but rather force them to express themselves. What a relief to have nothing to say, the right to say nothing, because only then is there a chance of framing the rare, and even rarer, thing that might be worth saying. (N 129)

To instill creativity into our lives, to become-revolutionary, does not then entail a constant, unceasing communication and expression of ourselves. To the contrary, it involves breaking with the flow of communications, interrupting them, so that one might force into play a problem that has transformative (that is, revolutionary) potential. For Deleuze, such interruptions are inseparable from experimental, creative processes, where the consequences are in no way known or predictable. One cannot target or call for the efficient and timely production of creativity. It always emerges in an untimely fashion, within conditions that are fragile precisely because they are inefficient and run counter to many of the pressures of society that resist such conditions (the capitalist desire for predictable, efficient sources of revenue from 'creative' work).

For Deleuze, then, the revolutionary potential to transform the current system involves a becoming-revolutionary of our desires. This requires taking a time out, an interruption, a self-imposed leave of absence from the continuous processes of control and communication. This is not in order to glorify a reclusive aestheticized existence, but rather to encourage the conditions whereby the problems that set revolutionary movements into effect can arise. In particular, by becoming-imperceptible within the voids that are not captured by the processes of the society of control, one is then able to affirm the social multiplicity, the power of the multitude, that is the creative, transformative force inseparable from social and political assemblages. It is precisely this creativity of multiplicities that interested Deleuze in Hume; and just as Hume sought, within the given, to account for the constitution of that which is irreducible to the given, so too Deleuze, by affirming multiplicities, by thinking a thought that entails an embrace of singularities (as is also Badiou's project), facilitates a creation that is irreducible to anything actual. Following through on his Humean transcendental empiricism, Deleuze is far from being afraid of politics; rather, he affirms an experimental method of philosophizing that begins with the actual and may, through frequent trials, force the transformation of the way things are, including the powers that be.

As an effort in experimental, empiricist philosophy, this book has also aspired to think through what Deleuze AND Hume have actually written in a manner inseparable from politics, in a manner that embraces multiplicity and the power of AND, and in the hope that a problematized Deleuze's Hume may transform our ways of thinking, feeling, and being in the world. As Marx makes the point in his eleventh thesis on Feuerbach: 'The philosophers have only interpreted the world, in various ways; the point is to change it' (Marx [1845] 1978, 145).

Notes

1. See Sam Gillespie, 'Placing the Void: Badiou on Spinoza,' (Gillespie 2001) where this criticism is made explicitly. Gillespie summarizes Badiou's criticism of Deleuze by saying that Deleuze fails to develop a thought that thinks 'above and beyond the immediacy of presentation' (p. 74). For Badiou's charge that Deleuze's writings are monotonous, see Badiou 2000, p. 15, where he 'unhesitatingly' characterizes Deleuze's conceptual formulations as 'monotonous.'
2. I am using the language of dynamic systems theory here, though Deleuze began to do so himself in his final writings. In *Essays Critical and Clinical*, for example, Deleuze will refer to language as 'a homogeneous system in equilibrium' in contrast to the stuttering, far-from-equilibrium conditions (CC 108). For more on the relation between dynamic systems theory and Deleuze, see Massumi 1992 and Bell 2006b.

3. See especially Isabelle Stengers' magisterial work, *Penser avec Whitehead* (Stengers 2002), where this claim is made on numerous occasions and where Stengers, for her part, borrows heavily from Deleuze.
4. For more on the multitude, see Hardt and Negri 2004, and Paolo Virno 2004.
5. Aristotle, *Politics* 1301b26. Cited by Badiou 2005b, 100.
6. As Badiou argues, 'For every real figure of evil is presented, not as a fanatical non-opinion undermining being-together, but on the contrary as a politics aiming to ground authentic being-together. No "common sense" can counter it, only another politics can do so' (2005b, 20).
7. *Economic and Philosophic Manuscripts of 1844* (Marx [1844] 1987, 41): 'Accumulation, where private property prevails, is the concentration of capital in the hands of a few, it is in general an inevitable consequence if capitals are left to follow their natural course, and it is precisely through competition that the way is cleared for this natural destination of capital.' Below we will discuss Deleuze's criticism of competition as it has come to prevail in what he calls the 'society of control.'
8. See also, Agamben 1998, 11: 'Bare life remains included in politics in the form of the exception, that is, as something that is included solely through an exclusion.'
9. The *Declaration of Independence*, for example, as an act of constitutive power nonetheless relies upon certain universal principles that are taken to be inalienable – namely, as already constituted; and Hannah Arendt, Agamben notes, discusses a similar case when she examines the French Revolution (1998, 41).
10. The essay Agamben is referring to is 'On Language as Such and on the Language of Man,' in Benjamin 1978.
11. Immanuel Wallerstein has argued that this capitalist process of deterritorialization/reterritorialization (though he does not use these terms) has become a world system that now includes most of the world's economies. See Wallerstein 1979.
12. See TP 327–8. Here Deleuze and Guattari stress the importance of consistency as integral to assemblages, and for reasons we have been arguing for throughout this study. In short, an assemblage entails a consistency of pre-individual singularities that enables the actualization of identifiable limits, and yet inseparable from these limits are the deterritorializing lines of flight. A functioning assemblage entails both movements, and it is precisely consistency that maintains the functioning, or evades the paranoiac and schizophrenic poles. For more on these two poles, see AO 370–1. For a brief but helpful discussion of assemblages, see Protevi and Bonta 2004, 54–5.
13. For Badiou's discussion of the 'fidelity operator,' see Badiou 1991.
14. Charles Tilly has defined capitalism as the effort of capitalists to capture the flows of capital: 'Capitalists, then, are people who specialize in the accumulation, purchase, and sale of capital. They occupy the realm of exploitation, where the relations of production and exchange themselves yield surpluses, and capitalists capture them' (Tilly 1990, 17).
15. Hardt and Negri develop this line of thought in their book *Empire*, where for them the multitude functions as the condition for the possibility/impossibility of Empire: 'The deterritorializing power of the multitude is the productive force that sustains Empire and at the same time the force that calls for and makes necessary its destruction' (Hardt and Negri 2000, 61).

16. There is a similarity here with the work of Bourdieu, and especially with his concept of the *habitus*. In his numerous works, Bourdieu argues that social institutions, primarily education, reproduce existing social positions and relationships, relationships that include an unequal access to power and wealth. These relationships are reproduced by the *habitus* in that the *habitus* is, for Bourdieu, a 'kind of practical sense . . . what is in "sport" a "feel" for the game' (Bourdieu 1998, 25). Those with this practical sense acquire the social positions where this is what is expected, and those who don't, don't. Politically, the *habitus* becomes the unquestioned obviousness of a situation – such as the largely unquestioned assumption that competition encourages innovation – and, moreover, 'State injunctions,' Bourdieu argues, 'owe their obviousness, and thus their potency, to the fact that the state has imposed the very cognitive structures through which it is perceived' (ibid. 55). A question Bourdieu leaves largely untouched, as Randall Collins and others have noted (see Collins 1994), is how change is at all possible. This question is central to Deleuze's concerns.
17. Nietzsche, *Thus Spoke Zarathustra*, 'On the Flies of the Marketplace': 'Where solitude ceases the market place begins; and where the market place begins the noise of the great actors and the buzzing of the poisonous flies begins too . . . Little do the people comprehend the great – that is, the creating. But they have a mind for all showmen and actors of great things' (Nietzsche 1968, 163).

Bibliography

Agamben, Giorgio. 1998. *Homo Sacer: Sovereign Power and Bare Life*. Stanford: Stanford University Press.
—. 1999. *Potentialities: Collected Essays in Philosophy*. Translated by D. Heller-Roazen. Stanford: Stanford University Press.
—. 2005. *State of Exception*. Translated by K. Attell. Chicago: University of Chicago Press.
—. 2007. *Infancy and History: On the Destruction of Experience*. Translated by L. Heron. London and New York: Verso.
Alliez, Eric. 2004. *Signature of the World, or, What is the Philosophy of Deleuze and Guattari?* London and New York: Continuum.
Althusser, Louis. 1969. *For Marx*. Translated by B. Brewster. London: Allen Lane.
American Psychiatric Association. 2000. *Diagnostic and Statistical Manual of Mental Disorders*.
Anderson, Benedict. 1991. *Imagined Communities*. London and New York: Verso.
Ansell Pearson, Keith. 1999. *Germinal Life: The Difference and Repetition of Deleuze*. London and New York: Routledge.
—. 2002. *Philosophy and the Adventure of the Virtual: Bergson and the Time of Life*. London and New York: Routledge.
Aune, Bruce. 1991. *Knowledge of the External World*. London and New York: Routledge.
Badiou, Alain. 1991. 'On a Finally Objectless Subject,' in *Who Comes After the Subject?* Edited by Eduardo Cadava, Peter Connor, and Jean-Luc Nancy. London and New York: Routledge.
—. 1994. 'Gilles Deleuze, *The Fold: Leibniz and the Baroque*,' in *Gilles Deleuze and the Theater of Philosophy*. Edited by C. V. Boundas and D. Olkowski. London and New York: Routledge.
—. 2000. *Deleuze: The Clamor of Being*. Translated by L. Burchill. Minneapolis: University of Minnesota Press.
—. 2001. *Ethics: An Essay on the Understanding of Evil*. Translated by P. Hallward. London and New York: Verso.
—. 2004. *Theoretical Writings*. Translated by R. Brassier and A. Toscano. London and New York: Continuum.
—. 2005a. *Being and Event*. Translated by Oliver Feltham. London and New York: Continuum.
—. 2005b. *Metapolitics*. Translated by J. Barker. London and New York: Verso.

Battie, William. 1758. *A Treatise on Madness*. London: printed for J. Whitson and B. White, in Fleet-street.

Baugh, Bruce. 1992. 'Transcendental Empiricism: Deleuze's response to Hegel.' *Man and World* 25:2: 133–48.

Baxter, Donald L. M. 2006. 'Identity, Continued Existence, and the External World,' in *The Blackwell Guide to Hume's Treatise*. Edited by S. Traiger. London: Blackwell, pp. 114–50.

Bell, Jeffrey A. 1995. 'Philosophizing the Double-Bind: Deleuze Reads Nietzsche.' *Philosophy Today* 39: 371–90.

—. 1998. *The Problem of Difference: Phenomenology and Poststructuralism*. Toronto: University of Toronto Press.

—. 2004. 'Immanence/Transcendence: Deleuze and Voegelin on the Conditions for Political Order,' in *Eric Voegelin's Dialogue with the Postmoderns: Searching for Foundations*. Edited by P. A. Petrakis and C. L. Eubanks. Columbia: University of Missouri Press, pp. 93–120.

—. 2006a. 'Charting the Road of Inquiry: Deleuze's Humean Pragmatics and the Challenge of Badiou.' *The Southern Journal of Philosophy* 44: 399–425.

—. 2006b. *Philosophy at the Edge of Chaos: Gilles Deleuze and the Philosophy of Difference*. Toronto: University of Toronto Press.

Bell, Martin. 2000. 'Sceptical Doubts Concerning Hume's Causal Realism,' in *The New Hume Debate*. Edited by R. Read and K. A. Richman. London and New York: Routledge, pp. 122–37.

—. 2001. 'Belief and Instinct in Hume's First *Enquiry*,' in *Reading Hume on Human Understanding*. Edited by P. Millican. Oxford: Oxford University Press, pp. 175–210.

—. 2005. 'Transcendental Empiricism? Deleuze's Reading of Hume,' in *Impressions of Hume*. Edited by M. Frasca-Spada. Oxford: Oxford University Press, pp. 95–106.

Benjamin, Walter. 1955. *Illuminations: Essays and Reflections*. Edited by H. Arendt. Translated by H. Zohn. New York: Harcourt Brace Jovanovich.

—. 1978. *Reflections: Essays, Aphorisms, Autobiographical Writings*. Translated by E. Jephcott. New York: Schocken Books.

Bennett, Jonathan. 2001. *Learning From Six Philosophers*, 2 vols. Oxford: Clarendon Press.

—. 2002. 'Empiricism about Meanings,' in *Reading Hume on Human Undestanding: Essays on the First Enquiry*. Edited by P. Millican. Oxford: Oxford University Press, pp. 97–106.

Berger, Peter L. and Thomas Luckman. 1967. *The Social Construction of Reality*. New York: Anchor Books.

Bergson, Henri. [1907] 1911. *Creative Evolution*. Translated by A. Mitchell. New York: Henry Holt and Company.

—. [1932] 1954. *The Two Sources of Morality and Religion*. Translated by R. A. Audra and C. Brereton. New York: Doubleday Anchor Books.

—. [1896] 1988. *Matter and Memory*. Translated by N. M. Paul and W. S. Plamer. New York: Zone Books.

—. [1903] 1999. *An Introduction to Metaphysics*. Translated by T. E. Hulme. Indianapolis: Hackett.

—. [1889] 2001. *Time and Free Will: An Essay on the Immediate Data of Consciousness*. Translated by F. L. Pogson. New York: Dover Publications.

Berry, Christopher. 1997. *The Social Theory of the Scottish Enlightenment.* Edinburgh: Edinburgh University Press.
Bertström, Lars. 1993. 'Quine, Underdetermination and Skepticism.' *The Journal of Philosophy* 90: 331–58.
Blanchot, Maurice. 1987. 'Foucault as I Imagine Him,' in *Foucault/Blanchot: The Thought from Outside and Foucault as I Imagine Him.* New York: Zone Books.
Bloch, Olivier. 1993. *Spinoza A Xx^e Siècle.* Paris: Presses Universitaires de France.
Bloor, David. 1983. *Wittgenstein: A Social Theory of Knowledge.* London: MacMillan Press.
—. 1991. *Knowledge and Social Imagery.* Chicago: University of Chicago Press.
Bogue, Ronald. 1989. *Deleuze and Guattari.* New York and London: Routledge.
—. 2004. *Deleuze on Music, Painting, and the Arts.* New York and London: Routledge.
Boundas, Constantin V. 1994. 'Deleuze: Serialization and Subject-Formation,' in *Gilles Deleuze and the Theater of Philosophy.* Edited by C. V. Boundas and D. Olkowski. New York: Routledge.
Bourdieu, Pierre. 1968. 'Intellectual Field and Creative Project.' *Social Science Information* 8: 89–119.
—. 1977. *Reproduction: In Education, Society and Culture.* Translated by Richard Nice. Beverly Hills: SAGE Publications.
—. 1984. *Distinction: A Social Critique of the Judgment of Taste.* Translated by R. Nice. Cambridge, MA: Harvard University Press.
—. 1993. 'Concluding Remarks: For a Sociogenetic Understanding of Intellectual Works,' in *Bourdieu: Critical Perspectives.* Edited by C. Calhoun, E. LiPuma, and M. Postone. Chicago: University of Chicago Press, pp. 263–75.
—. 1998. *Practical Reason.* Stanford: Stanford University Press.
Box, M. A. 1990. *The Suasive Art of David Hume.* Princeton: Princeton University Press.
Bricke, John. 1980. *Hume's Philosophy of Mind.* Edinburgh: Edinburgh University Press.
Broackes, Justin. 2002. 'Hume, Belief, and Personal Identity,' in *Reading Hume on Human Understanding: Essays on Hume's First Enquiry.* Edited by P. Millican. Oxford: Oxford University Press, pp. 187–210.
Broadie, Alexander. 2001. *The Scottish Enlightenment.* Edinburgh: Birlinn.
Bryson, Gladys. 1945. *Man and Society: The Scottish Enquiry of the Eighteenth Century.* Princeton: Princeton University Press.
Buchanan, Ian. 1997. 'Deleuze and Cultural Studies.' *South Atlantic Quarterly* 96:3: 483–97.
—. 2000. *Deleuzism: A Metacommentary.* Durham, NC: Duke University Press.
Buckel, Stephen. 2001. *Hume's Enlightenment Tract: The Unity and Purpose of An Enquiry Concerning Human Understanding.* Oxford: Oxford University Press.
Camic, Charles. 1983. *Experience and Enlightenment: Socialization for Cultural Change.* Chicago: University of Chicago Press.
Campbell, R. H. and Andrew Skinner. 1982. *The Origins and Nature of the Scottish Enlightenment.* Edinburgh: J. Donald.
Chitnis, Anand. 1976. *The Scottish Enlightenment: A Social History.* London: Rowman and Littlefield.
—. 1987. 'The Eighteenth-Century Scottish Intellectual Inquiry: Context and Continuities versus Civic Virtue,' in *Aberdeen and the Enlightenment.*

Edited by J. J. Carter and J. H. Pittock. Aberdeen: Aberdeen University Press, pp. 77–92.
Clastres, Pierre. 1987. *Society Against the State*. Translated by R. Hurley. New York: Zone Books.
Colebrook, Claire. 2002. *Deleuze*. London and New York: Routledge.
Collingwood, R. G. 1946. *The Idea of History*. Oxford: Oxford University Press.
Collins, Randall. 1990. 'Market Dynamics as the Engine of Historical Change.' *Sociological Theory* 8: 111–35.
—. 1994. *Four Sociological Traditions*. Oxford and New York: Oxford University Press.
—. 1998. *The Sociology of Philosophies: A Global Theory of Intellectual Change*. Cambridge, MA: Harvard University Press.
—. 2005. *Interaction Ritual Chains*. Princeton: Princeton University Press.
Craig, Cairns. 1996. *Out of History: Narrative Paradigms in English and Scottish Culture*. Edinburgh: Polygon.
Craig, Edward. 2002. 'The Idea of Necessary Connexion,' in *Reading Hume on Human Understanding: Essays on Hume's First Enquiry*. Edited by P. Millican. Oxford: Oxford University Press, pp. 211–30.
Cummins, Robert. 1978. 'The Missing Shade of Blue.' *Philosophical Review* 87: 548–65.
Davidson, Donald. 1980. *Essays on Actions and Events*. Oxford: Oxford University Press.
Davis, Lennard J. 1996. *Factual Fictions*. Philadelphia: University of Pennsylvania Press.
De Landa, Manuel. 1997. *A Thousand Years of Nonlinear History*. New York: Zone Books.
—. 2002. *Intensive Science and Virtual Philosophy*. London: Continuum.
Deleuze, Gilles. 1968. 'Spinoza et la méthode générale de M. Gueroult.' *Revue de Métaphysique et de Morale* 4: 426–37.
—. 1981. *Spinoza: Practical Philosophy*. Translated by R. Hurley. San Francisco: City Lights Books.
—. 1983. *Nietzsche and Philosophy*. Translated by H. Tomlinson. New York: Columbia University Press.
—. 1984. *Kant's Critical Philosophy: The Doctrine of the Faculties*. Translated by H. Tomlinson and B. Habberjam. Minneapolis: University of Minnesota Press.
—. 1986. *Cinema 1: The Movement-Image*. Translated by H. Tomlinson and B. Habberjam. Minneapolis: University of Minnesota.
—. 1988a. *Bergsonism*. Translated by H. Tomlinson and B. Habberjam. New York: Zone Books.
—. 1988b. *Foucault*. Translated by S. Hand. Minneapolis: University of Minnesota Press.
—. 1988c. *Périclès et Verdi*. Paris: Les éditions de minuit.
—. 1989. *Cinema 2: The Time-Image*. Translated by H. Tomlinson and R. Galeta. Minneapolis: University of Minnesota Press.
—. 1990. *Expressionism in Philosophy: Spinoza*. Translated by M. Joughin. New York: Zone Books.
—. 1991. *Empiricism and Subjectivity*. Translated by C. Boundas. New York: Columbia University Press.

De Landa, Manuel. 1993. *The Fold: Leibniz and the Baroque.* Translated by T. Conley. Minneapolis: University of Minnesota Press.
—. 1994. *Difference and Repetition.* Translated by P. Patton. New York: Columbia University Press.
—. 1995. *Negotiations.* Translated by M. Joughin. New York: Columbia University Press.
—. 1997. *Essays Critical and Clinical.* Translated by D. Smith and M. A. Greco. Minneapolis: University of Minnesota Press.
—. 2001. *Pure Immanence.* Translated by A. Boyman. New York: Zone Books.
—. 2004. *Desert Islands and Other Texts 1953–1974.* Translated by M. Taormina. New York: Semiotext(e).
—. 2006. *Two Regimes of Madness: Texts and Interviews 1975–1995.* Translated by A. Hodges and M. Taormina. New York: Semiotext(e).
Deleuze, Gilles and Félix Guattari. 1977. *Anti-Oedipus: Capitalism and Schizophrenia.* Translated by Robert Hurley, Mark Seem, and Helen R. Lane. Minneapolis: University of Minnesota Press.
—. 1986. *Kafka: Toward a Minor Literature.* Translated by D. Polan. Minneapolis: University of Minnesota Press.
—. 1987. *A Thousand Plateaus: Capitalism and Schizophrenia.* Translated by B. Massumi. Minneapolis: University of Minnesota Press.
—. 1994. *What is Philosophy?* Translated by H. Tomlinson and G. Burchell. New York: Columbia University Press.
Deleuze, Gilles and Claire Parnet. 1987. *Dialogues.* Translated by H. Tomlinson and B. Habberjam. New York: Columbia University Press.
Devine, T. M. 1999. *The Scottish Nation: A History.* New York: Viking.
Donaldson, Alexander. 1769. *A Letter from a gentleman in Edinburgh, to his friend in London; concerning literary property.* Edinburgh: s.n.
Douglass, Paul. 1992. 'Deleuze and the Endurance of Bergson.' *Thought* 67: 47–61.
Dreyfus, Hubert, and Paul Rabinow. 1982. *Michel Foucault: Beyond Structuralism and Hermeneutics.* New York: Prentice-Hall.
Evensky, Jerry, ed. 2007. *Adam Smith's Moral Philosophy: A Historical and Contemporary Perspective on Markets, Law, Ethics, and Culture.* Cambridge: Cambridge University Press.
Flew, Anthony. 1959. 'Hume's Check.' *Philosophical Quarterly* 9: 1–18.
—. 1961. *Hume's Philosophy of Belief.* London: Routledge & Kegan Paul.
Fodor, Jerry A. 2003. *Hume Variations.* Oxford: Clarendon Press.
Fogelin, Robert J. 1984. 'Hume and the Missing Shade of Blue.' *Philosophy and Phenomenological Research* 45: 263–71.
Forbes, Duncan. 1975. *Hume's Philosophical Politics.* Cambridge: Cambridge University Press.
Fosl, Peter S. 1993. 'Empiricism, Difference, and Common Life.' *Man and World* 26.
Foucault, Michel. 1977. *Language, Counter-Memory, Practice.* Translated by D. F. Bouchard and S. Simon. Ithaca, NY: Cornell University Press.
—. 2001. *Fearless Speech.* Los Angeles: Semiotext(e).
Frasca-Spada, Marina. 1998. *Space and Self in Hume's Treatise.* Cambridge: Cambridge University Press.
—. 2005. *Impressions of Hume.* Oxford: Oxford University Press.
Garrett, Don. 1997. *Cognition and Commitment in Hume's Philosophy.* Oxford: Oxford University Press.

Geiringer, Karl. 1968. *Haydn: A Creative Life in Music*. Berkeley: University of California Press.
Gerard, Alexander. 1758. 'Discourse on Genius.' Special Collections, Aberdeen University Library, *MS 3107/1/3*.
—. 1774. *An Essay on Genius*. Edinburgh: William Strahan; Thomas Cadell in the Strand; and William Creech.
—. [1759] 1963. *An Essay on Taste*. New York: Scholar's Facsimiles and Reproductions.
Gillespie, Sam. 2001. 'Placing the Void: Badiou on Spinoza.' *Angelaki* 6:3: 63–77.
Graham, Elspeth, Hilary Hinds, Elaine Hibby, and Helen Wilcox, eds. 1989. *Her Own Life: Autobiographical Writings by Seventeenth-Century Englishwomen*. London: Routledge.
Guattari, Félix. 1995. *Chaosmosis*. Translated by Julian Pefanis and Paul Bains. Bloomington: Indiana University Press.
Gueroult, Martial. 1968. *Spinoza I: Dieu (Ethique, I)*. Hildesheim: Georg Olms Verlagbuchhandlung.
—. 1974. *Spinoza II: L'Âme (Ethique, II)*. New York: Georg Olms Verlag.
Hacking, Ian. 1975. *The Emergence of Probability*. Cambridge: Cambridge University Press.
—. 1999. *The Social Construction of What?* Cambridge: Cambridge University Press.
—. 2002. *Historical Ontology*. Cambridge, MA: Harvard University Press.
Hallett, Harold F. 1930. *Aeternitas: A Spinozistic Study*. Oxford: The Clarendon Press.
—. 1973. 'Substance and its Modes,' in *Spinoza: A Collection of Critical Essays*. Edited by Marjorie Grene. Notre Dame: University of Notre Dame Press.
Hallward, Peter. 2006. *Out of This World*. London and New York: Verso.
—. ed. 2004. *Think Again: Badiou and the Future of Philosophy*. London: Continuum.
Hardt, Michael. 1994. 'Spinoza's Democracy: The Passions of Social Assemblages,' in *Marxism in the Postmodern Age*. Edited by A. Callari. New York: Guilford.
Hardt, Michael and Antonio Negri. 2000. *Empire*. Cambridge, MA: Harvard University Press.
—. 2004. *Multitude: War and Democracy in the Age of Empire*. New York: Penguin.
Hayden, Patrick. 1998. *Multiplicity and Becoming: The Pluralist Empiricism of Gilles Deleuze*. New York: P. Lang.
Haydn, Joseph. 1959. *The Collected Correspondence and London Notebooks*. Edited by H. C. Robbins Landun. London: Barrie and Rockliff.
Heraclitus. 1987. *Fragments*. Translation and commentary by T. M. Robinson. Toronto: University of Toronto Press.
Hobbes, Thomas. [1651] 1994. *Leviathan*. Edited by E. Curley. Indianapolis: Hackett.
Hodges, M. and J. Lachs. 1976. 'Hume on Belief.' *Review of Metaphysics* 30: 3–18.
Holland, Eugene W. 1991. 'Detteritorializing "Deterritorialization" – From the *Anti-Oedipus* to *A Thousand Plateaus*.' *SubStance* 66: 55–65.
Hont, Istvan and Michael Ignatieff. 1983. *Wealth and Virtue: the Shaping of Political Economy in the Scottish Enlightenment*. Cambridge: Cambridge University Press.
Horner, W. B. 1996. *Life Writing*. New York: Prentice Hall.

Houston, R. A. 2000. *Madness and Society in Eighteenth-Century Scotland.* Oxford: Clarendon Press.
Hume, David. 1748. *A true account of the behaviour and conduct of Archibald Stewart, Esq., late Lord Provost of Edinburgh: in a letter to a friend.* London: Printed for M. Cooper.
—. 1932. *The Letters of David Hume*, 2 vols. Edited by J. Y. T. Grieg. Oxford: Clarendon Press.
—. 1969. *New Letters of David Hume.* Edited by R. Klibansky and E. C. Mossner. Oxford: Oxford University Press.
—. [1739] 1978. *A Treatise of Human Nature.* Edited by L. A. Silby-Bigge. Oxford: Clarendon Press.
—. [1740] 1978. 'An Abstract of a *Treatise of Human Nature*,' in *A Treatise of Human Nature.* Edited by L. A. Selby-Bigge. Oxford: Clarendon Press.
—. [1741–2] 1985. *Essays, Moral, Political, and Literary.* Edited by E. Miller. Indianapolis: Liberty Fund.
—. [1748] 2005. *An Enquiry Concerning Human Understanding.* Edited by T. Beauchamp. Oxford: Oxford University Press.
—. [1751] 1975. *An Enquiry Concerning the Principles of Morals.* Edited by L. A. Silby-Bigge. Oxford: Clarendon Press.
—. [1754–62] 1983. *The History of England.* Indianapolis: Liberty Fund.
—. [1757] 1992. *Four Dissertations.* South Bend, IN: St. Augustine's Press.
—. [1779] 1947. *Dialogues Concerning Natural Religion.* Indianapolis: Bobbs-Merrill.
Hundert, E. J. 1994. *The Enlightenment's 'Fable': Bernard de Mandeville and the Discovery of Society.* Cambridge: Cambridge University Press.
Hunter, J. Paul. 1997. 'Protesting Fiction, Constructing History,' in *The Historical Imagination in Early Modern Britain: History, Rhetoric, and Fiction 1500–1800.* Edited by D. R. Kelley and D. Harris. Cambridge: Cambridge University Press, pp. 298–317.
Israel, Jonathan I. 2001. *Radical Enlightenment: Philosophy and the Making of Modernity 1650–1750.* Oxford: Oxford University Press.
Jacobs, Jane. 1969. *The Economy of Cities.* New York: Random House.
James, William. 1960. *The Selected Letters of William James.* Edited by E. Hardwick. New York: Farrar, Strauss, and Cudahy.
—. 1987. *William James: Writings 1902–1910.* New York: The Library of America.
Kafka, Franz. [1910–23] 1982. *The Diaries of Franz Kafka.* Edited by Max Brod. New York: Penguin Books.
Kant, Immanuel. [1784] 1983. 'Idea for a Universal History with a Cosmopolitian Intent,' in *Perpetual Peace and Other Essays.* Translated by Ted Humphrey. Indianapolis: Hackett.
Kemp Smith, Norman. 1905. 'The Naturalism of Hume.' *Mind* 14: 149–73.
—. 1941. *The Philosophy of David Hume.* London: Macmillan.
Lampert, Jay. 2006. *Deleuze and Guattari's Philosophy of History.* London and New York: Continuum.
Landon, H.C. Robbins. 1959. *The Collected Correspondence and London Notebooks of Joseph Haydn.* London: Barrie & Rockliff.
Latour, Bruno. 1987. *Science in Action: How to Follow Scientists and Engineers Through Society.* Cambridge, MA: Harvard University Press.

—. 1991. 'Technology is Society Made Durable,' in *A Sociology of Monsters: Essays on Power, Technology and Domination, Sociological Review Monograph*. Edited by J. Law. New York: Routledge & Kegan Paul, pp. 103–31.
—. 1999. *Pandora's Hope: Essays on the Reality of Science Studies*. Cambridge, MA: Harvard University Press.
—. 2000. 'On the Partial Existence of Existing and Nonexisting Objects,' in *Biographies of Scientific Objects*. Edited by L. Daston. Chicago: University of Chicago Press, pp. 247–69.
—. 2004. *Politics of Nature. How to Bring the Sciences into Democracy*. Translated by C. Porter. Cambridge, MA: Harvard University Press.
—. 2007. *Reassembling the Social: An Introduction to Actor-Network-Theory*. New York and Oxford: Oxford University Press.
Latour, Bruno and Shirley S. Strum. 1987. 'Redefining the Social Link – From Baboons to Humans.' *Social Science Information* 26: 783–802.
Latour, Bruno and Stephen Woolgar. 1986. *Laboratory Life: The Construction of Scientific Facts*. Princeton: Princeton University Press.
Law, John. 1993. *Organizing Modernity*. New York: Wiley.
Lawlor, Leonard. 2003. *The Challenge of Bergsonism*. London: Continuum.
Lecercle, Jean-Jacques. 2002. *Deleuze and Language*. New York: Palgrave Macmillan.
Loeb, Louis E. 1995. 'Instability and Uneasiness in Hume's theories of Belief and Justification.' *British Journal for the History of Philosophy* 3: 301–27.
Lynch, Michael. 1992. *Scotland: A New History*. London: Pimlico.
MacCormick, Neil. 1982. 'Law and Enlightenment,' in *The Origins and Nature of the Scottish Enlightenment*. Edited by R. H. Campbell and A. Skinner. Edinburgh: John Donald Publishers.
McCrone, David. 2001. *Understanding Scotland: The Sociology of a Nation*. New York: Routledge.
Macherey, Pierre. 1998. *Introduction à l'Éthique de Spinoza*. Paris: Presses Universitaires de France.
McKendrick, Neil, J. H. Plumb, and John Brewer. 1982. *The Birth of a Consumer Society: The Commercialization of 18th-Century England*. London: Europa.
McNeill, William. 1982. *The Pursuit of Power: Technology, Armed Force and Society Since A.D. 1000*. Oxford and New York: Oxford University Press.
Mandeville, Bernard. 1732. *The Fable of the Bees: or, private vices, publick benefits*. London: printed for J. Tonson.
Martelaere, Patricia de. 1984. 'Gilles Deleuze, Interprete de Hume.' *Revue Philosophique du Louvain* 84: 224–48.
Marx, Karl. 1978. *The Marx-Engels Reader*. New York: W.W. Norton & Company.
—. 1987. *Economic and Philosophic Manuscripts of 1844*. New York: Prometheus Books.
Massumi, Brian. 1992. *A User's Guide to Capitalism and Schizophrenia: Deviations from Deleuze and Guattari*. Cambridge, MA: The MIT Press.
May, Todd. 1991. 'The Politics of Life in the Thought of Gilles Deleuze.' *SubStance* 66: 24–35.
—. 2004a. 'Badiou and Deleuze on the One and the Many,' in *Think Again: Badiou and the Future of Philosophy*. Edited by Peter Hallward. London: Continuum.
—. 2004b. *Gilles Deleuze: An Introduction*. Cambridge: Cambridge University Press.

May, Todd. 2006. *The Philosophy of Foucault*. London: McGill-Queen's University Press.
Mengue, Philippe. 1994. *Gilles Deleuze, ou, Le systéme du multiple*. Paris: Editions Kimé.
Mill, John Stuart. 1991. *On Liberty and Other Essays*. Edited by J. Gray. Oxford and New York: Oxford University Press.
Millican, Peter. 2002a. 'Context, Aim, and Structure of Hume's First *Enquiry*,' in *Reading Hume on Human Understanding: Essays on Hume's First Enquiry*. Edited by P. Millican. Oxford: Oxford University Press, pp. 27–66.
—. 2002b. 'Reading Hume on Human Understanding.' Oxford: Oxford University Press.
Mossner, Ernest Campbell. 1954. *The Life of David Hume*. New York: Oxford University Press.
Mullarkey, John. 1999a. *Bergson and Philosophy*. Notre Dame: University of Notre Dame Press.
—. Editor. 1999b. *The New Bergson*. Manchester: Manchester University Press.
Negri, Antonio. 1991. *The Savage Anomaly: The Power of Spinoza's Metaphysics and Politics*. Translated by M. Hardt. Minneapolis: University of Minnesota Press.
Nietzsche, Friedrich. 1966. *Beyond Good and Evil*. Translated by Walter Kaufmann. New York: Vintage Books.
—. 1968. *The Portable Nietzsche*. Translated and edited by Walter Kaufman. New York: Viking Press.
—. 1984. *Human All Too Human*. Translated by Marion Faber and Stephen Lehmann. Lincoln: University of Nebraska Press.
Owen, David. 1999. *Hume's Reason*. Oxford and New York: Oxford University Press.
Patton, Paul. 1996a. 'Concept and Event.' *Man and World* 29: 315–26.
—. 1996b. *Deleuze: A Critical Reader*. Oxford and New York: Blackwell.
—. 2000. *Deleuze and the Political*. London and New York: Routledge.
Pears, David. 1990. *Hume's System*. Oxford: Oxford University Press.
Phillipson, Nicholas T. 1973. 'Towards a Definition of the Scottish Enlightenment,' in *City and Society in the 18th Century*. Edited by P. Fritz and D. Williams. Toronto: University of Toronto Press, pp. 125–45.
—. 1981. 'The Scottish Enlightenment,' in *Enlightenment in National Context*. Edited by R. Porter and M. Teich. Cambridge: Cambridge University Press.
Pittock, Murray. 1991. *The Invention of Scotland: The Stuart Myth and the Scottish Identity, 1638 to the Present*. New York: Routledge.
Pocock, J. G. A. 1975. *The Machiavellian Moment*. Princeton: Princeton University Press.
—. 1983. 'Cambridge Paradigms and Scotch Philosophers: a study of the relations between the civic humanist and the civil jurisprudential interpretation of eighteenth-century social thought,' in *Wealth and Virtue: The Shaping of Political Economy in the Scottish Enlightenment*. Edited by I. Hont and M. Ignatieff. Cambridge: Cambridge University Press.
—. 1985. *Virtue, Commerce and History*. Cambridge: Cambridge University Press.
Prestongrange, William Grant, Lord, et al. 1744. *Midwinter v. Booksellers*. Advocates Library, Edinburgh: Elchies Papers XV: A-B, case no. 45.
Protevi, John. 2001. *Political Physics*. London: Athlone.

Protevi, John and Mark Bonta. 2004. *Deleuze and Geophilosophy*. Edinburgh: Edinburgh University Press.
Quine, W. V. O. 1990. *The Pursuit of Truth*. Cambridge: Cambridge University Press.
Ramond, Charles. 1995. *Qualité et quantité dans la philosophie de Spinoza*. Paris: Presses Universitaires de France.
Rancière, Jacques. 1991. *The Ignorant Schoolmaster*. Translated by K. Ross. Stanford: Stanford University Press.
Reid, Thomas. [1764] 1997. *An Inquiry into the Human Mind on the Principles of Common Sense*. Edited by D. R. Brookes. University Park, PA: The Pennsylvania State University Press.
—. 1969. *Essays on the Intellectual Powers of Man*. Cambridge, MA: The MIT Press.
Rendall, Jane. 1978. *The Origins of the Scottish Enlightenment*. New York: St. Martin's Press.
Ringer, Fritz. 1969. *The Decline of the German Mandarins*. Cambridge, MA: Harvard University Press.
—. 1990. 'The Intellectual Field, Intellectual History, and the Sociology of Knowledge.' *Theory and Society* 19: 269–94.
—. 2000. *Max Weber's Methodology: The Unification of the Cultural and Social Sciences*. Cambridge, MA: Harvard University Press.
Rose, Mark. 1995. *Authors and Owners: The Invention of Copyright*. Cambridge, MA: Harvard University Press.
Schmidt, Claudia M. 2003. *David Hume: Reason in History*. Happy Valley, PA: Pennsylvania State University Press.
Scotland, Court of Session. 1791. *Decisions*. Edinburgh: Bell and Bradfute, William Creech, and Watson, Elder and company.
Shapin, Steven. 1974. 'Property, Patronage, and the Politics of Science: The Founding of the Royal Society of Edinburgh.' *The British Journal for the History of Science* 7: 1–41.
—. 1980. 'Social Uses of Science,' in *The Ferment of Knowledge: Studies in the Historiography of Eighteenth-Century Science*. Edited by R. Porter and G. S. Rousseau. Cambridge: Cambridge University Press.
—. 1994. *A Social History of Truth: Civility and Science in Seventeenth-Century England*. Chicago: University of Chicago Press.
Sher, Richard. 1985. *The Church and University in the Scottish Enlightenment*. Princeton: Princeton University Press.
Smith, Daniel W. 2003. 'Mathematics and the Theory of Multiplicities: Badiou and Deleuze Revisited.' *The Journal of Southern Philosophy* 41:3: 411–50.
—. 2007. 'The Conditions of the New.' *Deleuze Studies* 1:1: 1–21.
Smout, T. C. 1969. *History of the Scottish People: 1580–1830*. London: Collins.
Spinoza, Benedict de. 1677. *Opera Posthuma, quorum series post praesatinem exhibetur*. Edited by J. Jellesz. Amsterdam: Johannes Rieuwertsz.
—. 1951. 'Political Treatise,' in *Works of Spinoza*, vol. 1. Edited by R. H. M. Elwes. New York: Dover Publications, Inc.
—. 1985. *The Ethics*, in *The Collected Works of Spinoza, Volume I*. Edited by E. Curley. Princeton: Princeton University Press.
Stach, Reiner. 2005. *Kafka: The Decisive Years*. Translated by Shelley Frisch. New York: Harcourt, Inc.

Stengers, Isabelle. 2002. *Penser avec Whitehead*. Paris: Seuil.
Stewart, M. A. 2005. 'Hume's Intellectual Development: 1711–1752,' in *Impressions of Hume*. Edited by M. Frasca-Spada and P. J. E. Kail. Oxford: Oxford University Press, pp. 11–57.
Strawson, Galen. 2002. 'David Hume: Objects and Power,' in *Reading Hume on Human Understanding: Essays on Hume's First Enquiry*. Edited by P. Millican. Oxford: Oxford University Press, pp. 231–57.
Stroud, Barry. 1977. *Hume*. New York and London: Routledge.
Sudnow, David. 1978. *Ways of the Hand*. Cambridge, MA: Harvard University Press.
Swift, Johathan. [1704] 1970. *A Tale of a Tub. To which is added the battle of the books, and the Mechanical operation of the Spirit*. London: Fraser Press.
Temple, Sir William. 1690. *Miscellanea*. London: printed by T. M. for Ri. Simpson and Ra. Simpson.
Thoburn, Nicholas. 2003. *Deleuze, Marx, and Politics*. New York: Routledge.
Tilly, Charles. 1990. *Coercion, Capital, and European States, AD 990–1990*. Cambridge: Blackwell.
Traiger, Saul. 1987. 'Impressions, Ideas, and Fictions.' *Hume Studies* 13: 381–99.
—. Editor. 2006. *The Blackwell Guide to Hume's Treatise*. London: Blackwell.
Tweyman, Stanley, editor. 1995. *David Hume: Critical Assessments*, 6 vols. London and New York: Routledge.
Vinciguerra, Lorenzo. 2001. *Spinoza*. Paris: Hachette.
Virno, Paolo. 2004. *A Grammar of the Multitude*. Translated by by Isabella Bertoletti, James Cascaito, and Andrea Casson. New York: Semiotext(e).
Wallerstein, Immanuel. 1979. *The Capitalist World-Economy*. Cambridge: Cambridge University Press.
Warburton, William, Bp. of Gloucester. 1747. *A letter from an author, to a member of Parliament, concerning literary property*. London: John and Paul Knapton.
Watt, Ian. 1957. *The Rise of the Novel*. Berkeley: University of California Press.
Weber, Max. 1949. 'Objectivity in Social Science and Policy,' in *The Methodology of the Social Sciences*. Edited and translated by Edward Shils and Henry A. Finch.
—. 1959. *From Max Weber: Essays on Sociology*. Oxford and New York: Oxford University Press.
Williams, James. 2004. *Gilles Deleuze's Difference and Repetition: A Critical Introduction*. Edinburgh: Edinburgh University Press.
Winkler, Kenneth. 1991. 'The New Hume,' *Philosophical Review* 100: 541–79.
Wormald, Jenny. 1981. *Court, Kirk and Community*. Edinburgh: Edinburgh University Press.
Wotton, William. 1694. *Reflections upon Ancient and Modern Learning*. London: s.n.
Wright, John P. 1983. *The Sceptical Realism of David Hume*. Manchester: Manchester University Press.
—. 2000. 'Hume's Causal Realism: Recovering a Traditional Interpretation,' in *The New Hume Debate*. Edited by R. Read and K. A. Richman. London and New York: Routledge, pp. 88–99.
Žižek, Slavoj. 2004. *Organs Without Bodies: Deleuze and Consequences*. New York: Routledge.
Zourabichvili, François. 1994. *Deleuze, une philosophie de l'événement*. Paris: Presses Universitaires de France.

Index

Addison, Joseph, 109
Agamben, Giorgio, 21, 144–7
Althusser, Louis, 121–2
Alzheimer's disease, 44

Bach, Carl Philipp Emanuel, 66
Bach, Johann Sebastian, 66
Badiou, Alain, 2, 22–4, 65–6, 67–8,
    72–4, 109, 111, 125, 131–5,
    138–9, 142–5
Belief, 26–9, 36–7
    Belief in the world, 27–8, 38
Benjamin, Walter, 146–7
Bennett, Jonathan, 11–12, 13, 36–8,
    39, 49
Blacklock, Thomas, 13
Blair, Hugh, 118
Blanchot, Maurice, 79
Bloor, David, 68–9
Blue, missing shade of, 10–11,
    12–13, 15, 16
Bourdieu, Pierre, 101–2, 127
Broadie, Alexander, 108
Buchanan, George, 108
Burnet, Gilbert, 108
Butler, Bishop, 109

Cantorian set-theory, 133–4
Capitalism, 96–7, 112, 149–51
Carlyle, Alexander, 120
Charles I, 85
Cicero, 109–10

Clarke, Samuel, 109
Collingwood, R. G., 104n1
Commerce, 87–8, 90–1, 94–7
Conjunction, power of, 20
Consumer Society, 115–16
Counter-actualization, 50, 60–1
Cultural preconscious, 111–12

Dalrymple, James, Viscount Stair,
    108, 117
Deleuze, Gilles
    (and Félix Guattari) and apparatus
        of capture, 99–100
    and assemblages, 148–9
    and becoming-imperceptible,
        151–3
    and Bergson, 50–6
    and intellectual history, 107
    and linguistic multiplicity, 132–3
    (and Guattari) and private
        property, 113, 115–16
    and social multiplicity, 139, 147
    and societies of control, 151–2
    and traditional view of empiricism,
        19
    and transcendental empiricism,
        15–18
    nominalist Deleuze, 3
    realist Deleuze, 3–4
Descartes, René, 123
Devine, T. M., 115–16, 118
Dickens, Charles, 76–7

Don Quixote, 107
Double Articulation, 16, 125–6
Dualism, 4, 52–3, 70
  and empiricism, 29, 34, 35

Effect, autonomy of, 61
Empiricism, 1, 4, 19
  Deleuze as empiricist, 1
  see also radical empiricism, transcendental empiricism
Event, 4

Ferguson, Adam, 89, 118
Foucault, Michel, 64–5, 97–9, 122, 126, 139–41
Frege, Gottlieb, 11

Garrett, Don, 12–13, 38–9, 44, 49
Gorgias, 141–2
Gregory, James, 108

Hardt, Michael, 73
Haydn, Joseph, 65–8, 134–5
Heidegger, Martin, 65–6
Historical ontology, 5, 36–42, 54, 67, 79
History, 59
  problematizing history, 59–60, 64–5, 67, 71–2, 103–4
Hobbes, Thomas, 94
Holism, 11
Home, Henry, Lord Kames, 84, 114
Human Nature, principles of, 15
Hume, David
  and belief, 36–42
  and fictioning of identity, 14–15
  and *History of England*, 84–8
  and institutions, 6–7
  and personal identity, 42–8
  early influences on, 109–10
  historiography, 82–3
  letter to Dr. George Cheyne, 110–11
  on causation (necessity), 26–7, 29
  on ideas and impressions, 10–15
  rejection of *Treatise*, 82–4
  Thomas Reid's critique of, 123–4
Hutcheson, Francis, 109
Hutton, James, 118

Identity, 13–14, 27
Impressions (and ideas), 10–15
Improvizational jazz, 24–6
Institutions, 17, 86–8, 118
Intellectual property, 113–15

Jacobs, Jane, 124–5
James VI/I, 85, 108
James, William, 1–2, 18–22, 49
Justice, 91–2

Kafka, Franz, 73–80, 126
Kant, Immanuel, 34–5, 55, 75
Kemp Smith, Norman, 39–41, 45–6, 48

Latour, Bruno, 4–5, 41–2, 68–72, 91, 135–9, 141–3
Leibniz, G. W. F., 67
Locke, John, 109, 112, 123
Logical positivism, 11

Madness, 40, 46, 92–3, 94–7, 117; *see also* schizophrenia
Maier, John, 108
Mandevelle, Bernard de, 109
Marx, Karl, 113, 144, 150, 153
May '68, 98
Meaning, Fregean-Russellean theory of, 11
Memory, 53
Mercantilism, 88
Millar, Andrew, 113–14
Millar, John, 89
Monboddo, Lord, 89
Multitude, power of, 99–100

Negri, Antonio, 73
New Hume debate, 28–9, 34

Nietzsche, Friedrich, 109, 126
Nondenumerable sets, 99–100, 126
  contrasted with denumerable sets, 100–1

Overdetermination, 121–2

Pasteur, Louis, 69–71
Pears, David, 10–11, 13, 49
Personal identity, 42–8
Phillipson, Nicholas, 107–8, 117–18, 119–20
Pouchet, Félix-Archimède, 69–70
Private property, 113, 115–16; see also intellectual property
Problematizing history see history
Pure experience, 20

Quasi-cause, 60–1

Radical empiricism, 18–22
Rancière, Jacques, 65
Reid, Thomas, 10, 120, 123–4
Ringer, Fritz, 101–3
Russell, Bertrand, 11

Schizophrenia, 94–7
  schizoanalysis, 55, 96
Science studies, 68–72
Scotticisms, 120–1
Scottish Enlightenment, 103–4, 107–11, 117–22
Scotus, Duns, 108
Select Society, 119–20
Shaftesbury, Third Earl of, 109

Smith, Adam, 85, 89, 118
Social constructivism, 69–70
Spinoza, Benedict, 22–4, 126–7, 133
Statute of Anne (1710), 113, 114–15
Steele, Richard, 109
Strawson, Galen, 28
Stroud, Barry, 44–5
Strum, Shirley, 71
Sudnow, David, 24–5, 127
Swift, Jonathan, 116

Taste
  delicacy of, 106–7
  higher taste, 106–7, 122, 127–8
  standard of, 130n21
Temple, Sir William, 116
Title principle, 38–9
Tories, 85–7
Transcendental empiricism, 6, 9, 14, 15–18, 35, 42–3, 46, 55

Underdetermination, 30n6, 69

Virtual, 3, 5–6
  reality of, 22–6
  relationship to actual, 24–5, 46, 51–2, 108–9, 138–9

Weber, Max, 61–4
Whigs, 85–7
Whitehead, Alfred North, 67, 136–7
Whole Duty of Man, 116
Winkler, Kenneth, 28–9
Wittgenstein, Ludwig, 11

EU representative:
Easy Access System Europe
Mustamäe tee 50, 10621 Tallinn, Estonia
Gpsr.requests@easproject.com

www.ingramcontent.com/pod-product-compliance
Lightning Source LLC
Chambersburg PA
CBHW051101230426
43667CB00013B/2392